AF624368

India

A Splendour in Cultural Diversity

Books Written by Sir Paulias Matane

1. Kum Tumun of Minj
2. A New GuineanTravels Through Africa
3. My Childhood in New Guinea
4. What Good is Business?
5. Bai Bisniss! Helpim Yumi Oslem Wanem?
6. Aimbe the Challenger
7. Aimbe the Magician
8. Aimbe the School Dropout
9. Aimbe the Pastor**
10. Two Papua New Guineans Discover the Bible Lands
11. Chit Chat, Vol. 1
12. Let's Do it PNG#
13. To Serve With Love
14. Travels Through the Bible Lands*
15. East to West: The Longest Train Trip in the World
16. Trekking Through the New Worlds
17. Voyage to Antarctica
18. Laughter Made in PNG
19. Amazing Discoveries in 40 Years of Marriage
20. The Other Side of Port Moresby in Pictures
21. The Word Power
22. A Trip of a Lifetime
23. Waliling Community United Church: Then and Now
24. Coach Adventures Down Under
25. Management Problems in PNG: Some Solutions#
26. Further Management Problems in PNG: Some Solutions #
27. Chit Chat Vol. III
28. Management for Excellence #
29. Exploring South-East Asia, Vol. 1
30. Exploring South-East Asia Vol. 2
31. Exploring the Holy Lands*
32. Humour: The PNG Way
33. Ripples in the South Pacific Ocean**

Notes

* Reprinted under a different title (Sr. No. 30) with some changes

** Same title at Sr. No. 9 reprinted under new title at Sr. No. 32 in paperback

\# Titles at Sr. No. 25 and 26 combined at Sr. No. 28

India

A Splendour in Cultural Diversity

Sir Paulias Matane

M L Ahuja

Anmol Publications Private Ltd.

New Delhi - 110 002 (India)

Anmol Publications Pvt. Ltd.
4374/4B, Ansari Road, Daryaganj
New Delhi - 110 002
Ph.: 23261597, 23278000,23255577
Fax:91-11-23280289
E.mail:anmolpublications@vsnl.com
Visit us at: www.anmolpublications.com

Fortune Books
A House of Children's Books
(Unit of Anmol Publications Pvt. Ltd.)
4374/4B, Ansari Road, Daryaganj
New Delhi - 110 002
Ph.: 23261597, 23278000,23255577
Fax:91-11-23280289
E.mail:anmolpublications@vsnl.com
Visit us at: www.anmolpublications.com

© M L Ahuja
First Published, 2004
ISBN 81-261-1899-7 (HB)
ISBN 81-261-1837-7 (PB)

All rights reserved. No part of this publication may be reproduced, stored in a retrieval system or transmitted, in any form or by any means, mechanical, photocopying, recording or otherwise, without prior written permission of the publisher.

Designed by Aslam Parvez

Printed in India

Published by J.L. Kumar for Anmol Publications Pvt. Ltd., New Delhi - 110 002 and printed at G.K. Fine Art Press, Delhi-110031.

V.N. Khare
Chief Justice of India

Foreword

India is a vast democratic country having different religions and races. There are also regional differences among the same religious group. But, still the country is characterized by unity in diversity.

India is a secular country, which implies equal respect for all the people, irrespective of their religion, caste, race or sex. In the words of Former President of India Dr. S.Radhakrishnan, "It does not mean irreligion or atheism or even stress on material comforts. It proclaims that it lays stress on the universality of spiritual values which may be attained by a variety of ways". Secularism is enshrined in our Constitution, which gives full freedom to all to profess and practice their religious beliefs and rites so long as they are not repugnant to our ethical sense.

It is heartening to find that Sir Paulias Matane from Papua New Guinea and Mr. M.L. Ahuja from India, the authors of the book titled **India: A Splendour in Cultural Diversity** have dealt with different subjects like religions, festivals and marriage system in India which gives its importance in Indian society. Reading of this book creates love and affection for each other's religion.

This book is a repository of information for the Indians living within the country, non-resident Indians living outside India as well as all others to understand this sub-continent in its proper perspective. It should also be useful for the younger generation to know about our rich cultural and traditional values.

New Delhi:
December 4, 2003.

(V.N. Khare)

5, Krishna Menon Marg, New Delhi-110 011 Phone: 23015290

Preface

Though I never had an opportunity to meet Mahatma Gandhi, I have been considerably influenced by his simple life and pragmatic approach to economic, social and political problems. This, together with India being the biggest and successful democracy, evoked my interest in the land and people of India. Every time I had been to India, I felt that I have still to understand the real India.

Mr. M L Ahuja, who met me in Papua New Guinea, where I am based, offered to take me around in my next trip so as to see for myself the cultural diversity and understand India in its proper perspective.

I was in New Delhi in March 2003. Mr. Ahuja took me to the whole of old and New Delhi, Agra and Jaipur. With his help, I was able to know the historical importance of the monuments in these three cities. We visited various temples, Sikh shrines, mosques and churches. By chance, Holi, the festival of color, was then being celebrated. I had an opportunity to participate in this. Mr. Ahuja took me to various small scale industries, where I talked to men and women about their social and cultural environment in addition to the range and quality of the products manufactured by them.

While going through the Chandini Chowk and Jama Masjid areas in Delhi, I was really amazed to see the surging crowd either walking on foot or traveling through different modes of transport. I became more curious to know the educational opportunities available in the country, vis-a-vis the cost factor, the status of women, standard of living of the people in general and industrial development in the country to assess how far we, in the developing countries, can collaborate with the Indian entrepreneurs to improve our standard of living.

In Hindu temples, I found people worshipping a number of deities in their own characteristic way. This further raised my curiosity to know about the concept of their worship and expectation of the devotees from each deity that he or she worshipped. In the three cities, which I visited, I found everywhere many places of worship. Either it was a Hindu temple, a *gurudwara*, a mosque or a church. I was told that they are in the range of 2.4 million in whole of the country and the people have the freedom to practice their religion the way they like. But what surprised me most was the news item in almost every issue of the newspapers of the people fighting in the name of religion. This makes it essential for all of us to know the concept and principles underlying each religion and bring in us a spirit of tolerance towards the followers of all religions. This book, therefore, is intended towards this objective in view.

I was fortunate to have the company of Mr. Ahuja to respond to my various queries during my trip to three cities. I am always poised to share my experience and ecstasy with the people at large through my writings and presentations on EM-TV in PNG. I had been to the Latin American countries and my experiences are embodied in *Trekking Through the New Worlds*. I was in Bethlehem and Middle East and the result is my book, *Exploring the Holy Lands*. Similarly, I have recorded my observations in *Voyage to Antartica* after I returned from there. These books are also intended to share information with the people at large.

But, writing a good book about India, which should be informative, yet based on facts, requires not only the observation but also considerable research. I am grateful to Mr. M L Ahuja for undertaking this arduous task within a short time. He kept me abreast with the outcome of his study through e-mail and I thus had a chance to react at various points quickly. Thus, this book is an outcome of our joint efforts.

Writing a book on India is indeed a stupendous task. We have found numerous books on India. They deal with politics, economy, social and cultural aspects. There are separate books on Hinduism, Sikhism, Islam and other religions. There are also books meant for tourists explaining the historical background and grandeur of the monuments in Delhi, Agra and Jaipur. But our attempt has been to present to the readers an ideal synthesis of all this and much more, so as to comprehend India and its countrymen in their proper perspective. We feel that a study of India's cultural diversity is essential not only for the outsiders but also by the Indians themselves to understand the real India. Based on this premise, we decided to provide an overview of the land, people, education, religious groups and cultural diversity and yet limit our study to this small and handy book, which could easily be made accessible to the individual readers. If this can help the readers at far off places, we shall deem our efforts well-rewarded.

In our efforts to present to the readers maximum information, we have consulted all possible magazines, journals, newspapers and books. We are indeed thankful to their authors and publishers. We express our deep sense of gratitude to Justice V.N. Khare, Hon'ble Chief Justice of India for sparing his valuable time to contribute the illuminating Foreword to this book. Mr. S. Balwant, Mr. A. Pal, Mr. Raj Kumar Sethi, Mr. Sanjay Mehta, Mr. Surjit Pattnaik, Mr. Aslam Parvez, Mr. Inderlal Panjwani, Mrs. Manju Sethi, Mrs. Shamonu, Mr. Neeraj Budhiraja, Mr. Saurabh Bhagat, Dr. (Mrs.) Ravi Bala Dhingra, Mr. L.R. Bhutani and Mrs. Maya Ravindran have helped us in collecting photographs included in this book. Dr. B.N. Malhotra had also been of considerable help to us. We are grateful to him. Our thanks are due to them. We are also thanful to Dr. Rahul Malhotra for providing us some latest statistics.

The cover of this book as well as the illustrations within were prepared by Mr. Aslam Parvez, Propietor of Printplus. We would like to thank him for his painful endeavors. We are also thankful to Mr. J. L. Kumar, Managing Director, Anmol Publications Pvt. Ltd. for undertaking publication of this book and making it presentable.

Paulias Matane
December 15, 2003

of the land, people, agriculture, religious groups and cultural diversity and yet limit our study to this small and handy book, which could easily be made accessible to the individual readers. If this can help the readers in their places, we shall deem our efforts well-rewarded.

In our efforts to present to the readers up-to-date information, we have consulted all possible magazines, journals, newspapers and books. We are indeed thankful to their authors and publishers. We express our deep sense of gratitude to Justice V.N. Khare, Hon'ble Chief Justice of India for sparing his valuable time to contribute the illuminating Foreword to this book. Mr. [illegible] Pathak, Mr. A. Pal, Mr. Raj Kumar Sethi, Mr. Sanjay Mehta, Mr. Sumit [illegible], Mr. Aslam Parvez, Mr. Inderlal [illegible], Mrs. Manju Sethi, Mrs. [illegible], Mr. [illegible], Mr. Saurabh Singal, Dr (Mrs.) Pankaja Dhingra, Mr. I.K. [illegible] and Mrs. [illegible] have helped us in collecting photographs included in this book. Dr B.N. Malhotra had also been of considerable help to us. We are grateful to him. Our thanks are due to them. We are also thankful to Dr. Rahul Malhotra for providing us some latest statistics.

The cover of this book as well as the illustrations within were prepared by Mr. Aslam Parvez, Proprietor of [illegible]. We would like to thank him for his artistic endeavors. We are also thankful to Mr. J.L. Kumar, Managing Director, Anmol Publications Pvt. Ltd for undertaking publication of this book and making it presentable.

Paulias Matane
December [illegible], 2003

Contents

The Prologue

India is the cradle of the human race, the birthplace of human speech, the mother of history, the grandmother of legends, and the great grandmother of tradition. Our most valuable and most instructive materials in the history of man are treasured up in India only.

Mark Twain

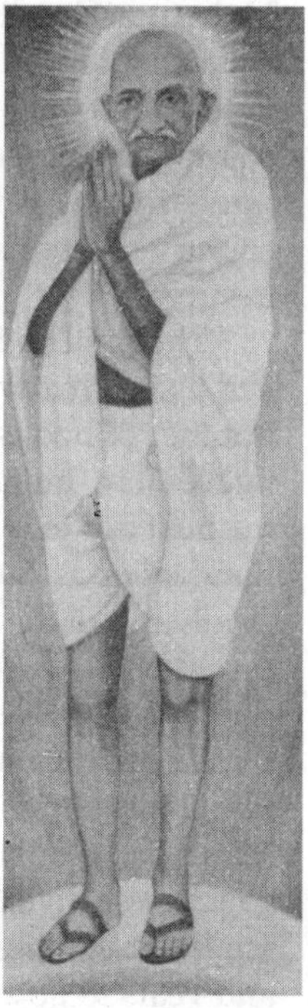

This kaleidoscopic view of India, as portrayed by Mark Twain in these lines, intensified my urge to go to India once again. Moreover, I had also an opportunity to read the life and philosophy of Mahatma Gandhi. Mohandas Karamchand Gandhi, whom the world called "Mahatma" or "Great Soul" spearheaded the non-violent movement first in South Africa and then in India. He navigated himself through the rapids of political activities by following Truth, which, for him, incorporated Love and Justice. He was anxious to show to the British that if Indians were conscious of their rights as British subjects they were equally eager to accept the corresponding responsibilities.

He laid emphasis on *khadi* (coarse cloth), village industries, a symbiotic relationship between human plant and animal life. The emphasis is relevant even today and a scheme of rural employment forms part of the Industrial Policy adopted by the Government of India. This policy envisages a dovetailing of heavy industries like steel, coal, oil, shipping, transport, power generation and a host of others which are capable of production through the rural and cottage sector. At the next stage, stands the medium industries, where mechanized production has obvious benefits of mass production and cost advantage. The small scale industries and the cottage and rural industries form the last rung of the ladder producing articles for local consumption with local raw materials on a decentralized basis.

For Mahatma Gandhi, religion was not a matter of orthodoxy, it was a matter of faith. All religions for him were equally worthy of man's respect. His inter-faith prayer meetings were symbolic of his spiritual position. He placed morality higher than everything else in life and insisted that Truth should form every individual's actions, whether political or economic. To him, a just cause did not justify unjust means and the means adopted for achieving a desirable end should also be fair and just. He used to talk of "inner voice", which is nothing more than conscience. A nation, he said, can hardly survive without character. This indeed is the quintessence of Mahatma Gandhi's philosophy, a man who fought for India's emancipation but didn't enjoy its fruits himself. He was a saint indeed. I bow to him and his ideals, which he espoused. How the country, which gave birth to this saint-politician—such persons are rarely found on this earth—should look like after 55 years of his country's freedom, for which he ceaselessly worked, was my keen desire.

Though I had been to India for the first time in the year 1967 and had visited many parts of this country several times, after reading a number of books about the country, I felt that I have yet to know many more things to understand what India is. I, therefore, planned my next trip to New Delhi, Agra and Jaipur. I carefully chose these three cities as they form a Golden Triangle to make the outsider familiar with the entire country.

India is a vast country with an area of 3,287,263 sq. km. and a population of over one billion, consisting of Hindus, Muslims, Sikhs, Buddhists, Jains and Parsis. Then there are people who speak Hindi, English, Bengali, Urdu, Punjabi, Marathi, Gujarati, Assamese, Manipuri, etc. How do they co-exist and interact? The more I read about these diverse elements, the more impatient I became to go and see for myself the life and culture of Indians. It should take months and years to go around the whole country. I, therefore, decided to visit only these three cities, which are often visited by most of the travelers who do not have the time and resources to go to the entire country, and yet are able to comprehend what India is all about.

Jenny, my daughter-in-law (wife of my first son Eddie) dropped me off at the International Departure Gate of Jackson's Airport of Port Moresby at 2 pm on March 6, 2003. Eddie was at the door of the B767 Air Niugini plane to bid me farewell on a 6-hour flight from Port Moresby to Singapore.

PX 392 took off at 3.40 pm. The flight, though long, was smooth and comfortable. Service offered by Air Niugini staff was excellent. Some fellow passengers, I met, were nice, helpful and friendly. These were pluses. Would my trip from Singapore to New Delhi be just as good? Would I be able to enjoy the trip? Answers to these remained to be seen.

When we arrived at Singapore's Changi Airport, I began to wonder where to stay and what to do, as I was to be there for 22 hours, right from 8.20 pm when I arrived there till 6.45 pm, the next day.

Instead of going out of that huge and most modern terminal, where you could find just about everything you need, I decided to check in at the Ambassador Transit Hotel for the night, which costs S$80 for a single room. But one has to share the toilet, shower and fitness facilities with other transit passengers.

I had been to Singapore many times since 1967 and had seen it blossoming from a poor third world nation to one of the fastest economically growing nations in the world under the dynamic leadership of Singaporean father and the first Prime Minister, Lee Kwan Yew (1959-1990). I have already recorded my impressions and reminiscences about Singapore in two of my 33 books and 4 articles in my column, "The Time Traveler" in the *National* newspaper, published during 2002.

The following day, I decided to use two hours in the morning of March 7 to tour "Little India" in Singapore, basically to prepare myself for the 2-week trip to the real India.

Clean and efficiently managed passenger buses operate in Singapore 24 hours a day. I boarded one outside Changi Airport and traveled directly to 141 Serangoon Road to visit the Sri Veeramakaliamman Temple. This is in the lively neighborhood, where one can see some of the island's finest Hindu temples. The particular temple was teeming with worshippers who were there to seek blessings from the Hindu Goddess Kali.

I strolled through narrow walkways to the blaring sounds of Hindi music. I admired the women as they pushed by in a rainbow of saris, leaving the sweet scent of jasmine flowers in their wake.

The famous Tekka Centre marks the threshold of Little India. A wet market, food and shopping complex rolled into one. Tekka means 'at the foot of the bamboo shoot' in a local dialect. The hawker centre on the ground floor offers an impressive spread of local favourites while the fresh produce markets attract loyalists who journey there for the wonderful array of vegetables and herbs.

By noon, I was back at Changi Airport to 'explore' its terminals. As mentioned earlier, Changi Airport is quite big and worth seeing. You can find there everything you need, or want to see: transit hotels, TV lounges/movie theatre, swimming pool, transpa, shower, fitness, nap, massage, oxygen therapy, gardens and koi ponds, snooze arcade, music lounges, free Singapore tour desk, business centre, money changers, prayer room, shops of all hues, restaurants, cyber cafe, post offices, and even the Sky Train. Isn't it amazing?

For those who are interested in nature, gardens in the terminals are available. I visited the following:

- **Cactus Garden**: This was voted Singapore's best rooftop garden at the Singapore Garden City Award 2001. This garden, located at the rooftop area, next to the Manna Restaurant, has 40 species of cacti and succulents found in the American, Asian and African regions.
- **Bamboo Garden**: A serene grove of supple-stemmed bamboo 'greeted' me as I entered the glass, granite sky-lit garden. Bamboo, commonly known to inspire architectural designs, is also a mystical plant that symbolizes strength, flexibility, endurance and modesty. The Bamboo Garden is located next to Gate D 46, Level 2.
- **Heliconia Garden:** This has more than 20 species of plants from the Heliconia and Ginger families. It is named after the mountain seat of the Greek God, Helican. Heliconia comes from as far as the Brazilian and South American plains. Speckled like jewels among the lush greenery of the garden, the red, yellow, orange, green and pink bracts of blooms truly filled me up with a sense of wonder and awe.
- **Sunflower Garden:** Strikingly colorful and vibrant, there were more than 14,000 species of flowering plants belonging to the

sunflower family in the world. I was spellbound by the happy and cheerful mood embodied by the sunflowers.

- **Fern Garden**: As I walked right into the canopy of overhanging fronds, I was enchanted by the majestic Tasmanian tree ferns, lush rosettes, of Bird's Nest ferns and feathery Boston ferns as I made my way through the diverse fern species.
- **Orchid Garden**: Orchid is Singapore's national flower. More than 15 species of orchids in colourful blooms were displayed in a natural landscape environment. As I stood there, I was mesmerized by the graceful orchid displays on natural drift wood species overhanging the Koi Pond.

I was still in the last garden when an announcement was made that Flight SQ408 from Singapore to New Delhi was soon to leave. I turned my mind away from the orchids and walked quickly to Gate E22. At 1545, I checked in, was issued Seat 87 D in a crowded Boeing 777-200, and, exactly at 1845, the plane lifted off. I was on my way to New Delhi, India's capital city. My mind was switched off from Singapore and was directed to the sub-continent of India.

I have visited parts of India many times since 1967. The more I visited the subcontinent, the more I find that I know less about it. Will this visit add more to my lack of knowledge about this great nation or will I know just a bit more about its land, environment, history, people, business, technology? These thoughts reverberated in my mind as I settled down in my seat.

As the flight was to take a little over 5 hours, I picked up several books and pamphlets about India and read some of them. One of these books was *Manorama Year Book 2003,* which provided me with an overview of the country. A study of the other book, *India's Continuity in Change*, gave me an insight into the land, people, culture and multifaceted development of the country. While going through some magazines, beautiful temples, *gurudwaras* and mosques as well as the marriage systems sparked in me the feelings to go and see them. By the way, I had two invitations to attend, one Hindu and another Muslim marriage, while I was to be in New Delhi.

If one were to capture the essence of the entire Indian sub-continent in a single word, it should be 'diversity'. There is a breathtaking range in every aspect of the country, from the very topography of the land, down to the array of snacks at its wayside stalls. This variety is manifest across the length and breadth of the land, and temporally with stone age tribes living in the shadow of atomic power plants. Overlaid on each other, one gets a multi-dimensional, multiple-colored tapestry of great richness and depth, as bewildering as it is beautiful, as subtle as it is exuberant.

Yet the diverse threads of this living tapestry, woven together in an underlying canvas of unifying shared experience and collective memory together provide one with a unique flavour that is unmistakably 'Indian'. This unity, too, permeates at every level, from geopolitical distinctiveness of the landmass to the film music that reverberates from teashops in every corner of the country.

The basis of this diversity indeed is the land itself, as I could gather. It has the highest mountain range in the world, as well as the low-lying mangrove swamps of the Sunderbans, which are daily submerged by the sea at high tide. To the west lie the sandy wastes of the Thar Desert, where the sand dumes and the camel ride attracts a number of tourists, while Mansynram in the Garo Hills of Meghalaya in the northeast is reputed to be the wettest spot on earth.

The diversity of India should further be manifest from its four main regions: the North, the South, the East and the West, each with its own characteristics—weather, environment, or even languages. Yet the whole country is well knit. It is a federal democracy and indeed the world's biggest democracy.

To the north of India, the Himalayas form an unbroken arc stretching 2400 kilomerers from the Pamir knot in the northwest to the Valley of the Brahmaputra River in the east. These, the highest and youngest mountains in the world, were formed when part of the ancient, prehistoric continent of Gondwana land (see my book, *Voyage to Antarctica,* Chapter 6) collided with the main Asian landmass, lifting it into gigantic fold mountains, some 17 million years ago. Geologically speaking, this is a fairly recent event, and the Himalayas are still rising under the continuing northward thrust of what is now the Deccan Plateau of Peninsular India.

The towering Greater Himalayas rise over 6000 meters in spectacular jagged peaks that include Mt. Everest in Nepal (8848 meters), the highest mountain in the world. In contrast, the Deccan Plateau is a stable mass of pre-Cambrian rocks, part of which are dated as 3.5 thousand million years old. It has been weathered over by wind, water and temperature differences into soft, rounded contours bounded by remnant hills. The plateau slopes gently to the east, and is drained by 4 rivers. These rivers have broken the Eastern Ghats into small, low hills, and their deltas have built up a relatively wide coastal plain bordering the Bay of Bengal. The Western Ghats fall steeply to a narrow coastal strip drained by many small streams running into the Arabian Sea, sometimes forming lovely inland lagoons and back-waters. The two coasts meet at Kanyakumari, the southernmost tip of India, at the confluence of the Bay of Bengal, the Arabian Sea and the Indian Ocean.

Between the Himalayas and the Deccan are the wide, flat and fertile Indo-Gangetic plains, formed by the silt carried down by the Himalayan rivers, and stretching 3330 kilometers between the two deltas. In the west, the five rivers were the cradle of Indian civilization. In the centre, the Yamuna at the sacred confluence at Allahabad joins the holy Ganga, worshipped as a manifestation of a Goddess. These rich alluvial plains supported successful empires and sophisticated civilizations. The mighty Brahamaputra flows north of the Himalayas for most of its length, then suddenly turns south, breaks through the mountains and does a U-turn through the Assam Valley, before joining the Ganga. The combined delta of these two rivers is the largest in the world. For South of the Sunderbans, where the Bay of Bengal merges with the Indian Ocean, lie the hauntingly beautiful Andaman and Nichobar Islands. The summits of a submerged chain of volcanic mountains, are covered with luxuriant tropical forests. Lakshadweep islands lie in the Arabian Sea of the South-West Kerala coast. Their crystal blue lagoons offer our eyes a feast of delicate corals and tropical marine life.

Diverse though is the land the subcontinent forms a self-contained geographical unit, bounded by the mountains to the north and by the seas to the south.

I was still engrossed in what the Indian land and environment could be when an announcement was made that we would soon land at Indira Gandhi International Airport at 9.50 pm (2.20 am PNG time on March 8, 2003). Immediately, I put my books away in a bag. The plane landed and taxied on to the arrival terminal. After checking out at Immigration and Custom, I walked to the Arrival Lounge as I had no unaccompanied luggage to collect. I stayed in Hotel Atithi Palace, 50 Darya Ganj, from where I was to explore India, as I had envisioned, during my brief sojourn. These 14 days, I must say, were quite rewarding when I could see for myself the 'unity in diversity'. Though one can discover India in its multifaceted aspects, I concentrated myself on the diversity of the people, their art and architecture, their culture and religion. I also visited a number of industries to tell the readers how best they can collaborate with the Indian entrepreneurs to benefit from their experience. I did this basically because there is already in place Papua New Guinea's Foreign Policy, which calls for us to 'Look North', nations to the north, to learn from their experiences in many areas, in my case, small to medium scale industries for our population. I will share these ideas with you in the last chapter of this book—the Epilogue.

1

Land, People and Governance

The Recent History

India, as I had learnt, is one of the oldest civilizations with astonishing variety and rich cultural heritage. After a prolonged struggle against British colonial rule, India became independent, within the Commonwealth, on August 15, 1947. The United Kingdom's Indian Empire was partitioned, broadly on a religious basis, between India and Pakistan. India emerged out of the long night of colonialism only to be feted in blood and hate. Freedom meant Partition, as India and Pakistan. The minds of the liberated too were partitioned, one of the most decisive mutilations in history. Kashmir remained a thorny issue. It has led to four wars between India and Pakistan and over 70,000 deaths in the mujahaideen-inflicted terrorism. A firm believer in Mohammed Ali Jinnah's two-nation theory, Pakistan refutes Kashmir's accession to India simply because it is a state with a Muslim majority.

The principal nationalist movement that had opposed British rule was the Indian National Congress, later known as the Congress Party. After Independence, the Congress leader, Jawaharlal Nehru, became India's first Prime Minister. Sectarian violence, the movement of 12 million refugees, the integration of the former princely states into the Indian federal structure and a territorial dispute with Pakistan over Kashmir, presented major problems to the new Government.

India became independent as a dominion, with the British monarch as Head of State, represented by an appointed governor-general. In November 1949, however, the Constituent Assembly approved a republican Constitution, providing for a president (with mainly ceremonial functions) as head of State. Accordingly, India became a republic on January 26, 1950, while remaining a member of the Commonwealth. France transferred sovereignty of Chandernagore to India in May 1950 and ceded its four remaining Indian settlements in 1954.

In 1956, the states were reorganized on linguistic basis. It was implemented in three waves: southern states in 1956 (birth of Andhra Pradesh), western states by 1960 (Gujarat), and north-western areas by 1966 (Punjab, Haryana and Himachal). The subsequent division of the north-eastern region (1964 and 1971) was on a tribal basis, as was the mini-reorganization of the Hindi heartland in 2000, creating Jharkhand, Chattisgarh and Uttaranchal. A unique experiment in unity in diversity, linguistic reorganization has provided robustness to Indian federalism.

The lack of effective opposition to Congress policies expedited industrialization and social reform. In December 1961, Indian forces overran the Portuguese territories of Goa, Daman and Diu, which was immediately annexed by India. Border disputes with the People's Republic of China escalated into a brief military conflict in 1962. Nehru died on May 24, 1969 and was succeeded by Lal Bahadur Shastri. India and Pakistan fought a second war over Kashmir in 1965. Following mediation by the USSR, Prime Minister Lal Bahadur Shastri and President Ayub Khan of Pakistan signed a joint declaration, aimed at a peaceful settlement of the Kashmir dispute on January 10, 1966. Shastri died on the following day, and Nehru's daughter, Indira Gandhi, became India's third Prime Minister.

Before Partition of the country, the pomp and pageantry of the erstwhile *Maharajas* (kings) were unrivalled, their wealth and indulgence being the stuff of legend and history. With their fabulous palaces, jewelry collections, elaborate *durbars* and fleet of luxury cars they became a definition for lavish hospitality and a privileged lifestyle. Some of them used priceless diamonds as paper weights. The fairy tale ended when Prime Minister Indira Gandhi introduced the 26th amendment to the Constitution of India in July 1971, abolishing privy purses and recognition granted to the rulers of Indian states. Privy purses, in proportion to the size of the revenue of former princely states, had been granted to the royal at the time of Independence as a *quid pro quo* for surrender of their ruling powers and dissolution of their states.

The March 1977 general election brought Jayaprakash Narain-led Janata Party to power. Morarji Desai became the Prime Minister. In 1979, a wave of defections by Lok Sabha members of the Janata Party paved the way to the resignation of Desai's Government and Charan

Singh became the leader of the Lok Dal and shortly afterwards the Prime Minister in a coalition with both the Congress parties. When Congress (I) withdrew its support, Charan Singh's 24-day administration collapsed, and Parliament was dissolved. 1980 general election again brought Indira Gandhi as Prime Minister, as her party secured an overwhelming majority.

There was unrest in the Sikh community of Punjab, despite the election to the Indian presidency in July 1982 of Giani Zail Singh, the first Sikh to hold the position. Demands were made for greater religious recognition for the settlement of grievances over water rights and the sharing of the state capital of Chandigarh with Haryana. In addition, a minority called for the creation of a separate Sikh State *(khalistan)*. The followers of an extremist Sikh leader, Jarnail Singh Bhindranwale, established a terrorist stronghold inside the Golden Temple (the Sikh holy shrine) at Amritsar. The Government sent in troops to dislodge the terrorists and the assault resulted in the death of Bhindranwale and hundreds of his supporters. In October 1984, militant Sikh members of her personal bodyguard assassinated Indira Gandhi. Her son, Rajiv Gandhi, was sworn in as Prime Minister.

In the November 1989 general election, the Congress (I) lost its overall majority. V P Singh of the National Front coalition was sworn in as the Prime Minister. In 1990, there was violence over the Government's populist decision to implement the recommendations of the 10-year old Mandal Commission and to raise the quota of the government and public-sector jobs reserved for deprived sections of the population. In October 1990, the BJP withdrew its support from the National Front. In November 1990, one of the Prime Minister's leading rivals in the Janata Dal, Chandrashekhar, formed his own dissident faction, known as Janata Dal (Socialist). V P Singh resigned and Chandrashekhar became the Prime Minister.

During the 1991 general election, on May 21, Rajiv Gandhi was assassinated. P V Narasimha Rao of the Congress took over as Prime Minister. The 1996 general election gave no party or group an overall majority. The largest party in terms of seats was the BJP. Atal Bihari Vajpayee of the BJP became the Prime Minister of the coalition government but had to resign after 13 days as he couldn't prove his majority on the floor of the House. The National Front and Left Front merged to form an informal coalition, known as the United Front, comprising of 13 parties. With the Congress offering external support the United Front formed the Government with H D Deve Gowda as the Prime Minister. In March 1997, Deve Gowda faced serious political crisis when the Congress threatened to withdraw its parliamentary support for the UF Government. On April 11, he resigned following the defeat of the UF administration in a vote of confidence by 158 votes to 292. A few days later, Inder Kumar Gujral, the Minister for External Affairs in the outgoing Government, was chosen by the UF to replace Deve Gowda as leader of the coalition and became the Prime Minister.

In the 1998 general election, the BJP and its regional allies established themselves as the pre-eminent force in Indian politics. On March 28, 1998, Atal Bihari Vajpayee became the Prime Minister of 14-party led coalition, which completed its 5-year term. The country has achieved multifaceted socio-economic progress since its Independence in 1947. The country claims to have become self-sufficient in agricultural production and is among the ten industrialized countries in the world and the sixth nation to have gone into outer space to conquer nature for the benefit of the people.

Physiography

India covers an area of 3,287,263 sq km, extending from the snow-covered Himalayan heights to the tropical rain forests of the south. It is bounded by the Himalayas in the north. It stretches southwards and at the Tropic of Cancer, tapers off into the Indian Ocean between the Bay of Bengal on the east and the Arabian Sea on the west. It has a land frontier of about 15,200 km. The total length of the coastline of the mainland, Lakshadweep Islands and Andaman and Nicobar Islands, is 7,516.6 km. Countries having a common border with India are Afghanistan and Pakistan to the north-west, China, Bhutan and Nepal to the north, Myanmar to the east and Bangladesh to the east of West Bengal. Sri Lanka is separated from India by a narrow channel of sea formed by the Palk Strait and the Gulf of Mannar.

Population

India's population, as on March 1, 2001, figured 1,027 million (531.3 million males and 495.7 million females). Of the total population, 16.48 per cent is of Scheduled Caste and 8.08 per cent of Scheduled Tribe. Though the latest figures are not available, according to 1991 Census, 74.3 per cent of the population is in rural areas while 25.7 per cent of the population lives in urban areas. The total number of villages is 580,781. The country accounts for a meager 2.4 per cent of the world surface area of 135.79 million sq km. Yet, it supports and sustains 16.7 per cent of the world population. The country has 28 States and 7 Union Territories. Delhi, the capital city of India, is the most thickly populated city with 9,294 persons per sq meter. West Bengal is the second most thickly populated State with a population density of 904 in 2001. Bihar is the highest densely populated state pushing Kerala to the third place. The sex ratio in the country had always remained unfavourable to females. It was 972 to 1000 males at the beginning of the twentieth century and in 2001 it is 933 to 1000 males.

In a country of over a billion people—with 20 million added every year—poised to take over as the world's most populous nation in another 20-odd years, the Government of India had to resort to measures for family planning. Launched in 1952, when the population was already a mammoth 369 million, the family planning program was designed primarily to get couples in the reproductive age to adopt safe contraceptive practices. Its symbol, the red inverted triangle, became as ubiquitous as the sign for fertilizers in rural India. Family planning became a bad word among politicians after Sanjay Gandhi's forceful sterilization drive during the Emergency, regarded as one of the major reasons for Indira Gandhi's defeat in the historic 1977 general elections. But, with the southern states showing the way with innovative schemes, the past two decades have seen a significant drop in population growth—the fertility rate dropped from 6 in 1951 to 2.85 in 1999. It is still a long way before India achieves zero population growth, but as a programme, it has an impact on every Indian couple's plans for a family.

Unity in Diversity

India is a secular state where we find Hindus, Muslims, Christians, Sikhs, Buddhists and others practicing their religions with equal freedom. According to 1991 Census, there are 82.41 per cent Hindus, 11.67 per cent Muslims, 2.32 per cent Christians, 1.99 per cent Sikhs, 0.77 per cent Buddhists. 0.41 per cent Jains, and 0.43 per cent of the population follow other religions. Though there are many languages, which are being spoken and written in 35 States and Union Territories, only 18 languages have been officially recognized. According to 1991 Census, Hindi is spoken and read by 39.85 per cent of the population, Bengali by 8.22 per cent, Telugu by 7.80 per cent, Marathi by 7.38 per cent, Tamil by 6.26 per cent, Urdu by 6.26 per cent, Gujarati by 4.81 per cent, Kannada by 3.87 per cent, Malayalam by 3.59 per cent, Oriya by

3.22 per cent, Punjabi by 2.76 per cent, Assamese by 1.55 per cent, Sindhi by 0.25 per cent, Nepali by 0.25 per cent, Konkani by 0.21 per cent, Manipuri by 0.15 per cent, and Sanskrit by 0.001 per cent.

National Symbols

India's national flag is a horizontal tricolour of deep saffron (kesaria) at the top, white in the middle and dark green at the bottom in equal proportion. The ratio of width of the flag to its length is two to three. In the centre of the white band is a navy-blue wheel, which represents the chakra. Its design is that of the wheel which appears on the abacus of the Sarnath Lion Capital of Ashoka. Its diameter approximates to the width of the white band and it has 24 spokes. The Government, through the provisions of the Emblems and Names (Prevention of Improper Use) Act 1950, regulates the display of the national flag.

The country's emblem is an adaptation from the Sarnath Lion Capital of Ashoka. In the original, there are four lions, standing back to back, mounted on an abacus with a frieze carrying sculptures in high relief of an elephant, a galloping horse, a bull and a lion separated by intervening wheels over a bell-shaped lotus. Carved out of a single block of polished sandstone, the Capital is crowned by the Wheel of the Law (*Dharma Chakra*). In the State emblem, adopted by the Government of India only three lions are visible, the fourth being hidden from view. The wheel appears in the centre of the abacus with a bull on right and a horse on left and the outlines of other wheels on extreme right and left. The bell-shaped lotus has been omitted. The words *Satyameva Jayate* from *Mundaka Upanishad,* meaning 'Truth Alone Triumphs', are inscribed below the abacus in Devanagari script.

The national bird of India is peacock, a colourful, swan-sized bird, with a fan-shaped crest of feathers, a white patch under the eye and a long, slender neck. The male of the species is more colourful than the female, with a glistening blue breast and neck and a spectacular bronze-green train of around 200 elongated feathers. The female is brownish, slightly smaller than the male and lacks the train. The elaborate courtship dance of the male, fanning out the tail and preening its feathers is a gorgeous sight.

Lotus (*Nelumbo Nucipera Gaertn)* is the national flower of India. It is a sacred flower and occupies a unique position in the art and mythology of ancient India. It is an auspicious symbol of Indian culture since time immemorial.

National Anthem

The national anthem of India is as under:

Jana-gana-mana-adhinayaka, jaya he
Bharata-bhagya-vidhata.
Punjab-Sindh,Gujarat-Maratha
Dravida-Utkala-Banga
Vindhya-Himachala-Yamuna-Ganga
Uchchala-Jaladhi-taranga.
Tava shubha name jage,
Tava shubha asisa mange,
Gahe tava jaya gatha,
Jana-gana-mangala-jaya he, jaya he,
Bharata-bhagya-vidhata.
Jaya he, jaya he, jaya he,
Jaya jaya jaya, jaya he!.

Translated into English, it reads as under:

Thou art the ruler of the minds of all people,
Dispenser of India's destiny.
The name rouses the hearts of Punjab, Sind, Gujarat and Maratha,
Of the Dravida and Orissa and Bengal;
It echoes in the hills of the Vindhyas and Himalayas,
Mingles in the music of Jamuna and Ganges and is
Chanted by the waves of the Indian Sea.
They prey for thy blessings and sing thy praise.
The saving of all people waits in thy hand,
Thou dispenser of India's destiny.
Victory, victory, victory to thee.

The song, Vande Mataram, composed in Sanskrit by Bankimchandra Chatterji, was a source of inspiration to the people in their struggle for freedom. It has an equal status with Jana-gana-mana. The first political occassion when it was sung was the 1896 session of Indian National Congress.

Vande Mataram,
Sujalam, suphalam, malayaja shitalam,
Shasyashyamalam, Mataram!
Shubhrajyothsna pulakitayaminim,
Phullakusumita drumadala shobhinim,
Suhasinim sumadhura bhashinim, Sukadam
varadam, mataram!

English translation of the stanza rendered by Sri Aurobindo (in Sri Aurobindo Birth Centernary Library, Popular Edition 1972, vol.8) is

I bow to thee, Mother,
richly-watered, richly-fruited,
cool with the winds of the south,
dark with the crops of the harvests, The Mother!
Her nights rejoicing in the glory of the moonlight,
Her lands clothed beautifully with her trees
in flowering bloom, sweet of laughter, sweet speech,
The Mother, giver of boons, giver of bliss.

Indian Economy

India entered the twenty-first century as a regional economic power, having recorded a sustained growth of 5-6 per cent on an average over the last two decades. It also accomplished a whole array of structural reforms in the area of trade, industry, taxation, exchange rate and financial sector to make itself financially competitive. Though, in the latter half of the 1990s, Asia and other regions faced financial crises, India's growth remained steady. The nineties saw India raise its per capita income by an annual average of 4 per cent. Its exports rose from 18 to 44 billion dollars in 2002. By March 2002, the country had the lowest rate of inflation in over two decades at around 2 per cent, based on the wholesale price index.

India's self-sufficiency in food production, achieved within the first three decades of independence, helped the country to do away with the imports of its basic needs. It reflected the success of the Green Revolution. By the end of 1990s, the country had built up a huge food reserve. The food stocks had mounted to around 60 million tones at the beginning of 2002.

This is because of Government's well-planned efforts through successive Five-Year Plans. The country embarked on planning for economic and social development in 1951 soon after independence in 1947. The planning is based on inspiration from the Soviet Union. Economic growth targets were set and the investments needed in different sectors of the economy to develop and facilitate the achievement of the physical targets were assessed. The plans embodied detailed framework for outlays in the public sector while the level of private investments in the rest of the economy was indicated in overall terms.

Enormous strides have been made in all fields in over 50 years of planned development. They are in per capita income, life expectancy, provision of basic services in urban and rural areas while the country made spectacular progress in diversifying and attaining the industrial base, ensuring food self-sufficiency and advancing a high technology, achieving capabilities in space and nuclear science and specialized skills in information technology. The financial sector saw a manifold expansion and the banking system, largely government-owned, has become competitive with the entry of Indian private and foreign entities.

The Tenth Five-Year Plan has raised the growth target to 8 per cent per annum and proposes monitorable targets on poverty reduction, primary education and raising of literacy rate, decline in infant and maternal mortality rates, and employment growth trends. The target for poverty reduction is 20 per cent, ensuring universal access to primary education and increase in literacy rate to 72 per cent in 2007 from 65 per cent at present. The present per capita income is US$2,230.

According to estimates of the World Bank, in 2001, India's gross national income (GNI), measured at average 1999-2001 prices, was US$474,323 million, equivalent to $460 per head (or $2,450 per head on an international purchasing power parity basis). During 1990-2001, it was estimated that the population increased at an average annual rate of 1.8 per cent, while gross domestic product (GDP) per head increased, in real terms, by an average of 3.5 per cent in 1990-2001. Overall GDP increased, in real terms, at an average annual rate of 5.4 per cent in 1990-2001. Growth reached 4.0 per cent in 2000-01 and 5.4 per cent in 2001-02.

Agriculture (including forestry and fishing) contributed an estimated 24.5 per cent of GDP in 2001. About 59.2 per cent of the economically active population were employed in agriculture in 2001. Industry (including mining, manufacturing, power and construction) contributed an estimated 27.1 per cent of GDP in 2001. According to World Bank estimates, about 12.9 per cent of the working population were employed in the industrial sector in 1995. Mining contributed an estimated 2.2 per cent of GDP during this period and employed 0.6 per cent of the working population in 1991. Manufacturing contributed an estimated 15.9 per cent and employed 10 per cent of the working population in 1991.

The services sector in India, which is dominated by the rapidly expanding data-processing business, the growing number of business call centres and the tourism industry, contributed an estimated 48.4 per cent and engaged 20.5 per cent economically active population in 1991. The average annual rate of population growth was an estimated 8.5 per cent in 1990-2001: consumer prices rose by 4.0 per cent in 2000 and by 3.7 per cent in 2001. In rural India, the number of people wholly unemployed, comprise about 6 per cent of the potential labour force for adult males, but the proportion is around 23 per cent when account is taken of underemployment.

India is a member of the Asian Development Bank (ADB), of the UN's Economic and Social Commission for Asia and the Pacific, of the South Asian Association for Regional Cooperation (SAARC), and of the Colombo Plan. Economic reforms undertaken by the then Finance Minister Dr Manmohan Singh in 1991 were the most momentous in Indian history. Along with major shifts in policies, they represented a bigger change in mindsets. Licence raj ended; almost all Central taxes were lowered and public-sector monopoly on the whole range of industries was broken. India began to taste economic freedom.

The process of wide-ranging economic reform initiated in 1991, including trade and investment liberalization, industrial deregulation, disinvestment by the Government in public sector enterprises and the gradual privatization, financial and tax reforms etc has continued despite several changes in the Government. Nevertheless, by the end of 2001-02, the Government had partially transferred a number of companies, including the telecommunications, monopoly of Videsh Sanchar Nigam Ltd. (VSNL) and Indian Tourism Development to the private sector. Restrictions on foreign participation in a number of sectors (including the pharmaceuticals industry) were eased or lifted to encourage greater foreign investment. In 2002-03, the Government negotiated the sale of stakes in Hindustan Zinc and car manufacturer, Maruti Udyog. In 2002, the Government decided to sell a stake in Hindustan Petroleum Corporation Ltd. to a strategic investor and portion on Bharat Petroleum Corporation Ltd. to the public through a share offering.

Despite the global economic slow down, software exports were forecast to expand by 30 per cent in 2002-03 to reach US$7000 million. The rapidly expanding industry presented increasing employment opportunities. Nevertheless, concern grew over the high number of qualified information technology professionals leaving the country for better-paid work elsewhere. In the early 2000, business call centres had become the faster growing industry in India, expanding by 70 per cent in 2002 and providing $1479 million revenue. An increasing number of multinational companies were moving their call centre operations to India, largely owing to cheaper labour costs and low long-distance telephone charges. Nasscum has estimated that the revenue from call centres would reach US$24,000 million by 2008.

Poverty

According to the NSSO Report 1999-2000, the percentage of people below the poverty line is 26.10 per cent nationwide. It was 54.09 per cent in 1973-74. The poverty situation in several states is appalling: Orissa 49.15 per cent, Madhya Pradesh 37.43, Sikkim 36.55 per cent and Tripura 34.44 per cent. In terms of numbers, Uttar Pradesh has 53 million, Bihar 43 million, Madhya Pradesh 30 million, Maharashtra 22 million, West Bengal 21 million, Orissa 17 million and Andhra Pradesh 12 million below the poverty line. It is based on the minimum required consumption expenditure level of items, such as food, clothing, shelter, transport and health care, which meets the average per capita daily calorie requirement of 2400 calories in rural areas and 2100 calories in urban areas, along with minimum of food expenditure. In 1999, the Planning Commission's Task Force worked out the monetary equivalent of the norms at Rs.327.56 per capita per month in the rural areas and Rs. 454.11 per capita per month in urban areas.

Transport

The transport system of the country comprises several modes, including rail, road, coastal shipping, air transport etc.

Railways form the major mode of transportation of passengers and goods. Indian railways are one of the largest systems in the world. It plays a vital role in the economic, industrial and social development of the country. Beginning in 1853, it has since grown into a vast network of 6,867 stations with a fleet of 7,517 locomotives, 35650 coaches, 5125 other coaching vehicles and 253,186 wagons. In 1999-2000, railways in India moved 431 billion passengers and 456.2 billion tones of freight.

India has one of the largest road networks in the world. It is growing at an average rate of 10 per cent. The Parliament approved the National Highways (Amendment) Bill 1995, which provides for

Car

Bus

Goods train

Truck

Tempo for goods

3-wheeler scooter

Motorcycle

2-wheeler scooter

Cyclericksaw

Cycle

Bullock cart

Tonga

Ship

Aeroplane

Camels

private investment, including foreign, in the building of national highways and their maintenance. The national highways network of 57,737 km (2001) constitutes less than 2 per cent of the total road network, but carries nearly 40 per cent of the total road traffic. In 2000, there were 6042000 private cars, jeeps and taxis, 559000 buses and coaches, 268100 goods vehicles, 33913000 motorcycles and scooters, and 5198000 other forms of transport like *rerha* (horse-driven vehicle for carrying mainly goods), bullock carts, bicycles, *rickshaws,* etc.

The Government has ended the monopoly of Indian Airlines and Air India on the scheduled operations by repealing the Air Corporation Act 1953. Indian Airlines, Alliance Air, private scheduled airlines and air taxis provide domestic service whereas Air India international service. At present, there are three private scheduled airlines operating on the domestic network giving passengers more choice of flights. Air India operates to 35 destinations and 12 additional destinations through arrangements with foreign airlines. In 1998, it owned a fleet strength of 23 aircrafts comprising of B747-400, B747-300, B747-200, A300-B4, and A310-300. Indian Airlines operated 69 domestic stations and 17 international stations. It then had a fleet of 57 aircrafts. Pawan Hans Helicopters Ltd. provides helicopter services to ONGC and to inaccessible areas and difficult terrain. It operates 30 helicopters. There are 47 air taxi operators providing non-scheduled air services.

Ports in India are governed by the Indian Ports Act 1908. At present, 90 per cent of the country's international trade in terms of volume and 77 per cent in terms of value is moved by sea. The country continues to have the largest merchant shipping fleet among the developing countries and ranks 17th in the world in terms of shipping tonnage. There are 12 major ports in India apart from 181 minor working ports along the coastline of 5,560 km. Kandla, Mumbai, Mormugoa, New Mangalore, Cochin and Jawaharlal Nehru Port are the major ports of West Coast. On the east coast, Tuticorin, Chennai, Visakhapatnam, Paradip and Kolkata-Haldia are the major ports. All the major ports are administered in accordance with the provisions of the Major Port Trust Act 1963. The major ports handled a total cargo traffic of 281 million tones during 2000-01. There were 122 shipping companies in India operating in April 2001, including Shipping Corporation of India, a public sector company and 10 other government agencies. There are 4 major and 3 medium size shipyards in the country in the public sector.

The Governance

The Constitution of India envisages parliamentary form of government, federal in structure with unitary features. President of India is constitutional head of executive of the Union. The Council of Ministers, headed by the Prime Minister, aids and advises the President who acts in accordance with such advice. Real executive power vests in the Council of Ministers. Council of Ministers is collectively responsible to the House of the People (Lok Sabha). Similarly, in states, Governor is head of executive, but it is the Council of Ministers with Chief Minister as head in whom the real executive power vests. Council of Ministers of a state is collectively responsible to the Legislative Assembly. The Constitution distributes legislative powers between Parliament and state legislatures and provides for vesting of residual powers in Parliament. Power to amend the Constitution also vests in Parliament. The Constitution has also provision for independent judiciary, Comptroller and Auditor-General, Public Service Commissions and Chief Election Commissioner.

As already explained, India comprises of 28 States and seven Union Territories. The country's Constitution offers all citizens, individually and collectively, some basic freedom. These are guaranteed in the Constitution and are contained in Part III of the Constitution, which deals with Fundamental Rights. They are: (I) right to equality including equality before law, prohibition of discrimination on grounds of religion, race, caste, sex or place of birth and equality of opportunity in matters of employment; (ii) right to freedom of speech and expression; assembly; association or union; movement; residence; and right to practice any profession or occupation. Some of these rights are subject to security of the State, friendly relations with foreign countries, public order, decency or morality; (iii) right against exploitation, prohibiting all forms of forced labour, child labour and traffic in human beings; (iv) right to freedom of conscience and free profession, practice and propagation of religion; (v) right of any section of citizens to conserve their culture, language or script and right of minorities to establish and administer educational institutions of their choice; and (vi) right to constitutional remedies for enforcement of Fundamental Rights.

The Indian Constitution lays down certain Directive Principles of State Policy which, though not justiciable, are 'fundamental in governance of the country' and it is the duty of the State to apply these principles in making laws. Accordingly, the State shall strive to promote the welfare of the people by securing and protecting as effectively as it may a social order in which justice—social, economic and political—shall form in all institutions of national life. The State shall direct its policy in such a manner as to secure the right of all men and women to an adequate means of livelihood, equal pay for equal work and within limits of its economic capacity and development, to make effective provision for securing the right to work, education and to public assistance in the event of unemployment, old age, sickness and disablement or other cases of undeserved want. The State shall also endeavour to secure to workers a living wage, humane conditions of work, a decent standard of life and full involvement of workers in management of industries. In the economic sphere, the State is to direct its policy in such a manner as to secure distribution of ownership and control of material resources of community to subserve the common good and to ensure that operation of economic system does not result in concentration of wealth and means of production to common detriment. Some of the other important directives relate to provision of opportunities and facilities for children to develop in a healthy manner, free and compulsory education for all children up to the age of 14; promotion of education and economic interests of scheduled castes, scheduled tribes and other weaker sections; organization of village panchayats; separation of judiciary from executive, promulgation of a uniform civil code for the whole country; protection of national monuments; promotion of justice on the basis of equal opportunity; provision of free legal aid; protection and improvement of environment and safeguarding of forests and wildlife of the country and promotion of international peace and security; just and honourable relations between nations, respect for international law, treaty obligations and settlement of international disputes by arbitration.

Legislature of the Union is called Parliament, which consists of President and two Houses, known as Council of States (Rajya Sabha) and House of the People (Lok Sabha). Rajya Sabha consists of 250 members, of which 12 members shall be nominated by the President from amongst persons having special knowledge or practical experience in respect of such matters as literature, science, art and social service, and not more than 238 representatives of the States and of the Union Territories. Elections to the Rajya Sabha are indirect. Members representing states are elected by elected members of legislative assemblies of the States in accordance with the system of proportional representation by means of the single transferable vote, and those representing Union Territories are chosen in such a manner as Parliament may, by law, prescribe. The Rajya Sabha is not subject to dissolution. One-third of its members retire every second year. At present, Rajya Sabha has 245 seats. Of these, 233 members represent the States and the Union Territories and the President nominates 12 members.

The Lok Sabha is composed of representatives of people chosen by direct election on the basis of adult suffrage. The maximum strength of the House, envisaged by the Constitution, is now 552. Of this, 530 members are to represent the States, 20 to represent Union Territories and not more than two members of Anglo-Indian community to be nominated by the President, if, in his opinion, that community is not adequately represented in the House. At present, Lok Sabha consists of 545 members. The term of the Lok Sabha, unless dissolved, is five years from the date appointed for its first meeting. However, while a proclamation of emergency is in operation, this period may be extended by Parliament by law for a period not exceeding one year at a time and not extending, in any case, beyond a period of six months after the proclamation has ceased to operate.

The year 2002 marked the fiftieth year of constituting the Lok Sabha. The first general elections under the new Constitution were held during the year 1951-52 and the first Prime Minister of India was Jawaharlal Nehru. The first President of India was Dr Rajendra Prasad. Since then there have been 13 more general elections.

The tenure of the first Lok Sabha was from May 13, 1952 to April 4, 1957. The Second Lok Sabha was from May 10, 1957 to March 31, 1962. The Third Lok Sabha was from April 16, 1962 to March 3, 1967. The fourth Lok Sabha was from March 4, 1967 to December 27, 1970. The Fifth Lok Sabha was from March 19, 1971 to January 18, 1977. The Sixth Lok Sabha was from March 25, 1977 to August 22, 1979. Seventh Lok Sabha was from January 21, 1980 to December 31, 1984. The Eighth Lok Sabha was from January 15, 1984 to November 27, 1989. The Ninth Lok Sabha was from December 18, 1989 to March 13, 1991. Tenth Lok Sabha was from July 9, 1991 to May 10, 1996. Eleventh Lok Sabha was from May 22, 1996 to December 4, 1997. Twelfth Lok Sabha was from March 23, 1998 to April 26, 1999. The Thirteenth Lok Sabha was constituted on October 20, 1999 and the next General Elections are likely to be held in 2004. The Ninth Lok Sabha was dissolved after having been in existence for a period of one year, six months and 13 days. The Eleventh Lok Sabha was also dissolved after having been in existence for a period of one year, one month and four days.

India has over 550 registered political parties who represent different shades of ideologies and factors. They are categorized as National, State and Registered Parties. A party, which gets 4 per cent of the valid polled votes or 1/25th of the total seats in a State is considered as a State or Recognized Party. A party, which gets 4 per cent of the total valid votes or 1/25th of the seats in four or more States, is recognized as a National Party. The National Party has the same election symbol all over the country. While the poll symbols of the State parties differ from State to State, the Registered parties can pick up any symbol. There were 6 National Parties, 40 State Parties and over 504 Registered Parties in 1998.

Indian National Congress, established in 1885, is the oldest political party in India with a track record of great sacrifices made by its leaders. It had been in power both at the Centre and the States during the prime ministership of Jawaharlal Nehru and Indira Gandhi, except during Emergency when Indira Gandhi lost power to Janata Party in 1977. It was for the first time that Indian National Congress was routed out of power. Within three years, the seventh general elections in 1980 brought the Congress back to power under the leadership of Indira Gandhi. After her assassination, the Congress Party opted her son, Rajiv Gandhi, as the Prime Minister, but the Party lost power in the 1989 general elections. For the first time since Independence in 1947 a 'Hung Parliament' was thrown in with no party or group getting a clear majority, though the Congress (I) had 193 seats followed by the Janata Dal with 141 seats and the Bharatiya Janata Party with 88 seats.

Therefore, the National Front, a combination of five parties, became the party in power with V P Singh as the Prime Minister. Since then no political party has been able to get absolute majority and the country is being ruled by coalition governments. In the 12th Lok Sabha, the Bharatiya Janata Party and its 18 political allies formed the coalition government. The BJP-led coalition government was in power for about 18 months, including five months as caretaker government at the Centre. However, the coalition failed to win the vote of confidence in February 1999. In the 13th general elections, the BJP and its allies unitedly worked under the umbrella of National Democratic Alliance (NDA). The BJP-led 13-party coalition, headed by Atal Bihari Vajpayee, has, however, been able to complete its term of 5 years due to the charisma and statesmanship of Prime Minister Vajpayee.

In addition to the Congress and the BJP, the other major political parties are: the Communist Party of India, the Communist Party of India (Marxist), Janata Dal (United), Bahujan Samaj Party, Telugu Desam Party, Rashtriya Janata Dal, Lok Shakti, Samata Party (now merged in Janata Dal-United), Samajwadi Party, Dravida Munnetra Kazhagam (DMK), All India Anna Dravida Munnetra Kazhagam (AIADMK), Akali Dal, and National Conference.

There has been a growing trend of regional parties making an impact on the Indian political scene. It became evident when in 1996 the United Front government was formed at the Centre with the support of 13 parties. The Congress, which had been assiduously fostering the concept of majority government and stability, is no more averse to this coalition politics. This became apparent in a number of states. As a result of these new trends in Indian politics, regional parties have held sway. They are: AIADMK in Tamil Nadu, Telugu Desam in Andhra Pradesh, Rashtriya Janata Dal in Bihar, Sikkim Democratic Party in Sikkim, Arunachal Congress in Arunachal Pradesh, and Manipur People's Party in Manipur, the Communist Party of India (Marxist) in West Bengal and Tripura. The BJP had partnership with Bahujan Samaj Party in Uttar Pradesh.

The Congress and the Janata Dal have mainly contributed to the growth of regional parties. Trinamool Congress, the Karnataka Vikas Party, and Bihar Jan Congress, for instance, are offsprings of the Congress. The Janata Dal had always been vulnerable to splits. An influential section of the party in Orissa broke away to launch the Biju Janata Dal. The party also suffered its worst setback after the entire Bihar unit broke away with Laloo Prasad Yadav launching the Rashtriya Janata Dal and Ramakrishna Hegde floated the Lok Shakti in Karnataka. In 1999, it further split, thus making it Janata Dal (Secular) and Janata Dal (United). However, on the eve of Assembly elections in 2003, Samata Party merged in Janata Dal (United).

The rise of the regional parties has been mainly because of the substantial failure of the High Command system in the Congress, the BJP or the Janata Dal. Many of the regional forces have been the offshoots of the Congress, whether it was Charan Singh's Bharatiya Kranti Dal in Uttar Pradesh or Ajoy Mukherjee's Bangla Congress in West Bengal or Bansi Lal's Haryana Vikas Party in Haryana. All of them have been the outcome of a rebellion against the central leadership favouring the rival faction within the State Congress.

Similarly, Waghela's party was born out of a revolt against the BJP President who had sided the rival faction in Gujarat BJP. The other regional parties had their anti-Congress attitude as their basic foundation. Shiv Sena in Maharashtra, Telugu Desam in Andhra Pradesh, Akali Dal in Punjab and Asom Gana Parishad had always been opposed to Congress and this paid them electoral dividends. Control of the Central Government and domination of a majority of the states also gave a big impetus to regionalism. The regional parties too have kept themselves strong by a mixture of regionalism and pragmatism. The flexibility helped them to stay ahead of their national or regional levels. Therefore, what is required is the balancing of ideology. This is where the present BJP-led National Democratic Alliance has succeeded by completing its full tenure of five years under the leadership of Atal Bihari Vajpayee.

Elections in India are conducted by the Election Commission of India, which is an independent constitutional authority set up to superintend, direct and control the preparation of electoral rolls and conduct elections. The Commission is guided by the Representation of People Act 1950, Representation of People Act 1951, Presidential and Vice-Presidential Elections Act 1952, Government of Union Territories Act 1963, Government of the National Capital Territory of Delhi Act 1991 and the Rules and Orders made under them.

In 1999, the Commission started its experiment for the use of electronic voting machines for the first time in State Legislative Assembly of Goa. These machines were later used in 45 parliamentary constituencies across the country during the 13th General Election, covering more than 65,000 polling stations and an electorate of over 60 million, in selected constituencies during state assembly elections and in all the assembly constituencies in December 2003. This process, it has been felt, facilitates quick election results.

There has been a steady growth in the electorate and the contesting candidates. In 1952, for an electorate of 173,213,635 there were 1864 contestants for 489 seats and 196,084 polling stations were set up. In 1988, the number went up to 605,884,103 with 773,494 polling stations and 4,750 candidates were in fray for 543 seats. Of these, 271 were women contestants but only 43 won.

A good deal of money and muscle power is used in elections. The Election Commission has introduced the system of Identity Cards to curb the malpractice of impersonation. Every candidate is required to submit an account of his expenses for the election in a particular manner. It has been stated that in 1993, the Commission sent video camera crew at several places in many constituencies to record scenes of ostentatious election activities. The Commission ordered that political parties, which splashed their slogans and symbols on private or public walls, should wash them off after elections. Central and state governments were asked not to take policy decision after the polls are announced. Television programs to analyze the election trends and results before the counting of votes were banned. Strict codes of conduct were laid. The election laws have undergone some important changes. To discourage the increasing number of contestants, especially the independents, the amount of security deposit has been enhanced. There is a restriction on contesting election from more than two constituencies. Prohibition has been imposed on going armed to or near a polling station. The Law Commission has proposed some fundamental changes to overcome political instability in the coalition era.

If one gets an opportunity to cover elections in India, it is difficult to believe that India is a poor country. There was a time when political parties used to hold rallies, organize meetings, and communicate their messages through banners and posters. The election campaigns in India have acquired new dimension. The political parties hire special planes for their leaders and advertising agencies are engaged for their campaigns. Celphones, pagers, fax machines, e-mails and slick documentaries are the normal means of communication. A carefully orchestrated machinery is put to work with proper assignments. In 1996, television only covered the news. Advertising agencies were used and there were restrictions on the use of banners and posters, the candidates fought their individual battles through the medium of newspapers and electronic media. A host of private channels joined the fray, bombarding the viewers with news programmes and special election bulletins to reach viewers at the national level. The 12th General Elections became a television election. Posters and hoardings being virtually banned and limit on loudspeakers having been imposed by the Election Commission after 10 pm, elections became no longer the road shows. The various political parties also made use of film stars to attract people in their meetings. Special audiocassettes and video films are prepared.

Standard of Living

What's the general standard of living of the Indian people and how much is the gap between the urban and rural India? I was curious to know. Luckily, I was able to get official information from the Census 2001. The Census 2001 was different from the earlier ones. Instead of using the traditional category of population, gender, religion and urban/rural break-up, this time it expanded itself into household amenities, which could facilitate proper planning for the Government. Ordinary Indians were asked questions about their surroundings—their homes, the amenities they enjoyed and the consumer products they acquired in their households. The scenario, as portrayed by *India Today*, August 1, 2003, is as follows:

> By 2001, there were 179 million residential houses in India, that is about 6 people to each house. Of these, 53.7 million were in urban India and 5.5 million in rural areas. Among the urban houses, 15 millions (29 per cent) had been rented. Only 21 per cent of the houses had concrete roof—31.8 million (44 per cent) in urban areas and 21.1 million (12 per cent) in rural areas. 82.2 million (35 per cent) houses had cement roof—50 per cent in urban areas. 73.8 million Indians (39 per cent) lived in one room—18.9 million (35 per cent) urban and 55 million (40 per cent) rural. There were 220 million married couples in India—57 million urban and 163 million rural. Of these, 38.6 million (68 per cent) had independent rooms in urban and 95.4 million (58 per cent) in rural areas. Only 23 per cent of the rural families had bathrooms in their houses. 70 per cent of the urban households had bathrooms in their houses.

The Census 2001 has also revealed some more interesting results.

> Some households in India at that time were without kitchen or toilets but they had television sets and two wheelers. 61 million families had television in their homes. Families in India generally view television as a priority item. They will walk for miles from their homes to bathe and to attend nature's call, but would watch television within the confines of their homes. In 2001, rural India had 260mTV sets, one in every five families. That explains why there are more brands of television than any other consumer electronic product in India. 35 per cent families had radio at that time. 22.5 million (12 per cent) Indians then had two wheelers. Of them, 13.3 million (25 per cent) were in urban areas and 9.2 million (7 per cent) in rural areas.

> By 2001, India had 5 million private cars, not counting those owned by the government or used for commercial purposes. The sale of car zoomed up in 2003 with a monthly sale of 50,000. On two-wheeler ownership, rural India is fast catching up with cities. Almost every second home in India has a bank account. In 2001, 68 million households (35 per cent) had bank account—26.6 million (50 per cent) in urban areas and 41.6 million (30 per cent) in rural areas.
>
> For the population of over one billion there are about 12,500 screens, which translate into a minuscule of less than 13 screens per million. Urban Indians are reportedly spending over Rs.100 each on tickets plus the mandatory coke and popcorn break. On an average, about 4000 people see movies in one multiplex every day.

There has been a vast revolution in the field of communication. The cable industry has been in existence for over a decade, though the Cable Television Networks (Regulation) Act was passed in 1995. The entertainment revolution began innocuously enough with local channels telecasting Hindi movies. But the 1991 Gulf War made CNN a household acronym in India. In July 1993, Rupert Murdoch's $525 million acquisition of a 63.6 per cent stake in Star TV made viewers swap aerial antennae for satellite dishes. A 50:50 joint venture between NewsCorp and Zee TV in 1995—dissolved in 1999—changed the destiny of Indian TV, propelling it into the global village, allowing the viewer to make the transition from one terrestrial channel to 70 satellite networks. By the middle of 2003, there were 70 satellite channels and 30,000 cable operators to provide access to 40 million households.

For years, Indians used to live by the maxim, *utne paon pasariye jitni lambi chaadar* (stretch your legs such that your legs don't stick out of the blanket). Keeping this in view, purchases used to be limited to savings or income. Similarly, one could create assets either out of savings or through inheritance. To be in debt was considered unwise and mortgage the future. This is no longer so now. Indians would rather stretch their legs beyond the blanket to live like a king. The DSP Merrill Lynch Indian Economics report reveals that bank lending to individuals have trebled from Rs. 536,000m to over Rs.1600,000m in five years as Indians borrow and spend on homes, cars, consumer goods, durable items, marriages and even holidays. It is simply because the banks in India have become quite liberal in giving loans and the interest rates have gone down considerably.

There has also been a fundamental shift in the economics architecture. The services sector, which needs little capital, is blooming. The DSP Merrill Lynch India Demographics report states that the number of households in the upper middle and high income groups has shot up and is set to double from 25m to 44m in 2007. Banks are now in a race to use psychological means to acquire clientele. One can get anything, big or small, and pay it in easy instalments.

It is now hard to believe the slogan *roti, kapada aur makan,* which we once used to hear from the political parties in India during the election campaigns. Cell phones are now considered to be flashy toys. In New Delhi, we can see almost every fourth person holding it whether he or she is young, old or a student even. It has even reached the Indian villages. Till a few years before 1999, even a basic telephone was a rationed asset, which only a privileged could possess. Today, over 20 million Indians—including farmers and fishermen—don't leave their homes without their cell phones. This is largely due to the opening up of the telecom sector to the private sector in the mid-1990s, which not only brought choices of different service providers but also introduced the concept of customer service. In a country where for 40 years owning a phone was more difficult than owning a house, a basic telephone connection is finally just a call away. The 1999 shift from the license fee era to the one of revenue sharing between the government and the telecom operators triggered crashing of cell phone tariffs from Rs.16 a minute to one Indian rupee.

An Emerging Developed Nation

By exploding the first nuclear device on May 18, 1974 in the Pokhran desert in Rajasthan India joined the club of nuclear powers, then the exclusive preserve of the Big Five. It earned for India respect from much of the world but made it a pariah with the US. The explosion also triggered a nuclear race in the subcontinent. The launch of SLV-3, India's pencil-thin satellite launcher, on July 18, 1980 changed India's image as a country driven by bullock-cart power. As a rocket, it may not have been much when compared with those made by space giants. But SLV-3 was a forerunner of a series of giant rocket launchers that by the 1990s had propelled India as a space power to reckon with. The rocket, which also thrust its team leader Dr A P J Abdul Kalam (now President of the Republic of India) to fame, could punch a satellite,

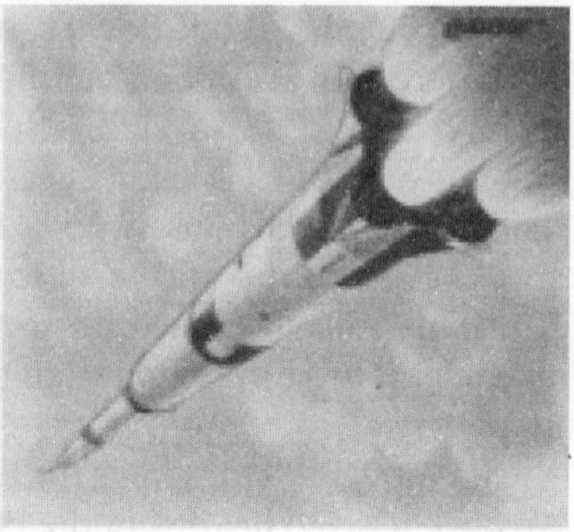

weighing only 30 kg, about 300 km into the space. But today India has the capability to hurl satellite, weighing two tones or as much as a truck, 36,000 km, into space. India's telephone companies and television channels now largely depend on satellites, that are built indigenously, saving the country substantial foreign exchange. More than this, the space program changed the way Indian scientific establishments could be run by introducing the mission approach to management. For the Indians now 'Made in India' is no longer a tag to be ashamed of and they can now boast of their country's accomplishments in social, economic, political, scientific and technical fields for promoting their goods in the overseas markets.

2

The Golden Triangle

On March 8, 2003, I was still fast asleep in Room No.113 of Hotel Atithi Palace in New Delhi, when a copy of that day's newspaper, *The Hindustan Times*, was pushed in under the door of my room. I rubbed my sleepy eyes, recollected my thoughts and realized that I was not in my Viviran village house in the Toma LLG, but in Delhi, the National Capital Territory of India, formed in the 11th century A D by a Rajput Chieftain of the Tomara Clan. From the Hindu King in the 11th century to the citadel of the biggest democracy of the world must have necessarily ushered in a substantial change for visitors, like me, to cherish, I thought.

While I was thinking of this, the hotel boy slipped a pamphlet in my room describing a daily trip to Delhi, Agra and Jaipur. The cities of Delhi, Agra and Jaipur, in fact, are popularly known as the Golden Triangle of India, as the largest number of tourists to India go to these cities. These areas are well equipped with places to stay. The choice of accommodation ranges from up-market luxury hotels run by international or leading Indian chains to small guesthouses and youth hostels. In addition, there are state-run hotels in several towns, with comfortable boarding and lodging facilities at reasonable rates. Then, there are grand old palaces and monuments, which re-create the lavish lifestyles of former rulers and aristocracy. One can also stay in *ashrams* and small guesthouses, which provide at least the basic facilities. Again, in this region one comes across people of all religions following different professions. It is indeed a mini India. On knowing this, I decided to see as much as possible in these cities and share this information with the readers at large.

Delhi

Delhi, as I was told, is, undoubtedly the fine mosaic of old and new. It is the only city where one can see everything that one wants to see in

India. Not the high Himalayas or the palm-fringed sea beaches, but everything else: people of all races, religions and languages, a history that spans centuries, beginning a thousand years before the advent of Christ to the present day. The city has ancient temples, mosques, mausoleums, palaces and castles, congested *bazaars* seething with humanity, huge parks, spacious gardens, wide-open vistas lined by flowering trees, a baffling variety of flora and fauna, and even slums. It is a vibrant city, full of activity. It is a major cultural center of the country with music, dance and art events held throughout the year.

Delhi, with its present name of National Capital Territory (NCT), is spread over an area of 1,483 sq km and has a population of 13,782,976, according to 2001 Census, speaking Hindi, Punjabi, Urdu and English. It has 214 villages but more than 90 per cent of Delhi's population lives in the urban area. The urban area of Delhi is mostly thickly populated with 9,294 persons per sq km. and literacy rate of 81.82 per cent. It has been ranked as the second-most affluent state of India with a per capita income of Rs 26,600 a year, against the national average of Rs. 13,000.

The city of Delhi was founded in the 11th century A D by a Rajput Chieftain of Tomara clan. The Chauhans obtained possession of the city from Tomaras. Prithvi Raj, the Chauhan ruler of Ajmer and Delhi, made the city of Delhi famous by his heroic valour and romantic adventures. The city under Prithvi Raj and Kanauj under Jai Chand was the principal kingdom of north India at that time. In 1192, Delhi passed into the hands of Muslim rulers for the next six centuries. Under the Mughal Emperor, Delhi became a world famous city. In 1857, following the mutiny of the Indian troops, the British deposed the titular Emperor Bahadur Shah and formally annexed Delhi. In 1912, the capital of British India was transferred from Calcutta to Delhi. A new city—New Delhi—of imposing dimensions was laid out by the side of the old city,Old Delhi, by the British Indian Government. Independent India has retained this historic capital.

When we talk of Delhi, it is both Old Delhi as well as New Delhi. What is known as Old Delhi today was originally the Mughal capital of Shahjahanabad, built by Shah Jahan when he moved the imperial court from Agra to Delhi. Construction began in 1638. Rubble wall pierced Delhi by 14 gates of which three survive. Old Delhi has now been considerably expanded to accommodate the refugees from West Pakistan after partition in 1947. The large number of migrants from many states, who come here either in search of job or for education, have further resulted in an increase in population. Travelling through the city, I discovered that Delhi is the largest commercial hub in Northern India. I was able to see a number of small industries located in the residential areas. People seem to be quite hard working. These small industries manufacture TV sets, musical systems, electrical goods, textiles, hosiery, leather goods, soft drinks, etc. There are also units for metal forging, casting, galvanizing, electroplating, printing and warehousing. I was told that around 900,000 people work in approx. 89,000 units.

I then turned my attention to the newspaper of the day. As usual, there were many reports on the World Cup which was being competed for in South Africa, negative reports on the possible war headed by the USA/UK against Iraq, social, political and economic problems of the world. But what struck me most was a small 12-line news item with the heading "Delhi Most Polluted" out of 10 Indian cities. And I was to visit three of these polluted cities. As a matter of fact, the statement was attributed to the Minister of State for Environment and Forests, Dileep Singh Judev. But when one is reminded of the above facts of Delhi, the growing population, the expanding industries, and the large number of vehicles on roads, pollution becomes inevitable. Is there any escape from this growing pollution and is the Government seized of this?

While I was thinking of all this, my eyes glanced at a small column of Khushwant Singh, the prominent journalist of India. In his column titled "India in Miniature", he stated:

> My India is now confined to my little backyard. I spend most of my day from sunrise to sunset watching life go by. No one misses me; I miss no one. My patch of garden tells me how things are going on in the country. Seasons change with alarming suddenness ... For a couple of days, strings of yellow jasmines hang down over my verandah and cherry trees come into blossom. They fade and the fragrance of orange blossom pervades the atmosphere, while fluffs of pale white flowers sprout on my mango trees .... My little garden of Eden has high-rise buildings on three sides. Two are occupied by upper middle-class families, one by their servants. I have India in miniature in my own backyard. Anyone, who does not earn his living by honest labour, drapes himself in saffron or white robes, goes stark naked or dressed in ashes and ... becomes a saint or a *mahatma* ... We Indians hold saints and *sadhus* in awe ... Once a person declares himself a saint, his life becomes much easier. If

> he has any wits about him, he gathers followers who look after his worldly needs. He is a *nikhattoo* (non-earner) and a *kaamchor* (work-shy). Akbar Illahabadi put it neatly.

The writer Khushwant Singh is about 94 and he has to spend his last days at home, though he had been quite active so far. Like Khushwant Singh, there are many people who are fortunate to enjoy beautiful ambience in spite of the fact that Delhi is a congested city and many people, especially in the walled city, cannot breathe fresh air.

On March 11, 2003, *The Times of India* carried a news item, "Is Delhi a Safe City for Senior Citizens?" written by Dependra Pathak and M N Bhattacharjee. The column reads:

> Senior citizens have always been considered vulnerable by criminal elements ... Senior citizens living with their families are far less vulnerable than those living alone ... A few years ago, Delhi witnessed a spate of crimes against senior citizens ... Ensuring safety for the elderly has always been a priority for the Delhi Police. It has been effectively running the senior citizens scheme for decades.

Though there have been cases of murder and rape in Delhi, police in Delhi is quite vigilant and sympathetic. Why Delhi has become so much polluted and congested? Rapid economic development and urbanization has inevitable concomitant growth with congestion on roads in Delhi. The traffic is obviously not smooth and one is not expected to reach one's destination in time. This is despite the fact that Delhi has a road length of 25,948 kms and an increasing number of over-bridges and sub-ways have eased the congestion on roads. The congestion is due to the phenomenal growth in vehicles. According to the traffic police, the number of vehicles registered by them till the end of 2001 were in the range of 3.6 million as compared to 0.20 million in 1972 with an annual growth of about 3.5 per cent. They range from animal-driven vehicles (*tonga,* driven by horse, and bullock cart) to bicycles, tricycles (*rickshaws*) to 2-wheeler and 3-wheeler scooters to private cars of all hues and standards, tempos (goods vehicles) to buses, each with a capacity of 30 to 70 persons. By the end of 2001, the total number of registered vehicles was 133,169. Out of these, 63,370 were private cars, 61,372 were m/cycles/scooters, 880 taxis, 800 3-wheeler scooters (at present more than 2600), 3,797 goods vehicles, 4,550 buses each with a capacity of 30 to 70 persons. Apart from these, by the end of 2001, there were 148,056 slow-moving vehicles, including 36,544 cycle rickshaws (tricycles), 305 *tongas* (horse-driven passenger vehicle with a seating capacity of four persons), 46 *rehras* (horse-driven vehicle generally for transporting goods), 4694 handcarts, 216 bullock carts and 106,251 c-rickshaw trollies. The government has undertaken a big project of Metro Railway and the entire city is likely to be connected with the network of railways by the year 2010. This should ease the congestion and do away with the problem of pollution.

The National Capital Territory has become the largest hub of northern India. It is also the largest centre of small industries manufacturing TV sets, musical systems, electrical goods, light engineering machines, automobile parts, sports goods, bicycles, plastic and pvc goods, textiles, fertilizers, medicines, hosiery, leather goods, soft drinks, etc. There are also units for forging, casting, galvanizing, electroplating, printing and warehousing. About 89,000 units are in operation engaging about 0.9 million persons. The polluting manufacturing units are being shifted outside Delhi.

Delhi has more private vehicles than the other three metros combined and the highest per capita ownership of consumer goods. Its infrastructure has drawn business people. Much of Delhi's acclaim for its infrastructure is due to the good work of the governments of neighbouring states in the sprawling suburbs of Noida, Gurgaon and Faridabad. With the intervention of the Supreme Court and the Delhi High Court, the state's once notorious problems of pollution and transport have all abated. In spite of the fact that the city has over 100 art galleries, a dozen-odd golf courses and a number of five-star restaurants, one-third of its population lives in slums and unauthorized colonies, and a number of posh areas are facing water and power problems.

Places to be Visited

What should attract the tourist like me? The most frequented monument of Delhi is **Lal Qila** (Red Fort), built by Emperor Shah Jahan (1628-65), perhaps the greatest builder of all times. When he decided to shift his capital from Agra to Delhi, where it belonged, he first enclosed the city by high battlements and bastions with eight gates for entrance and exit. Then he built the Red Fort inside it, along the banks of the Jamuna river. Within the Fort, he built a hall of public audience (*Diwan-i-Am*). The emperor gave daily audiences to all his subjects in this 60-pillared hall. The intricately carved throne canopy stands on a platform, while the low marble bench was for the chief minister (*wazir*). The emperor met his most trusted nobles in *Diwan-I-Khas* (hall for private audience). The walls and pillars of this were once inlaid with gems and the ceiling was of silver inlaid with precious stones. He also laid out a garden, which he called *Hayat Baksh* (life-giving), criss-crossed with canals and fountains. Every morning, he would appear in a latticed window of his palace for his subjects to have a view of them. On formal occasions, he sat on the Peacock Throne inlaid with precious stones. Yet, *Khas Mahal* (royal apartments) in the Red Fort has a prayer room (*Tasbih Khana*), which was flanked by his sleeping chamber (*Khwabgah*) and sitting room (*Baithak*). This overlooked the Yamuna and led to a balcony where the emperor appeared before his subjects at sunrise. The Red Fort had several buildings added to it by Shah Jahan's successors. The most attractive of them is the small, white marble *Moti* (Pearl) Mosque built by Aurangzeb (1658-1707).

Red Fort was commissioned by Shah Jahan in 1639. It took nine years to build and was the seat of Mughal power until 1857, when the last emperor, Bahadur Shah Zafar, was dethroned and exiled. Lahori Gate, one of Fort's six gateways, leads on to the covered bazaar of Chatta Chowk, where brocades and jewels were once sold. Beyond this lies the *Naqqar Khana* (apartments for servants), from where musicians played three times a day.

Shah Jahan also built the royal mosque, **Jama Masjid**, reckoned by many people as the most beautiful and the largest mosque in the world. This grand mosque, built in 1656 by the Emperor Shah Jahan on a natural rocky outcrop, took six years and 5,000 workmen to construct it at the cost of nearly a million rupees. A magnificent flight of red sandstone steps leads to the great arched entrances where, in Aurangzeb's time, horses were sold and jugglers performed. At present, sweet-sellers, cobblers and beggars mill around here. The huge 28m (300 ft) square courtyard accommodates upto 20,000 people at prayer times, especially during Friday prayers and on *Id*, when it looks like a sea of worshippers. Next to the ablution tank in the centre is the *dikka* platform where, before loudspeakers took over, a second prayer leader echoed the

Imam's words and actions for worshippers too far from the pulpit. The three imposing black and white marble domes surmount the enormous prayer hall, and two minarets frame the great central arch.

What remains to be seen by an outsider in Old Delhi is the **Chandini Chowk** (Moonlit Square), extending from Red Fort to Fatehpuri Masjid, lying in the heart of Old Delhi, where both religious activity and commerce mix happily together. It was once a grand processional thoroughfare that led from Red Fort to Jama Masjid. When Jahanara Begum, Shah Jahan's favourite daughter, laid it out in 1648, a canal ran down the centre of the tree-lined stately avenue. Chandini Chowk, or the "silvery, moonlit square", was then lined with merchants' shops and the grand residences or *havelis* of noblemen. All along its length are the shrines, sacred to various communities. The first is the Digamber Jain Mandir. Next to it is the Bird Hospital for sick and wounded birds. Loud chants and calls of vendors, selling flowers and vermilion powder, surround the Gauri Shankar Mandir, dedicated to Siva and Parvati, which has a linga, said to be 800 years old. Further, close to the Sisganj Gurudwara, is the Kotwali (police station), the scene of British reprisal after 1857. The actual Chandni Chowk is the open spaces in front of the British Town Hall, now the Hardayal Library. Further down, and commanding the end of this charming quarter, stands the Fatehpuri Masjid, constructed in 1650 by Fatehpuri Begum, one of Emperor Shah Jahan's wife.

While in Old Delhi, one must go to **Rajghat**, the symbol of patriotism and the site of Mahatma Gandhi's cremation. All visiting heads of state are taken to Rajghat to lay wreaths in memory of the "Father of the Nation". On Gandhi's birthday (October 2) and death anniversary (January 30), the nation's leaders gather here for prayer meetings. I found it a peaceful place.

From Raj Ghat I drove to **Purana Qila**, literally "old fort". It is located on the busy Mathura Road and is believed to be the place where Indraprastha, the Pandava capital mentioned in the epic, *The Mahabharata*, once stood. It was here that Humayun, the second Mughal emperor, began to construct his city, *Dinpanah* (Asylum of Faith) just four years after his father, Babur, established the Mughal dynasty in 1526. Today, of the many palaces, barracks and houses that once existed, only Sher

Shah's mosque and the building, said to be Humayun's library, remain. The Yamuna once flowed on the Fort's eastern side. The present entrance, an imposing red sandstone gate on the Western Wall, called the *Bara Darwaza*, is one of the three principal gates of Shergarh.

New Delhi didn't exist before the Britishers came. King George V announced in a *durbar* that the capital would be shifted from Calcutta to Delhi where it had always belonged. After the First World War was over, the government got down to the job of building a new capital. Two renowned architects—Edwin (later Sir) Lutyens and Herbert (later Sir) Baker—were commissioned to make blueprints of the city and the major buildings. Lutyens made the masterplan of the Viceregal (later Presidential) palace, Rashtrapati Bhawan, and the War Memorial Arch (India Gate). Gradually, a new city began to rise in what was once a sparsely inhabited wilderness of *keekar*, camel thorn and cactus.

Once New Delhi used to boast of having more trees per square kilometre than any world capital. But, after Partition of the country, new colonies had to be built to accommodate the unending stream of refugees and other newcomers. Blocks of high-rise apartments came up, making the capital the most congested and polluted city.

In New Delhi, one should go to **Nehru Memorial Museum and Library**. It was once called the **Teen Murti Bhavan** where India's first Prime Minister, Jawaharlal Nehru, lived during 1947 to 1964. On his death, the house was converted into a national memorial, comprising of museum and a library for research scholars. Originally, the residence of the Commander-in-Chief of British Forces in India and designed by Robert Tor Russell, the architect of Connaught Place, its design follows the established Lutyen's-style classicism with a teak paneled interior and vaulted reception rooms. The extensive grounds are home to the **Nehru Planetarium**, which also needs to be visited. What is worth seeing is the show of constellation of stars with lucid commentary in English and Hindi.

Jantar Mantar

British-built shopping complex in New Delhi, **Connaught Place**, offers a pleasant atmosphere to stroll in and to browse through beautiful shops, designed by Robert Tor Russell after the Duke of Connaught, an uncle of King George V. It has many restaurants and a number of cinema halls. Yet, in this area, one needs to go to **Jantar Mantar**, which reminds us of the interest of Sawai Jai

Singh II of Jaipur in astronomy. This observatory was built in the year 1724 by Sawai Jai Singh II and was commissioned by the then Mughal Emperor Muhammed Shah. Sawai Jai Singh was a keen astronomer and he felt that the existing instruments were not accurate enough to calculate the eclipses and planetary positions required for setting the timings of his *pujas* and other sacred rituals. To solve the problem, he erected five observatories with instruments. They are large and are fixed to the cite to be both exact and not prone to vibration. The instruments are the Samrat Yantra, a right-angled triangle whose hypotenuse is parallel to the earth's axis. This is, in fact, a gigantic sundial, and there are two brick quadrants on either side, which measure its shadow. The others are the Jai Prakash Yantra, Jai Singh's invention, which, among other functions, verifies the time of the spring equinox, the Ram Yantra which reads the altitude of the sun: and the Misra Yantra, a group of instruments for a variety of purposes.

From Jantar Mantar one can reach the area where **Parliament House** (*Sansad Bhawan)*, circular in shape, is situated. It is located to the north of Vijay Chowk. This is the circular building where 552 Members of Lok Sabha and 245 Members of Rajya Sabha, constituting Parliament, debate issues concerning the nation. The Parliament House was built following the Montagu-Chelmsford Reforms of 1919 to house the Legislative Assembly. The Constitution of India was drafted here in the early days of the Independence. Nowadays, both the Rajya Sabha (Upper House) and the Lok Sabha (House of the People) meet here when Parliament is in session.

From Parliament House one comes to **Vijay Chowk**. It was planned as a commanding approach to the Viceroy's House. It is at this place that the President of India takes salute of the Republic Day parade on 26 January. Again, it is at this place that one can witness on 29 January the Beating Retreat ceremony. Rising impressively from the leveled top of Raisina Hill are the two virtually identical Central Secretariat buildings designed by Herbert Baker and known as the **North and South Blocks**. These long classical edifices house the Home and Finance ministries and the Ministry of Foreign Affairs.

From Vijay Chowk, one can witness the large trees and fountains lining the lawns of Rajpath up to **India Gate**. India Gate is at the eastern end of Rajpath. It was built to commemorate the Indian and

British soldiers who died in World War I and those who fell in battle in North-West Frontier Province and the Third Afghan War. An eternal flame burns in memory of unknown soldiers who died in the 1971 Indo-Pakistan war. Facing India Gate is the sandstone canopy where King George V's statue was installed after his death in 1936. Around India Gate are the stately homes of erstwhile Indian princes, including Hyderabad House where official state banquets are held. Then there are Jaipur, Bikaner, Patiala and Baroda Houses. Close to Vijay Chowk is **Rashtrapati Bhawan,** the residence of the President of India. It was designed by Edwin Lutyens to be the focal point of New Delhi during the British rule. This 20th century architectural masterpiece cover an area of 4.5 acres (2 ha) of land. Built at a cost of £877,136.00, involving 23,000 labourers, 700 million bricks, 3 million cubic feet of stone and 3000 stone cutters, it has 340 rooms and numerous splendid gardens. It has 14-hole golf course, a polo ground and a cricket field. The whole building is a blend of Gothic and Indian architecture and second in size only to the Palace of Versailles.

The panoramic view of Rashtrapati Bhawan consists of superbly trimmed trees and lush verdant lawns. It has more than 600 variety of trees, including mango, *neem, jamun, peepal* and banyan, adding majesty to the highest office in India, who, beside presiding over ceremonial functions, has much more to deal with political events of great significance, both at the national and political level. The most prominent and distinguishing aspect of Rashtrapati Bhawan is its dome which is superimposed on its structure. It is visible from a distance and has the most eye-catching round roof with circular base. The dome is believed to be structured on the pattern of the great Stupa of Sanchi. When Chakravarti Rajagopalachari assumed the office as the first Governor General of India and became the occupant of this building he preferred to stay in few rooms which now form the family wing of the President. He converted the then Viceroy's other apartment to be the Guest Wing where the Heads of State of other countries stay during their visit to India.

The other place, worth seeing in New Delhi, is the **National Museum** where one can see a collection of more than 150,000 pieces of Indian art. Spread over three floors, the museum has 30 galleries. The impressive collection includes sculptures, paintings, jewellry, decorative arts and textiles. They represent the finest examples of each time and period from all over the country. One can also go to **Lakshmi Narayan Mandir**, popularly known as **Birla Mandir**. The prominent industrialist G.D. Birla built it in 1938. It is the country's first temple where there is no caste restriction. The main shrine has images of Visnu and his consort, Lakshmi. Other shrines in this temple are dedicated to Radha-Krsna, Ḥanuman, Siva and Durga and on the walls are inscriptions from Hindu scriptures, often with English translations. They are also decorated with paintings from *The Mahabharata* and *The Ramayana.*

Qutab Minar in Mehrauli area is reminiscent of the grand Islamic architecture. It is world's highest single tower where Qutbuddin Aibak laid the foundation of Delhi sultanate. This five-storeyed Victory Tower was started by Qutbuddin Aibak and was completed by his successor, Iltutmish. In this complex, there is a 4th-century pillar, originally made as a flagstaff in Visnu's honour, a tribute to ancient Indian metallurgy.

Jusf opposite the Kalkaji Temple is the **Baha'i House of Worship**, a place where silence and order prevails. Because of its magnificent shape of unfurling 27-petalled white marble lotus, it is popularly known as **Lotus Temple**. The edifice, circled by nine pools and 27 acres (92 ha) of green manicured lawns, is one of Delhi's most innovative modern structures. The Baha's sect originated in Persia and this temple was designed by Iranian architect, Fariburz Sahba. Its construction began in 1980 and was completed in 1986. Inside, the lofty auditorium can seat 1,300 persons. All are welcome to meditate there and attend the daily 15-minute services. The temple looks spectacular after dark when the lighting

gives the marble panels a luminous quality.

There is little disagreement that human history is strongly influenced by the founders of the world's great religions. The powerful impact on civilization of Lord Krsna, the Buddha, Zoroaster, Moses, Jesus Christ and Prophet Muhammad is seen by Baha'is not only in the cultural forms and value systems, which arise from their works and teachings, but is also reflected in the impact that the example of their lives has on human kind. The writings of Baha'u'llah describes their devine intermediaries as "manifestations of God". Just as humans are superior to the animals and possess capacities that the animal world does not have, so the "manifestations" are endorsed with superior powers. The "manifestations" are not simply great human thinkers, or philosophers, with greater understanding or knowledge than others. They are, by their very nature, superior to those who do not possess a similar capacity.

The founder, Baha'u'llah, was born in Persia on November 12, 1817. His father was an influential minister in the Shah's court in Persia. Yet Baha'u'llah declined a position in the government. He chose to devote himself to help the poor. From childhood, Baha'u'llah was extremely kind and generous and a lover of outdoor life. When he was hardly 14 he became famous for his learning. He could speak on any subject and solve any problem presented to him. He rejected the dogma of materialism. He gradually captured the imagination and loyalty of several million people from virtually every race, culture and nation on earth. He asserted that the wars, exploitation, injustices and prejudice that have marked immature stages in the process of human advancement should not be a cause of despair but a stimulus to assume the responsibilities of collective maturity.

Baha'u'llah's entire life, however, changed when he become a leading follower of the movement of the Bab. Bab was a messenger of God. In 1844, he announced that the human race was on the threshold of an era that would transform its moral and spiritual life. His own mission was to prepare humanity for the coming of that universal messenger of God awaited by the followers of all religions. This claim provoked violent hostility from the clergy and the authorities, and thousands of followers of the new faith were massacred. The Bab himself was publicly executed shorlty thereafter. Baha'u'llah was arrested as he supported Bab's cause. He was brought to Tehran where he was held prisoner. Here he recieved the first intimation of his mission. His personal reputation and social position saved his life, but he was banished from his native land after his wealth and properties were confiscated. For four years he lived in exile in Baghdad, braving through immense hardship and bitter persecution.

On the eve of his further exile to Constantinople, Baha'u'llah announced in 1863 that the 'Day of God' had dawned and that he, Baha'u'llah, was the one foretold by the Bab, promised in the scriptures of the past. To Judaism he was the "Lord of Hosts", to Christianity, the Return of Christ; to Islam the "Great Announcement", to Hinduism, the new incarnation of Krsna, to Buddhism, the "Maitreya Buddha", to Zoroastrianism, the advent of "Shah Bahrain". Successive banishments took Baha'u'llah and his family from Constantinople to Adrianople, and finally the grim penal colony of Akka in the Holy Land, where he lived the rest of his life in exile and died on May 29, 1892.

The present progressive restructuring of society gives Baha'u'llah's message a new dimension of meaning. Baha'u'llah's followers, numbering five-and-half million world-wide, uphold the divine origin of all the religions and consider Baha'u'llah to the "Promised One". He restored to a scientific age belief in the divine, while revealing the indestructible unity of religion and science.

Close to Lotus Temple in East of Kailash, the International Society of Krishna Consciousness has built up a magnificent and impressive structure, which is known as **ISKCON Temple**. Its sanctum sanctorum displays colourful frescoes and statutes of Lord Krsna. The temple provides a lavish display of light and sound at night. Next to the auditorium, there is a lavish life size statutes of Krsna and Arjuna with discourses on the evils of the world and how to overcome them. The temple provides a fine moment of coupling religion with entertainment that gets the targeted audience flocking to it almost on daily basis, especially in the evening. A beautiful restaurant in the temple's precincts serves food at reasonable cost. I enjoyed the delicious vegetarian lunch.

I tried to know the concept behind this International Society for Krishna Consciousness (ISKCON). Its Chairman is His Holiness Gopal Krishna Goswami who studied business administration from Sorbonne, France, and Canada, and joined ISKCON in 1968, leaving a prestigious position in a multinational firm. He said that there is "so much stress and violence because of great ambition and great greed. If we live by the teachings of the *Bhagwad Gita*, each person will act unselfishly. In Vedic times, rulers were concerned about their subjects.

They would give away their own belongings for their people". He felt that the leaders today rarely set an example for the masses to follow on their footsteps. He wants the people to understand the teachings of Lord Krsna and the *Bhagwad Gita*. This will contribute to their personal prosperity and nature's bounty. ISKCON seeks to promote this.

Delhi is also the largest **educational centre**. It has about 100 colleges, numerous high schools, both in the public and private sectors, and 15 universities. The universities are: All India Institute of Medical Sciences, Guru Govind Singh Indraprastha Vishwavidyalaya, University of Delhi, Indian Agricultural Research Institute, Indian Institute of Technology, Indira Gandhi National Open University, Jamia Hamdard, Jamia Milia Islamia, Jawaharlal Nehru University, National Museum Institute of History of Arts, Conservation & Museology, School of Planning & Architecture, Lal Bahadur Shastri Sanskrit Vidyapeeth, and TERI School of Advanced Studies.

When to go to Delhi and what's the best time to visit Delhi? I asked my host. I was told that weather-wise, of course, it is late autumn (October) through winter to early spring (April), when Delhi is full of flowers, blue sky and bright sunshine. Most tourists prefer to come to Delhi during these months because there is so much going on by way of festivals—Dussehra, Diwali, Republic Day celebrations, and the water festival, Holi. But in Delhi, there is always something going on by way of festivals and there is a constant change of landscape: the scorching heat of May and June, the monsoon showers of July and August, followed by the quiet change into autumn.

Agra

Agra is 223 km (139 miles) on southeast of Delhi and can be approached from Delhi in three ways. One can either go there by transport or by train. Luxury coaches take tourists in the morning and bring them back at night. Travelling by train is a truly unforgettable experience, involving lot of fun or frustration. If we can spare some time, it is the best way of getting to know Indian people and seeing the countryside. India has a well-organized railway network but it is also extremely busy. Therefore, one has to plan in advance. Nowadays, there are computerized ticket counters at railway stations. There are reservation counters in various parts of the city and we can book our ticket from any such centre. One can also get it through travel agents. The journey between Delhi and Agra takes only a few hours, depending on the train, which you take. One can go to Agra from Nizamuddin Railway Station by Taj Express and by Shatabti Express from New Delhi Railway Station. Both these trains will drop you to Agra or bring you back within three hours. However, Shatabdi Express is a luxurious train, but one has to be at New Delhi station at 6 am. One can also go to Agra by air.

The Shatabdi Express or Taj Express leaves us at Agra Fort Railway Station. The Railway Station building itself is a colonial building built in 1891 as a stopping-off point for colonial tourists visiting Agra's monuments. This is one of Agra's most frequently used stations, the other two are located in the Cantonment and at Raja-ki-Mandi.

The city of Agra, though close to Delhi, is comparatively warm. After I came out of the station, I was surrounded by *rickshaw-wallas* (those who drive tricycles manually), scooter drivers and taxi drivers. One needs to do a lot of bargaining before fixing a suitable conveyance. A stroll through the narrow alleys in the city can be a rewarding experience, offering glimpses of a close-knit way of life reminiscent of Mughal Agra. One finds in the city the followers of all religions—Hindus, Sikhs and Muslims. This is also the crafts and trade center where a staggering array of products, such as jewellry, *zari embroidary*, dried fruit, seeds, shoes and kites are available.

The city of Agra is on the West Bank of the river Yamuna and has become famous because of the Mughal monuments, particularly the **Taj Mahal**. Agra was the imperial capital of the Mughal court during the 16th and 17th centuries before it was shifted to Delhi. The Moghuls were prolific builders and nowhere is this more evident than in the picturesque riverine region along the Yamuna, which is the backdrop for its palaces, tombs, forts and gardens. Three

of these, the Taj Mahal, the Agra Fort and Akbar's abandoned capital of Fatehpur Sikri, have been declared World Heritage Sites by UNESCO. The imperial Mughal highway, which still runs along the Yamuna between Delhi and Agra, is a link to the region's historical past. The city of Agra lies in the centre of a rich and varied cultural territory. At one end of this region are the pastoral fields around Yamuna, and at the other, the stark and awesome ravines of the Chambal River. Between these two rivers are a number of towns, monuments and sanctuaries, making this one of the most popular travel circuits in north India. In mythology, Mathura was the sacred territory of Krsna, the Hindu deity, while in history it was the centre of an important Buddhist kingdom, and the imperial Mughal highway ran through it. This region contains some of the best examples of Indian art and architecture, while the riverine wetlands around Bharatpur provide a natural habitat for a range of wildlife and migratory birds.

The best way to explore this region, I was told, is by car. The National Highway, which runs from Delhi to Agra, goes through Mathura. A network of smaller roads link the region beyond Mathura and Brindavan. Except in patches, particularly after the monsoon, these roads are generally in a good condition. Once in Mathura, a boat trip along the Yamuna is a good way to see the *ghats* (river banks). The Keoladeo Ghana Sanctuary provides tourists with cycle-rickshaws and guides on payment. The area is also well serviced by trains, including the high speed Shatabdi Express, which goes from New Delhi to Bhopal via Gwalior and Jhansi and the Taj Express between Delhi and Agra. Several trains pass through Jhansi from where easy car trips can be made to Datia and Orchha. Like Agra, Gwalior also has domestic airport.

Agra has become a tourist place. **Taj Mahal** is, in fact, one of the world's most famous buildings and is known as seventh wonder of the world. Built in AD 1634 by Mughal Emperor Shah Jahan in memory of his favourite wife, Mumtas Mahal, it was built at a cost of 41 million rupees and 500 kilos of gold. Around 20,000 workers worked for almost 22 years to complete it in 1653. It is believed that the Taj Mahal was designed to represent an earthly replica of one of the houses of Paradise. It has been described as one of the most elegant and harmonious buildings in the world. It manifests the wealth and luxury of Mughal art, as seen in architecture and garden design, painting, jewellry, calligraphy, textiles, carpet weaving and furniture.

The Mughals were great admirers of nature. They believed that flowers were the "symbols of the divine realm". Flowers of varying nature have been extensively used to decorate the walls and create aesthetic look. The Florentine technique of *pietra dura* is said to have been imported by Jahangir and developed in Agra as *pachikari*. Minute precious and semi-precious stones were arranged and complex stylized floral designs made into a marble base. Even now also, one can find Muslim artisans in the old city maintaining paternal books, containing the intricate motifs used on the Taj who can re-create 17th century designs. Decorative panels of flowering plants, foliage and vases are realistically carved on the lower portions of the walls, while inlaid calligraphy in black marble has been used as a form of ornamentation on undecorated surfaces. The exquisitely detailed panels of inscriptions of Quranic passages, that line the recessed arches like banners, were designed by the Persian calligrapher, Amanat Khan. The size of the Quranic verses increases as the arch gets higher, creating the subtle optical illusion of a uniformly flowing script. Inside the building, one finds Mumtas Mahal's cenotaph raised on a platform placed next to Shah Jahan's. The actual graves, in a dark crypt below, are closed to the public.

The four minarets, each 40m (131 ft) high, and each crowned by a *chhatri*, framing the tomb, highlight the perfect symmetry of the complex. These minarets tilt outward so that they should not damage the building at the time of earthquake. In front of the Taj building, one finds the Lotus Pool, named after its lotus-shaped fountain spouts, the pool reflecting the tomb. Almost every visitor is photographed sitting on the marble bench here.

Next to Taj Mahal, I visited **Agra Fort**. I entered the Fort through the impressive Amar Singh gate. To its right is the Jahangiri Mahal, the only major palace that dates to Akbar's reign. The complex arrangement of halls, courtyards and galleries with dungeons below, were once the *zenana* or main harem building. In front of Jahangir Mahal is a large marble pool which, according to legend, was filled with thousands of rose petals during Nur Jahan's time, so that the empress could bathe in its scented waters. Along the river front or the Khas Mahal is an elegant marble hall within exuberantly painted ceiling, characteristic of Shah Jahan's style of architecture, and the two golden pavilions. These pavilions were associated with the princesses Jahanara and Roshanara. Facing them is *Anguri Bagh* (grape garden) with its lily-pools and candle-niches. The Sheesh Mahal and royal baths are to the northeast near the gloriously inlaid Musamman Burj, the double storeyed octagonal tower with clear views of the Taj. This was where his son Aurangazeb imprisoned Shah Jahan. Shah Jahan spent the last years of his life there. From a mirror installed in this room he used to have a glimpse of his wife's Tomb in the Taj Mahal.

This Fort is situated on the West Bank of the river Yamuna, and was built by Akbar between 1565 and 1573. Its imposing red sandstone ramparts form a crescent along the riverfront, and encompass an enormous complex of courtly buildings, ranging in style from the early eclecticism of Akbar to the sublime simplicity of Shah Jahan. The barracks to the north are 19-century British additions. A deep moat, once filled with water from the Yamuna, surrounds the Fort.

After the Agra Fort, I visited **Jama Masjid.** It is a magnificently proportioned building, also known as a Friday Mosque. Shah Jahan's favourite daughter, Jahanara Begum, who also commissioned other buildings and gardens, built it in 1648. The mosque's sandstone and marble tombs, with their distinctive zigzag chevron pattern, dominate the section of the town. The British demolished the eastern courtyard wing in 1857. Of interest to the visitors is the tank with its *shahi chirag* (royal stove) for heating water within the courtyard, and the separate prayer chamber for ladies.

The Mughal Emperor, Akbar, buried on the outskirts of Agra, and the building to commemorate him is known as the mausoleum of **Sikandra**. It has been named after Sikander Lodi, one of the last of the Delhi Sultan. It is widely believed that Akbar designed and started the construction of his own mausoleum which, after his death, was modified and completed by his son and successor, Jahangir.

The main gateway to the south is a magnificent red sandstone structure with a colossal central arch, finished with an exuberant polychrome mosaic of inlaid white marble, black slate and coloured stone. On each corner of the gateway are four graceful marble minarets. The garden, where deer and monkeys frolic, is a typical *charbagh*, enclosed garden, divided into four quarters representing the four quarters of life. The actual tomb is within the building, illuminated by shapes of light from arched window. A low door at the end of the ramp ensures that every visitor bows his head with respect on entry. Just outside the complex is the *kanch mahal*, a double storied red sand stone mansion with an ornamented facade and fretted balconies. Further down, on Mathura Road, is Mariam

Zamani's Tomb, where one of Akbar's wives is buried in a square building set on a high plinth within a small garden. It was used as an orphanage by the Church Missionary Society in 1812. A church has been constructed in the compound. Further along the Agra-Delhi highway is the *Guru-ka-Tal*, a unique example of the many tanks constructed by Jahangir for collecting rainwater. The reservoir is now part of *Gurudwara* complex dedicated to the ninth Sikh Guru, Teg Bahadur.

I was able to see the prominent monuments by 4 pm. Still there was enough time for my return journey to Delhi by Taj Express. I decided to go to the market. I was able to see some of the workshops of master craftsmen. Many call themselves as the descendents of those craftsmen who worked in the construction of Taj Mahal. They are mostly Mohammedans. Their showrooms display artifacts which have been exquisitely designed but their cost is prohibitive.

Jaipur

Shatabdi Express from New Delhi Railway Station took me to Jaipur. The pink soil and houses at the outskirt of the city heralded the vicinity of the Pink City, as it is known. As a matter of fact, from New Delhi, there is a special train, known as Pink City Express, which can take us there.

Jaipur, now the capital of Rajasthan state, is located in north India and has a distinct position in Indian history. What we see in this capital of Rajasthan is a dynamic blend of the old and the new, a proudly social structure with a modern liberalized economy. It had been an independent state before partition of the country. It had been the capital of the Kachawa kings from 1729 to 1749. Its birth and growth has been inextricably linked with that of its rulers. The city is a combination of a splendid creation of architecture, a genius in town planning, and intellectual, cultural, artistic and religious pursuits. From 1036 to 1727, Amber remained the Kachawa capital.

The new generation of Amber kings continued their territorial expansion and included Raja Man Singh I, a brilliant general and Commander-in-Chief of the Mughal army, and one of the nine gems of Akbar's court. Even while his campaigns took him to distant Kabul, Kandhar, and Bengal, he was able to start building the magnificent **Palace at Amber.** The Palace is a perfect specimen of Rajput architecture and his *bhojan shala*, or dining room, was decorated later with paintings of the cities of Delhi, Agra, Mathura and other holy places. His

architectural genius is evident not only in the Palace at Amber but in the remains of the old city beyond the citadel. His great grandson, Mirza Raja Jai Singh, further embellished the Palace in the form of the *Ganesh Pol*, the beautiful mosaic gate, the *Diwan-i-Am*, built with red sandstone pillars in the Mughal style, and Jai Mandir, with its square panels of ivory white marble. The Sheesh Mahal is a wonderful example of the mirror-inlay work of the period.

To the north of Jaipur, one finds **Amber Fort**, which was the Kacchawaha citadel until 1727. Protected by Jaigarh Fort, the massive ramparts of the Fort follow the contours of a natural ridge. One has to go there riding an elephant or by jeep. Successive rulers continued to come there on all important occasions to seek the blessings of the family deity, Shila Devi. Man Singh I established the citadel in 1592 on the remains of an old 11th century fort. Various buildings were added by Jai Singh I. Among these is **Sheesh Mahal,** where the flame of a single candle reflected in the tiny mirrors, embedded in this chamber, transforms it into a starlit sky. Jas Mandir in the Fort has latticed windows, a floral ceiling of elegant alabaster relief work and glass inlay. The main entrance to the historic Amber Fort is through the imposing Suraj Pol (Sun Gate), so called because it faces the direction of the rising sun. This gate leads into a huge flagged courtyard, Jaleb Chowk, literaly "the square where elephants and horses are tethered". Originally, it was Fort's parade ground. Its central area is surrounded on three sides by guard rooms, but now one can see there the souvenir and refreshment shops. A flight of steps leads to the Shila Devi Temple, which contains the image of the Kachhawaha family deity, a stone (*shila*) goddess Kali, brought here by Man Singh I from Bengal in 1604. The next courtyard has the *Diwan-I-Aam*, the space for public audience. The magnificent Ganesh Pol is the gateway to the three private palaces.

Towering above Jaipur are the two fortresses of **Nahargarh Jaigarh** that guard the approach from the north to both amber and the new capital of Jaipur. They now remind one of the warrior clans who fought for supremacy. The hill-top fort of Nahargarh ("tiger fort")

stands in what was once a densely forested area. Its fortifications have been strengthened by the successive rulers. Madhu Singh II added a lavish palace called Madhavendra Bhavan, for his nine queens. It has a cool, airy upper chamber from which the ladies of the court could view the city. Its walls and pillars are an outstanding example of *aravish*, a plaster work technique that is hand-polished with a piece of *agate* to produce a marvelous finish.

To the east of Nahargarh one can see the Brahmpuri area, where the grand *havelis* of the *pundits* and scholars of the Jaipur court once stood. One mention was the residence of Pandit Retnakar Pundarik, Brahmin courtier during the reign of Sawai Jai Singh II, who, it is said, conducted the *puja* that appeased the spirit of Nahar Singh. In a portion of the *haveli* (courtyard) one can see the super frescoes decorating the walls and ceilings of the living rooms. These lively paintings depict gods and goddesses, courtly scenes and festival processions.

It was Maharaja Sawai Jai Singh II who had the **Fort of Nahargarh** constructed in 1734. However, Maharaja's most enduring legacy is the city of Jaipur itself. Crowned in 1700 as the ruler of Amber at the young age of 12, he grew into an astute politician and a great general, and was well read. He fully deserved the title of Sawai (one-and-a-quarter) bestowed upon him by Emperor Aurangzeb. The Maharaja found Amber small, and its rocky terrain restricted his expansion. It was imperative, therefore, to plan and build a new city where a larger, more prosperous settlement could be established. He chose the open plains at the foot of Nahargarh to build his new capital. He was a proficient astronomer and well versed with Hindu texts. His city, therefore, conformed to the modes of town planning, as dictated by the Hindu *shilp-shastras*.

Work on the new city began on November 18, 1727. The rectangular shape of the town was divided into eight blocks, known as *chowkrisk*, including one block for the palace. The palace block, known as *Chowkri Sarhad*, *Purani Basti* and *Ramchandraji* occupied the road on the north and *Topkhana Hazuri* and the road on the south. Thus, Jaipur became the first planned city of India. Shops were of uniform size and shape. All buildings were made of stone, brick and lime, and positioned in such a way that rooms were well lit without being subjected to the glare of the desert sun. The height of the building was controlled. The pattern of the houses was usually the same. The Maharaja's successors continued to enhance Jaipur's beauty, adding to it beautiful buildings, temples and palaces.

In Jaipur's old walled area, **Hawa Mahal** (Palace of Winds) provides a fascinating look. Built in 1799 by Sawai Pratap Singh (1778-1803), this five-storeyed building is painted pink. It is said that this palace, built of lime and mortar, was so designed as to enable the ladies of the harem to watch unnoticed the coloruful street scenes and state processions below on Sireh Deori Bazaar.

Pratap Singh, the poet, composer and patron of the arts, was a devotee of Krsna and he dedicated the Hawa Mahal to him. Many believe that when seen from a distance, the building looks like the *mukut* (crown) that adorns Lord Krsna's head.

The **Hawa Mahal**, with its unique architecture, has made Jaipur famous throughout the world. It is exquisitely fretted with screens, allowing a play of breezes in the warm summer months. Its screens made it ideal for the women of the royal family to look out on to the streets without themselves being seen. The poet-king, Sawai Pratap Singh, who was a great devotee of Radha-Krsna and who authored a large number of books under the pen name of Brijnidhi, built it.

Sawai Pratap Singh's great grandson, Maharaja Sawai Ram Singh II, laid the beautiful Ram Niwas Bagh. During his time, the streets were paved and the gas-works introduced for street lighting. He was a great patron of arts and started the Maharaja School of Arts and Crafts. He also started the first high school for boys and girls, the first modern hospital, and a theatre in Jaipur. It was during his reign that Prince Albert, the consort of Queen Victoria, visited Jaipur and is said to have had the city painted pink for the occasion. He was a brilliant photographer, and was also very keen on flying kites. He invited a potter to his kingdom and his community to live in his city and practice their trade. This is how the blue pottery, for which Jaipur is famous, first came to Jaipur.

His successor was Maharaja Sawai Man Singh II, the last ruling king of the Kachawa clan. He was responsible for modernizing Jaipur and expanding it beyond the city walls in a well thought out plan, like his forefather Sawai Jai Singh. Educational institutions, like the

Maharaja College, the Maharani College, SMS Medical College and Hospital, and later the Maharani Gayatri Devi School and the Bhagwan Das Barracks, which now house the Rajasthan Government Secretariat, etc. were added. He expanded the Rambagh complex into a magnificent palace.

On Amber Road, opposite Trident Hotel, one can see the picturesque **Jal Mahal** (Water Palace) inside a lake. Built in the mid-18 century by Madho Singh I it was based on the Lake Palace at Udaipur where the king spent his childhood. Later, it was used as a lodge for duck shooting parties, and even now also a large number of waterbirds can be seen here. A terrace garden is enclosed by arched passages, and at each corner is a semi-octagonal tower, capped by an elegant cupola.

Jaipur is now home of all communities and the people participate enthusiastically in all festivals. During Moharrum, many beautifully decorated *tazias* are taken out in processions through the city to the **Jal Mahal,** the cremation place for the *tazias.* Jaipur is also an important place of pilgrimage among Vaishnavites as their principal divinities are located in the temples of Galtaji and Govindji. Once the city was also famous for its horses. The palace stables or *atish,* which contained 170 horses, have now been converted into a crowded market place. From the 1930s till the end of the '60s, the name of Jaipur was synonymous with polo. The city is also famous for its *Gunjan Khana,* the centre of music and performing arts, which gave birth to the Jaipur *gharana* or school of Dhrupad music and Kathak dance. Even now, in the early hours of the morning or in the afternoon, when traffic stills for a moment, music emanates from the City Palace, capturing the magic of Jaipur in that instant.

In the city of Jaipur, one finds fascinating markets, opulent palaces and historic sights. The city offers a chance to see the medieval alongside the modern. On its colourful streets one finds camels jostling for space with motorbikes and turbaned village elders rubbing shoulders with youngsters in blue jeans. The city is often rightly called the Pink City, because its prominent buildings are washed with this colour.

The **City Palace** in the heart of the city is worth seeing. It has been the home of the rulers of Jaipur since the first half of the 18th century. The sprawling complex is a superb blend of Rajput and Mughal architecture, with open, airy Mughal-style public buildings leading to private apartments. The opulence and exquisite craftsmanship is a tribute both to the wealth of the former *maharajas* and their lavish patronage of the arts. At present, part of the complex is open to the public, as the Maharaja Sawai Man Singh II Museum. It is popularly known as the City Palace Museum, where the beautiful Chandra Mahal remains the residence of the erstwhile Maharaja. Inside this, one finds erstwhile armoury houses among the museum's collections, the four delicately painted doorways, representing the seasons, the giant silver urns in *Diwan-I-Khas* listed in the *Guiness Book of Record*s as the largest silver objects in the world. They carried water of the sacred Ganges for Madho Singh II's visit to London in 1901. In the Art Gallery, one comes across *Takth-e-Rawal* (Golden Throne) on which the Maharaja sat when he appeared in public. It was either put on an elephant's back or carried by *palanquin* bearers. A glittering collection of textiles and *costumes* from the royal *toshakhana* is displayed on the first floor. They include exquisitely embroidered and handloom-woven shawls from Kashmir. Flanking the gateway are the two huge elephants, each carved from a single block of marble.

Of the five observatories built by Sawai Jai Singh II, the one in Jaipur, i.e. **Jantar Mantar**, is the largest and best preserved. Others are in Delhi, Ujjain, Mathura and Varanasi. Jai Singh had undertaken the latest astronomical studies in the world. Based on his knowledge he built this observatory between 1728 and 1734. It resembles a giant sculpture composition of 16 instruments and has been described as "the most realistic and logical landscape in stone". These instruments could help in forecasting how hot the summer months will be, the expected date of monsoon's arrival, duration and the intensity of the monsoon, and the possibility of floods and famine. One of them is Laghu Samrat Yantra, which calculates Jaipur's local time up to an accuracy of 20 seconds. Another one is Chakra Yantra, where a brass tube passes through the centre of two circular metal instruments through which the angle of stars and planets from the equator can be observed. Unnatansha Yantra used to determine the positions of stars and planets at any time of the day or night. Jai Singh believed that gigantic instruments would give more accurate results. Therefore, he designed Samrat Yantra to forecast the crop prospects for the year. Rashivalaya Yantra is composed of 12 pieces, each of which represents a sign of the zodiac and so faces a different angle and constellation. This *yantra*, used by astrologers to make accurate horoscopes, is only available here. In Jai Prakash Yantra, two sunken hemispheres map

out the heavens. This instrument is believed by some historians to have been invented by Jai Singh himself to verify the accuracy of all the others in the observatory.

In south of the walled city, the **Government Central Museum** (Albert Hall) was commissioned by Sawai Ram Singh II to honour the visit of Albert, the Prince of Wales, in 1876. It combines modern European with traditional Indian elements to create a highly ornamental style used for many public buildings during the British Raj. Its ground floor displays decorative shields and embossed salvers in Jaipur's famed metalware, life-sized models of rural scenes, glazed pottery, and even an Egyptian Mummy. The first floor has a fine collection of Mughal and Rajput miniature paintings.

Journey to Jaipur is quite tiring but it is most rewarding. Unlike Agra, the city's architecture is most impressive.

Maharaja

To make us comfortable, it should be better to stay at night. While traveling back to New Delhi by Shatabdi Express, the pomp and pageantry of the erstwhile *maharajas* (kings) flashed in my mind again and again. I became curious to know what has happened to them and to their successors. Mr M L Ahuja, who traveled with me to the monuments in New Delhi, Agra and Jaipur, told me that all the princely states, numbering 562, were brought together in India by a plan conceived by Sardar Vallabhbhai Patel at the time of Independence. It was by granting them privy purses in proportion to the size of the revenue of former princely states as a *quid pro quo* for surrender of their ruling powers and dissolution of their states. With their fabulous palaces, jewelry collections, elaborate *durbars* and fleet of luxury cars these *maharajas* had become a definition for lavish hospitality and a privileged lifestyle. The fairy tale ended when Prime Minister Indira Gandhi introduced the 26th Amendment to the Constitution of India in July 1971, abolishing privy purses and recognition granted to the rulers of Indian states.

3

Educational Opportunities

Education in India, after the Constitutional Amendment of 1976, has been included in the Concurrent List. The substantive, financial and administrative implications require the sharing of responsibility between the Union Government and the States. The Central Government plays the lead role in the evolution and monitoring of educational policies and programs. It lays down the National Policy on Education. Its policy envisages a National System of Education to bring about uniformity in education, making adult education programs a mass movement, providing universal access, retention and quality in elementary education, special emphasis on education of girls, establishment of pace-setting schools like Navodaya Vidyalayas in each district, vocationalization of secondary education, synthesis of knowledge and inter-disciplinary research in higher education, starting more open universities in states, strengthening of the All India Council of Technical Education, encouraging sports, physical education and yoga, and adoption of an effective evaluation method, etc.

Literacy

The latest Census in India was in 2001. For the purpose of knowing whether a person is literate or not, a person aged seven and above, who can both read and write with understanding in any language, is treated as literate. A person, who can only read but cannot write, is not literate. The provisional results of 2001 census reveal that there has been an increase in literacy in India. The literacy rate in India is 65.38 per cent (75.85 per cent for males and 54.16 for females). Kerala is on top with 90.92 per cent literacy rate, closely followed by Mizoram (88.49 per cent) and Lakshdweep (87.52 per cent). Bihar, with a literacy rate of 47.53 per cent, ranks last in the country preceded by Jharkhand

(54.13 per cent) and Jammu & Kashmir (54.46 per cent). Kerala also occupies the top spot in the country both in male literacy with 94.20 per cent and female literacy with 87.86 per cent. On the contrary, Bihar has recorded the lowest literacy rate, both in case of males (62.32 per cent) and females (33.57 per cent).

Language of Communication & Instruction

India never had a common language, which was intelligible to the masses. For many years, Sanskrit remained a common medium. But it was the language of the learned classes and not of the masses. Under the British, English became a sort of lingua franca. But it was restricted to the educated few. Language being the most important medium of communication and education, its development occupies an important place in the National Policy on Education and Program of Action. India is believed to have 1652 mother tongues of which 33 are spoken by the people numbering over a hundred thousand. These languages have interacted with one another through the centuries and have produced the major linguistic division of modern India. Among the major groups, the Aryan and the Dravidian are dominating families.

Indo-Aryan, the Indic-branch of the Indo-European family, came into India with the Aryans. It is the biggest of the language groups in India, accounting for about 74 per cent of the entire population. Dravidian languages, on the other hand, form a group by themselves and unlike the Aryan, Austric or Sino-Tibetan speeches, have no relations outside the Indian sub-continent, i.e. India, Pakistan and Bangladesh. The Dravidian family is the second largest group in India, covering about 25 per cent of the total population. Though the languages listed in the Constitution in independent India remain the official languages in the respective states, Hindi and English continue to be used for inter-State correspondence.

The languages listed in the Constitution are: Assamese, Bengali, Gujarati, Hindi, Kannada, Kashmiri, Konkani, Malayalam, Manipuri, Marathi, Nepali, Oriya, Punjabi, Sanskrit, Sindhi, Tamil, Telugu, and Urdu. According to 1991 Census, Hindi is the mother tongue of 39.85 per cent of the population, Bengali of 8.22 per cent, Telugu of 7.80 per cent, Marathi of 7.38 per cent, Tamil of 6.26 per cent, Urdu of 5.13 per cent, Gujarati of 4.81 per cent, Kannada of 3.87 per cent, Malayalam of 3.59 per cent, Oriya of 3.32 per cent, Punjabi of 2.76 per cent, Assamese of 1.55 per cent, Sindhi of 0.25 per cent, Nepali of 0.21 per cent, Manipuri 0.15 per cent, Kashmiri 0.46 per cent and Sanskrit of 0.01 per cent.

Elementary Education

The National System of Education is based on a national curriculum framework, which contains a common core along with other flexible, region-specific components. While the policy stresses widening of opportunities for the masses, it calls for consolidation of the existing system of higher and technical education. Universalization of Elementary Education has been accepted as a national goal. By the year 2002, 94 per cent of the country's rural population had primary schools within one km. At the upper primary stage, 84 per cent of the rural population had schools within a distance of three km. The central and state governments have, over a period of time, evolved strategies to check drop out rates and improve levels of achievement in the schools. These strategies include the creation of parental awareness and community mobilization, involvement of communities, economic incentives, improvement in the infrastructure facilities in schools, District Primary Education Program initiative, National Program of Nutritional Support to Primary Education (Mid-day Meals Scheme), Education Guarantee Scheme and Alternative and Innovative Education, Teacher Education Schemes, and Sarva Abhiyan initiative.

As a result of the consistent efforts of the Government at national level, enrolment ratio at primary stage has gone up from 40.60 per cent in 1950-51 to 94.90 per cent in 1999-2000. Number of primary and upper primary schools has gone up from 0.223 million in 1950-51 to 0.839 million in 1999-2000 and the number of teachers in primary and upper primary schools is 3.22 million in 1999-2000. In addition to all this, there are 0.292 million non-formal education centres covering about 7.3 million children in 25 States and Union Territories. A total number of 0.233 million centres were run through State government/ Union Territories. About 58,788 centres are being run by 816 voluntary agencies. Of the total number of centres, about 0.115 million centres are exclusively for girls. Since 1979-80, the Department of Education is running this scheme for children of 6-14 age group who remain outside the formal system due to various reasons.

The Government of India has made special provision for the education of women to ensure their equality. The Government is committed to bring about this change in the status of women through education. The major schemes are Mahila Samakhya, Sarva Shiksha Abhiyan, etc. By the year 2001, the scheme was in operation in 8000 villages in 53 districts, spread over 8 states: Andhra Pradesh, Assam, Bihar, Gujarat, Karnataka, Kerala, Madhya Pradesh and Uttar Pradesh.

Secondary Education

Secondary education serves as a bridge between the elementary and higher education to prepare young persons of the age group of 14-18 for entry into higher education. In 1999, there were 0.11 million secondary and senior secondary schools with 27.8 million enrolment, including 10.1 million girls. There were 1.54 million teachers. A scheme envisages the continuous upgradation of knowledge, competence, pedagogical skills, etc. of the teachers.

The Government of India set up National Council of Educational Research and Training (NCERT) as an apex resource organization in 1961 with headquarters at New Delhi. It assists and advises the Central and State governments on academic matters related to school education. It provides academic and technical support for qualitative improvement of school education through its constituents, i.e the Department of National Institute of Education at New Delhi, Central Institute of Educational Technology at New Delhi, Pandit Sunderlal Sharma Central Institute of Vocational Education at Bhopal, Bhubaneshwar, Mysore and Shillong. The Council conducts, aids, promotes and coordinates research in school education and teacher education, organizes pre-service and in-service training of teachers, extension services for institutions, develops and experiments with improved educational techniques, practices and innovations, collects, compiles, processes and disseminates educational information, assists the States/UnionTerritories in developing and implementing programs for qualitative improvement of school education, collaborates with international organizations, serves as the academic secretariat of the National Development Group for the Asia and the Pacific Program of Education, Innovation for Development, UNESCO, Bangkok, and develops, prints and distributes textual material, etc. NCERT has recently created National Resource Centre for Value Education, International Centre for Special Needs of Children, National Centre for Computer Extended Education/Multimedia Laboratory in addition to a Centre of International Project on Technical and Vocational Education.

University and Higher Education

University education in India is coordinated by the University Grants

Commission (UGC), which was established in 1956 by an Act of Parliament for the promotion and coordination as well as determination and maintenance of standards of teaching, examination and research in universities. The UGC serves as a coordinating body between the Union and State governments and the institutions of higher learning. It also acts as an advisory body to the governments and institutions on issues relating to higher education. To fulfil its objectives, the Commission can enquire, *inter alia*, into the financial needs of the universities, allocate and disburse grants to universities and colleges for the maintenance and development, establish and maintain common services and facilities, recommend measures for improvement of university education, make rules and regulations consistent with the Act, and give advice on allocation of grants and establishment of new universities.

By the year 2002, there were 291 university-level institutions, including 70 deemed universities. Of these, 17 are central universities under the administrative control of the Ministry of Human Resource Development, 162 are traditional universities, including 34 institutions for specialized studies in disciplines, while the others are professional/ technical institutions. Of these, 40 provide education in agriculture, including forestry, dairy, fisheries and veterinary science, 18 in medicine, 33 in engineering and technology, and three in information technology. The total number of colleges, by the year 2002, were 12,342 including 1,525 women's colleges. The total enrolment of students in universities and colleges were 8 million while the number of teachers in the year 2002 was 0.395 million.

Technical Education

The Government of India, through an Act of Parliament in 1987, set up an All India Council for Technical Education (AICTE). It is a statutory body to ensure proper planning and coordinated development of technical education system throughout the country, the promotion of qualitative improvement of such education in relation to planned quantitative growth and regulation and proper maintenance of norms and standards in technical education system.

The technical education spectrum at Central level comprise of All India Council for Technical Education, seven Indian Institutes of Technology (IITs), which are institutions of national importance, six Indian Institutes of Management (IIMs), three deemed-to-be universities, namely, Indian Institute of Science in Bangalore, Indian

School of Mines in Dhanbad, School of Planning and Architecture in New Delhi, and seventeen Regional Engineering Colleges. Ten Regional Engineering Colleges have since been converted into National Institutes of Technology. Other technical institutes at Central Sector are National Institute of Foundry and Forage Technology in Ranchi, National Institute of Industrial Engineering in Mumbai, Sant Longowal Institute of Engineering and Technology in Longowal, North-Eastern Regional Institute of Science and Technology in Itanagar, Indian Institute of Information Technology and Management in Gwalior, Indian Institute of Information Technology in Allahabad, four Technical Teachers Training Institutes, four Boards of Apprenticeship Training. There is one public sector undertaking also, namely, Educational Consultants India Ltd. There are numerous polytechnics and industrial training institutes to impart knowledge and training in carpentry, welding, motor mechanic, surveying and other vocations.

In the year 2001-03, the total number of AICTE approved engineering colleges was in the range of 1195 with a total intake capacity of 356,268. There has been a major thrust in increasing intake in related courses. In the year 2002-3, the number of institutions, granting Master of Computer Application (MCA), was 49,576.

Medical Education

The Indian Council of Medical Research (ICMR), New Delhi, is the apex body in India for the formulation, coordination and promotion of biomedical research. ICMR was constituted as an autonomous organization responsible for planning, organization, implementation and coordination of medical research in the country. The major functions of the Council are maintenance of uniform standard of medical education, both at the undergraduate and the postgraduate levels, maintenance of Indian Medical Register, reciprocity with foreign countries in the matter of mutual recognition of medical qualifications, continuing medical education and granting of provisional/permanent registration of doctors with recognized medical qualification, registration of additional qualification and issue of Good Standing Certificate to doctors for going abroad to commonwealth countries.

By the year 2002, there were 193 medical colleges in India. Out of these, 157 medical colleges have been recognized by MCI and 36 new medical colleges have been permitted by the Central Government to conduct MBBS course. The admission capacity in these colleges is approximately 21,450 students per year. In addition to these, there are 154 dental colleges with an admission capacity of approximately 9,000 students in the BDS course, 352 institutions imparting Diploma in Pharmacy to 20,534 students per annum, 155 institutions offering degree in Pharmacy to 8,361 students per annum, 739 general nursing and midwifery schools, 340 auxiliary nurse midwifery schools, 11 impart diploma in nursing education and administration. There are 18 colleges at B.Sc level in nursing and 19 colleges at M.Sc level in nursing. On an average, 13-15,000 nurses qualify every year. In 2002-03, 775812 general nurses and midwives were registered with various State Nursing Councils.

In post-Independence India, the Government of India recognized the merit of each of the Indian Systems of Medicine and Homoeopathy (ISM&H) and made attempts to develop them as viable systems of medicine for the health care needs of the people. It was felt that the goal of the World Health Organization of "Health for All" cannot be achieved through the modern Allopathic system alone and there is need to involve the ISM&H practitioners in the national mainstream for achieving this goal. This resulted in the recognition of traditional systems of Ayurveda, Siddha & Unani, Homoeopathy, Yoga and Naturopathy as National Systems of Medicine along with Allopathy. A separate Department under the Ministry of Health & Family Welfare in the year 1995 was established for this purpose. This paved the way for the organized development of all these six systems of medicine.

The institutional framework consists of central level Department of Indian Systems of Medicine and Homoeopathy, Statutory Regulatory Councils, Research Councils, National Institutes, Pharmacopoetal Laboratories and Drug manufacturing units. The health care infrastructure under ISM&H available in India consists of 3,841 hospitals with 65,753 bed capacity, 23,597 dispensaries, 412 undergraduate colleges, 88 colleges having Post Graduate Departments, 9,832 licensed manufacturing units and 68.9 million practitioners of Indian Systems of Medicine and Homoeopathy in the country. Under Siddha System, there are five Siddha medical colleges. Out of these five, two colleges are having the postgraduate teaching facility. The Government has set up national-level educational institutions of each system as model institutes to promote excellence in ISM&H education. In the field of Yoga and Naturopathy education, course content has been worked out. The feasibility of having an independent regulatory body for the education and practice of Yoga and Naturopathy is being examined. A mechanism is being evolved for granting accredition to institutes conducting diploma/degree course pending establishment of a Statutory Regulatory Body.

The Government of India has initiated many steps for popularization of ISM&H in foreign countries. There is a scheme for international exchange program/seminars/workshops with the objective to promote and develop Indian Systems of Medicine and increase involvement of professionals/researchers for dissemination of the proven work on research and developments. Delegations from Russia, Malaysia, South Africa, South Korea, Hungary, Myanmar and Brazil visited the Department during the year 2001-02. The Government of India has also entered into memoranda of understanding with Russia and Hungary for bilateral cooperation and collaboration in the field of Ayurveda education and research.

Major Research Institutes

The Government is encouraging research in physical sciences, chemical sciences, biological sciences, engineering, and information sciences. For this purpose, Central Electronic Engineering Research Institute is functioning in Pilani, Central Scientific Instruments Organization in Chandigarh, National Institute of Oceanography in Goa, Central Electrochemical Research Institute in Karaikudi, Central Leather Research Institute in Chennai, Central Salt and Marine Chemical Research Institute in Bhavnagar, Indian Institute of Chemical Technology in Hyderabad, Regional Research Laboratory in Jorhat, National Chemical Laboratory in Pune, Central Drug Research Institute in Lucknow, Central Food Technological Research Institute in Mysore, Central Institute of Medicinal and Aeromatic Plants in Lucknow, Centre for Biochemical Technology in Delhi, National Botanical Research Institute in Lucknow, Indian Institute of Chemical Biology in Kolkota, Industrial Toxicology Research Institute in Lucknow, Institute of Microbial Technology in Chandigarh, Institute of Himalayan Bioresource Technology in Palampur, Central Building Research Institute in Roorkee, Central Fuel Research Institute in Dhanbad, Central Glass and Ceramic Research Institute in Kolkota, Central Mining Research Institute in Dhanbad, Central Road Research Institute in New Delhi, National Aerospace Laboratories in Bangalore, National Metallurgical Laboratory, Jamshedpur, National Environmental Engineering in Nagpur, Regional Research Laboratory in Thiruvanthapuram, Regional Research Laboratory in Bhubanesvar, Structural Engineering Research Centre in Ghaziabad, Central Mechanical Engineering Research Institute in Durgapur, National Institute of Science, Technology and Developmental Studies in New Delhi, National Institute of Science Communication in New Delhi, and Indian National Scientific Documentation Centre (INSDOC) in New Delhi. In addition to all these, a number of research centres are affiliated to the Indian Council of Agricultural Research.

Book Promotion & Readership

For publishing, promotion of books and reading, promotion of Indian books abroad, assistance to authors and publishers, and promotion of children's literature, the National Book Trust was set up in 1957. It is an autonomous organization. It produces books in Hindi, English and fifteen other major Indian languages under its various series and also in Braille. Every alternate year, NBT organizes the World Book Fair, which is the largest in Asia and Africa. The Trust also observes 14-20 November every year as National Book Week.

According to the findings of the National Readership Survey 2002, India's print media readership base has expanded by 10 per cent over the last two years. Since the last NRS survey in 1999, the print media has acquired 17 million more readers. According to the survey, India's vast media industry reaches 180 million readers, 383.6 million television viewers, 680.6 million radio listeners and six million Internet users. The survey revealed that India's 428 million literate adults do not read any periodical publication. Besides India's vast illiterate adult population, there are 248 million literate adults who are unexposed to newspapers and magazines, in comparison to the 180 million who do read publications. Readers from nearly 600,000 villages make up only 48 per cent of the readership base, although rural India is home to 62.6 per cent of the country's literate population. This could be due to the urban-centric nature of most publications, which do not cater to the interests of rural residents. Thus, the NRS points to a vast, untapped readership base in rural India. Newspaper readership has grown by about 20 per cent from 0.131 million in 1999 to 0.155 million in 2002. Readership growth has been faster than literacy growth, which expanded by 13 per cent during the same period. Newspapers belonging to English, Hindi, Marathi and Kannada were mainly responsible for this rise in readership. The Hindi dailies, *Dainik Bhaskar* and *Dainik Jagran* have the highest readership with 1.3

million and 12.6 million readers respectively. In urban India, *The Times of India* is amongst the top 10. The fastest growing dailies are the Assamese dailies in urban areas (51.8 per cent increase) and the Bengali dailies in rural areas (129 per cent rise). Other high growth dailies are published in Oriya, Hindi, Punjabi, Kannada and Marathi. The highest readership was found to be in Kerala.

The reach of the press is higher in the southern, western and northeastern states, which have higher literacy rates. The northern states, barring Punjab, Himachal Pradesh and Haryana have lower exposure to the press. Television reach patterns are also along the same lines as press exposure, except in northeastern states where television reach is low but press reach is high. Kerala, the state with the highest literacy rate, has a 70 per cent readership. But in Bihar, which has one of the lowest literacy level, only 15 per cent of the population reads periodicals.

People in urban India spend less time in media-print, television, radio and the Internet. Most media time is taken up by television, which commands 72 per cent of the urban India's time spent on media. Around half of all homes in India with televisions now have cable and satellite subscriptions. The Internet has grown in terms of access by over 30 per cent in the last year. At present, 6.02 million people have an access to the Internet. Most of the Internet users are from urban India. There has been a sudden increase in the growth of Internet cafes, making the World Wide Web accessible to a larger audience. Radio still has the largest reach among all the media. It has 680.6 million listeners. All India Radio (primary channel) is still the most popular channel, drawing 61.8 per cent of the listeners. Vividh Bharati and FM garner 13.3 per cent and 14 per cent of the listeners respectively.

4

Gender Equality

On March 8, 2003, I was taken to Jama Masjid, located in the walled city of Delhi. Since it happens to be the most congested area in Delhi, we decided to take a *rickshaw* (tricycle, pulled by a man). The *rickshaw* puller, who appeared to be very hungry, struggled with our weights. As he pushed his tricycle along, his left wheel caught a woman's bag, which fell to the ground. In fury, she picked up her bag, shouted abuses at the *rickshaw*-puller and, at the same time, mercilessly hit him repeatedly all over the body and head with the bag. The *rickshaw*-puller became calm all along when being hit. I just could not believe this. My mind went back to my own country, Papua New Guinea. Anything like this, even if one is wrong, would retaliate. Others watching would join the fight and some would be badly hurt or even killed.

This incident made me think of women's status *vis-à-vis* men in India as distinct from Papua New Guinea and other countries. What prompts such women to show courage before men? I saw a number of *burqa*-clad (veiled) women moving either in *rickshaws* or walking around the Jama Masjid area. There must be many women, I thought, who may not be as aggressive as the woman was. Then, what should be the general status of women in India? It became a subject of lengthy discussion for me with some people. I also studied the reports of National Commission for Women to know the legal setting, the Constitution, the legislation, the attitude of the courts and the social realities to define the position of Indian women.

I had already heard that India has taken out a patent on international beauty crowns. Rita Faria was the first Indian to win the Miss World crown in 1994. Sushmita Sen, Aishwarya Rai, Diana Hayden, Yukta Mookhey, Priyanka Chopra, and Lara Dutta followed. However, the concluding decades of the last millennium has seen the emergence of a strong movement for women's empowerment all over the world. The years following Indian Independence have also been momentous ones for India. During this period, not only India marched ahead from foreign domination to independence, but also witnessed the country launching a series of development plans aimed at the socio-economic transformation. How have the women of India fared in this economic and social change?

I have read and have been told of the exciting developments like women becoming Supreme Court Judges, chief ministers, ministers, space scientists, and industrialists. Some of them have distinguished themselves in literature, science and arts, while some others have flown aircrafts and driven train engines. Women have also been inducted in army. Women officers, as I was told, were recruited in Indian army in as early as in 1990s. At present, they serve in all non-combat armed forces. Women officers are granted only Short Service Commission for 5 years, extendable by another 5 years. In Indian Air Force and Navy, their initial 10-year tenure can be extended by another 4-5 years. Doctors or nursing officers can, however, hope for a permanent Commission. IAF has women as pilots, albeit restricted to helicopters and transport aircrafts. Of the 424 women officers in the IAF at present, only 46 are pilots. It has no plan to have women fighter pilots like Israel, the US, UK and some other countries. The Navy doesn't allow women officers on board sea-faring warships. On the other hand, I heard about the large multitudes of women suffering indignities at home and outside. There have been media reports of criminal assault on women.

Towards Resurgence

Though in India's long history, individual women had risen to the levels of eminence—literary, religious, social or even political—Mahatma Gandhi's mass-mobilization of India's freedom had also involved women in large numbers from all strata of society. The leaders of women's movement, as it then existed, also had international linkages with the suffragist and anti-imperialist lobbies of the West. But this touched only a very small minority of women and the mass involvement of women. The overwhelming majority of them represented the most backward face of Indian citizenry. Hardly 7 per cent of them were literate. Life expectancy was barely 37 years and the women were subject to debilitating diseases and suffered maternal mortality of a rate as high as 1000 per hundred thousand live births. In

1931, Mahatma Gandhi said that "I shall work for India in which there shall be no high class and low-class of people ... women shall enjoy the same rights as men ..."

In keeping with this resolve of Mahatma Gandhi, Government of India's innovative forward looking National Policy for Empowerment of Women 2001 and the declaration of the Year 2001 for the Empowerment of Women are indicative of the things to follow. Gone are the days when the dictum of Manu, the Father of Indian Legal System, prevailed. Chapter 9 of Manu's *Manusmriti* ordains that men must make their women dependent day and night and keep them under their own control. They had to be guided by their fathers in childhood, by their husbands in youth and by their sons in old age.

Before independence, in the year 1947, a memorandum from the representative women's organization called for an adult franchise without sex discrimination. In 1931, the Karachi session of the Indian National Congress committed itself to political equality of women regardless of their status and qualification. The Government of India Act of 1935 paved the way for women above the age of 21 with property and education to exercise franchise, deleting the conditions of marriage. In 1950, the Constitution of India pledged the nation to achieve a just society, based on the principle of equality and dignity of the individual. It proclaimed the right to political and legal equality as fundamental rights of all Indians. The guarantee against discrimination in employment and office under the State opened the avenues to offices of power and dignity. The Committee on the Status of Women in India (CSWI) has used three indicators to test the efficacy of the political status of women. They are: (1) turnout of women voters and number of women candidates in each election, (2) the level of awareness, commitment and involvement of women participating in politics, (3) assessment of women's views about their own roles and efficacy in the political process and society's attitude to the new roles of women. Constant efforts are being made at all levels towards this objective.

Political Status

By the turn of the century, aspirations of educated women in India enlarged to cover political participation. The proportion of women members in the Lok Sabha has doubled over the half century since the first general election from 22 to 48 members, indicating an increase from 4.4 per cent to 8.9 per cent in 1999. After increasing in the second and third elections it started declining during the fourth and fifth elections touching a low of 3.4 per cent in 1977. Since then it has been rising. One of the two members to be nominated by the President in the Lok Sabha under Article 331 has been a woman in the 11th, 12th and 13th Lok Sabhas. Though there has been a perceptible increase of women MPs, yet it has not reached the world average of 10 per cent and does not necessarily make the "critical mass" required for influencing decisions. It has been observed that the membership in the Rajya Sabha is treated as a special preserve of the political parties who would like to bring in important candidates of their choice and who may be successful in popular electoral contests to the Lok Sabha. Bill for the reservation of seats for women is still pending before the Parliament.

Seeking Reservation in Parliament

The women's participation in political process, though less than that of males, is increasing. It ranged between 51.2 per cent in 1980 to 55.6 per cent in 1999. The difference between male and female participation has been 11 per cent to 8.4 per cent. In the past, political parties depended on the male heads of families to guide their women folk during election campaigns. But now, with increasing awareness of women on various social development issues and the need for fulfillment of various priorities of women, political parties have become conscious of addressing women voters exclusively. One example of this is the promise on the introduction of prohibition in several states in India during the election campaigns. This is in response to women's demands to curb domestic violence, mainly due to alcoholism. Other important specific issues on which political parties have come to undertake electoral commitments are those relating to education and health care of women, their access to skills, employment, income, economic assets etc. During 1998 and 1999 general elections, all major political parties committed in their manifestos to secure one-third reservation for women in the Parliament and State legislative bodies, but the Bill for reservation of women in the Parliament is still pending for want of consensus.

Government Machinery

The Department of Women and Child Development under the Ministry of Human Resource Development looks after the various programs and schemes and monitors them for effective implementation. The Department coordinates with various ministries to ensure that women get a fair share of the benefits under all development programs. In this way, in the agriculture and allied sectors, attention is given for improvement of the existing skills of women and imparting new skills under the program of farmers' training. The Central Social Welfare Board also extends grant-in-aid to voluntary organizations to set up income generating units. In villages, greater share of employment for women in small scale industries and *khadi* industries has been envisaged. The Research, Reference and Training Division of the Ministry of Information & Broadcasting has made a compilation of certain Codes of Conduct and also various laws governing women. The Ministry of Labour, through legislation, has ensured welfare and protection of women's rights. The Supreme Court, in the case of Writ Petition (Criminal) Nos.666-70 of 1992, filed by *Visaka and Others versus the State of Rajasthan and Others* has laid down certain guidelines for the prevention of sexual harassment of women employees in their workplaces. The guidelines have the force of law under Article 141 of the Constitution of India.

Legal Immunities

During the British India, Family law had been stagnant, incapable of adjustment to socio-economic dynamics. The Law Commission of India and the National Commission for Women have done extensive work on women-related laws. There has also been perceptible change for the better, especially in recent years, in the role of the judiciary in the matter of addressing women's issues. The Government of India has ratified the UN Convention on the Elimination of All Forms of Discrimination against Women (1993). But, still Personal laws continue to be diverse because of the overburden of traditional practices linked to the faiths of various communities. Implementation of Uniform Civil Code, as envisaged in Article 44 of the Constitution, has not come about as yet. It is principally because the orthodox sections in some communities have looked at it as violative of their faith. It has an impact on the policy makers from time to time. They have either desisted from legislative measures or have been inclined to put off consideration of such measures to an uncertain future.

Despite legislation and efforts of the Government as well as the judicial pronouncements, the social reality in the country is different.

Large numbers of girls continue to be married before the age of 18 years. This is despite the legal stipulations. This is also due to strong and deep-rooted social pressures. The minimum age for girls for marriage was raised to 18 years and 21 years for boys in 1976. But the legislation doesn't seem to be adequate to change the mindset. Nearly 20 per cent of the females still get married before 18 years. Over 50 per cent of the girls marry between 18 to 20 years in India. The proportion of girls marrying before 18 years is generally higher in rural areas compared to urban areas. The proportion of girls getting married after 21 years is significantly higher in urban areas compared to rural areas. In some parts of the country, there is a gap between the age of marriage and the consummation of marriage—'*gauna*', which usually takes place after a few years. However, with social awareness the mean age at marriage has gone up to 19.4 years in 1994 from 17.1 years in 1971 thereby recording an increase of 2.3 years against the increase of 1.7 years between 1951 and 1971.

Punishment for marriages in violation of age limit is relatively inadequate. If a male above 18 years and below 21 years of age marries a minor girl below 18 years, the punishment is 15 days' imprisonment or a fine of Rs 100. If a male contracts a marriage over 21 years of age, the punishment is 3 months' imprisonment and fine. According to the Hindu Marriage Act, a girl can opt out of marriage and can get divorce if she was below 15 years of age at the time of marriage and repudiates the marriage between 15 and 18. Under the Muslim law, marriage with minor girl poses yet another problem. Among Muslims, marriage is a contract. A contract with a minor is void. Again, under the Muslim Personal Law (Shariat) Application of 1937, minor girl can't enter into a contract of marriage despite her consent.

Dowry Prohibition Act, as amended, tantamounts to the demand of dowry with cruelty. Under section 304 B of the Indian Penal Code the husband and in-laws are liable to punishment in case of death of a woman preceded by dowry-related cruelty or harassment. Causing of dowry death was also made punishable with imprisonment for a period of not less than seven years. As a measure against the practice of dowry amongst the government servants, its acceptance has been made misconduct punishable under the Government Servants Conduct Rules.

In India, *Sati* (the practice of burning a wife with husband's dead body) had been largely practiced in the past. This practice, in fact, originated to protect widows from falling in the hands of enemies when their husbands were martyred in the bettelfield. But this practice continued for a long time till it was banned through the efforts of social activists like Raja Ram Mohan Roy. However, in the recent history, the isolated case has been that of Roop Kunwar.

Roop Kunwar was an 18-year old university student. Her husband was an unemployed university graduate. He died of cancer. On September 4, 1987, she was burnt alive on her husband's funeral pyre in Deorala in Rajasthan state. There were different versions regarding the incident. According to one version, it was Roop's voluntary act. There was yet another, that she was forced into the pyre. Women's activist groups were outraged. They organized demonstration in Rajasthan. The local people, however, retaliated/arguing that the incident was quite consistent with their ethnic culture. There was even a local media report that Roop's act was a reflection of her faith in "reincarnation". After initial delays, Roop's father-in-law and certain other members of the family were arrested for abetment to suicide. As a result of this, the Indian Parliament enacted Sati Prevention Act 1987.

The judiciary in India has been quite progressive and protective in interpreting the law relating to maintenance. In the *Shah Bano* case, the Supreme Court upheld the maintenance right of divorced Muslim women (AIR 1985 SC 945). Under Section 125 of Cr.PC, any man who deserts or divorces a wife, who cannot support herself, is liable to pay a stipulated compensation. This protection under the general law was held by the Court to be applicable to the *Shah Bano* case. Earlier, it had held that the *Mehr* could not be construed as exhausting a divorced Muslim woman's right to maintenance, especially if the *Mehr* did not tantamount to be adequate maintenance. The Muslim Women (Protection on Divorce) Act was enacted in 1986.

Shah Bano happened to be an obscure 62-year-old Muslim woman from Indore in Madhya Pradesh. She became a national cause celebrity and a political tool for the then government when all she wanted was alimony to support her five children. She filed a case, which eventually reached the Supreme Court. Muslim fundamentalists were outraged when the courts decided an issue that had traditionally been under the Muslim Personal Law. The core issue was that personal laws of all religions were intrinsically anti-women. The case set a precedent. The apex court's latest call to enact a common civil code also questions the legal recognition of "personal laws" relating to marriage and divorce in various religious communities. Her husband divorced Shah

Bano in 1978. Under the personal law she was entitled to only *Mehr,* an amount fixed at the time of marriage, and three months of maintenance. In 1985, the court imposed a liability on the husband to pay maintenance as long as the divorced woman could not take care of herself. Under pressure from the fundamentalists, the then Prime Minister Rajiv Gandhi came up with the Muslim Women (Protection on Rights of Divorce) Act in 1986, which pitted women's individual rights against the rights of a minority group. The apex court's call in 2003 seeks to correct that anomaly.

In terms of the Indian Christian Marriage Act 1872, the Parsi Marriage and Divorce Act 1865 and the Hindu Marriages Act 1955, monogamy has virtually become the principle amongst the majority of the Indian population. Only the Muslim law has not undergone any change so far. Polygamy continues to be in practice only under Muslim law, where marriage is a matter of contract. However, in practice, while bigamy is an offence under the Hindu Marriage Act, the practice still continues. Non-enforcement of law by the Government, social ostracism of the wife in the event of prosecution of the husband etc. are the principal reasons for the continuance of the practice of bigamy. To escape the rigours of law, some Hindus converted themselves as Muslims to have a second wife. Certain women's organizations have been agitating for Uniform Civil Court or are engaged in creating mass awareness about the issue. Community organizations have also been deliberating on Personal Law issues. The All India Muslim Personal Law Board, for example, is itself reported to be seriously seized of several of the Muslim women's problems like *'triple talaq'*, dowry, inheritance and succession.

The Supreme Court of India, interpreting the scope and extent of Section 494 (bigamy) of the Indian Penal Court, in *Sarla Mudgal* case, held that "...the second marriage of a Hindu husband, after conversion to Islam, without having the first marriage dissolved under the law, would be invalid. The second marriage would be void in terms of the provisions of Section 494 IPC and the apostate husband would be guilty of offense under section 494".

Both the husband and the wife, among the Hindus, can seek divorce on common grounds, be it under the Hindu Marriage Act 1955 or the Special Marriage Act 1954. Among the Christians also, under the Indian Divorce Act 1869, there are stipulated grounds for seeking divorce. Among the Muslims, the wife has been given restricted rights to dissolve marriage according to traditional laws.

She has the rights for such dissolution under the Muslim Marriage Act 1939 on stipulated grounds. But the husband has the entitlement to give *talaq* to the wife, without assigning any reason, whenever he wishes. While there are different forms of *talaq*, the triple *talaq* is both instantaneous in effect and is irrevocable. However, some aggrieved Muslim women, under Articles 14,15 and 21 of the Constitution, have contested this.

The Indian Succession Act 1925 provides for uniform succession to all other than Hindus, Sikhs, Jains, Buddhists and Muslims. The Hindu Succession Act 1956 establishes the inheritance right of women equally with men and abolishes life estate of female heirs, the retention of Mitakshara coparcenary (joint family) with its attendant inequality between female and male heirs. In the case of a joint family, a daughter gets only a smaller share than the son. While sharing of father's property between brother and sister is equal, the brother—in addition—is entitled to a share in the coparcenary from which the sister is excluded. Further, if the family owns a dwelling house, the daughter's right thereon is confined only to the right of residence.

Crimes against women are on the increase. According to *Crime in India*, 1996 and 1998, in 1990, there were 68,317 incidence of crimes against women. In 1994, the figure was 101,657, in 1995 it was 109,259, in 1996 it was 115,723, and in 1997 it was 131,338. These incidents related to rape, kidnapping and abduction, dowry death, torture, molestation, sexual harassment, importation of girls, *sati*, immoral traffic, dowry, etc.

A very serious and technology-based problem concerning women addressed by legislation after the report of the CSWI has been sex selection. Sex ratio was 972 per thousand at the turn of the century. This came down to 927 by 1991. In urban areas, it was even worse—893 per thousand. Census 2001 has revealed an improvement in the sex ratio to 933 females per 1000. However, the juvenile sex ratio has slipped down to 927 from 945. It is as low as 793 in Punjab, 820 in Haryana and 865 in Delhi. Deliberate practice of female foeticide has been causing these sliding ratios. The law against sex determination was first enacted in 1987 in the State of Maharashtra. Seven years thereafter, in 1994, a national law, the Prenatal Diagnostic Techniques (Regulation and Prevention of Misuse) Act was enacted with precedence over laws enacted by the states. It provides the application of the prenatal diagnostic techniques only for detection of abnormalities. It prohibits individuals or genetic clinics, using the techniques, to determine the sex of the foetus. It stipulates penalty of three years' imprisonment and fine of Rs.10,000 apart from suspension of registration of the doctor who violates the law. In spite of this, clandestine sex determination tests go largely unreported.

Section 354 of the Indian Penal Code deals with sexual assault, i.e. outraging the modesty of women. This carries the penalty of imprisonment, which may extend to two years. All kinds of sexual assaults, other than rape, are now dealt with under this provision. The punishment of rape of minor below 12 years of age has been enhanced to the minimum of 10 years. Under Section 376 of IPC, when the wife is below 12 years of age, the penalty is the same as provided for rape generally. But, where the wife is 12 or 12+ years of age, but below 15 years, it is construed as a lesser offence and the punishment is milder. In such cases, the penalty is imprisonment, which may extend to 2 years or fine or both. Under Section 375 of the Indian Penal Code, in the case of child wife, if she is above 15 years of age, infliction of sex on her against her will by the husband is not construed as rape at all.

As per the Indian Penal Code, in cases of adultery, the husband can prosecute his wife's paramour. The wife does not have a corresponding right, i.e. to prosecute her husband's paramour. In *Soumithri vs. Union of India* (AIR 1985 SC 1618), this legal position was challenged as violative of Article 14 of the Constitution. The Court held that the wife "is a victim and not the author of the crime". The Supreme Court also held that the provision relating to adultery was not discriminatory, as neither the wife nor the husband could sue each other. The legal provision was directed against the outsider who violated the sanctity of the matrimonial home. The situation of the wife not having the right to get the outsider prosecuted for violation of the matrimonial home was treated as reverse discrimination in favour of the woman.

The Immoral Traffic Prevention Act was enacted in 1986 under which child prostitution is an offence. There are also constitutional and other legal provisions, which prohibit trafficking in women and children. This prohibition is subsumed in Article 23 of the Constitution, which guarantees the fundamental right against exploitation. Sections 366, 366A, 372 and 373 of the Indian Penal Code provide for penalties for the criminal offence of trafficking in children.

The Indecent Representation of Women (Prohibition) Act 1986 prohibits indecent representation of women through advertisements or publications, writings, paintings, figures or in any other manner. It further prohibits sales, distribution and circulation of material containing indecent representation of women.

In western-style jurisprudence, *salus populi suprema lex esto* (let the welfare of the people be the final law) forms the bedrock of civil law. In 1986, the then Chief Justice P N Bhagwati introduced public interest litigation (PIL) in the Indian judicial system. The original idea was to give marginalised citizens access to justice, but by the mid-1990s PILs had transformed the legal landscape with a flurry of high-profile cases. By 1997, the trickle had turned into a flood, with over 300 PILs pending before the Supreme Court and another 2,000 in high courts, many either of a frivolous nature or the result of political or personal motivation. Many of them relate to women-related issues as well.

However, for the purpose of legal aid, women, as a class, fall under special category and are entitled to free legal services under Section 12 of the Legal Services Authorities Act 1987, irrespective of their income. The income ceiling prescribed under Section 12(h) of the Legal Services Authorities Act is not applicable to them. Women are entitled to free legal services right from the Munsif Court to the Supreme Court of India.

The judiciary has also contributed to its share to the promotion of women's cause through some creative interpretive judgements and historic rulings which have either themselves become law or have led to suitable legislation being enacted.

Educational and Economic Status

The National Policy on Education 1986 (as revised in 1992) recognizes the need to redress the traditional gender imbalance in educational access and achievement. Women were at low level of literacy at the beginning of this century. The advancement and literacy for women were only about 8 per cent in the first half century, and about 13.11 per cent between 1951 and 1971. The pace of improvement has been more significant between 1971 and 1991 raising it by 17.32 per cent to reach 39.32 per cent. The achievement between 1991 and 1996 has been a record at 11 per cent, taking it to 50 per cent between 1997 and 2001, intensifying programs under the Technology Mission for Literacy and specialized programs for promoting women's literacy.

The status of women is obviously connected with the economic position and their opportunities for participation in such activities.

In India, there has been an increasing awareness amongst the policy makers, the society and the women themselves about the need for enhancing women's economic participation as means of advancing their status. The women's movement has also been persistent in its efforts at generating awareness about the importance of women's economic participation through the grassroots action as well as their interaction with the Government at the national and state levels. The perspectives of women's human rights as well as human development are also getting increasing articulation and are being pressed through.

The Constitution of India not only provides for equal rights and privileges for women and men but also for making special provision for women. The successive Five Year Plans have consistently placed special emphasis on providing minimum health facilities integrated with family welfare and nutrition for women and children, acceleration of women's education, the increase in the labour force and welfare services for women in need.

Women face several barriers in attaining economic autonomy and sustainable livelihoods for themselves and their dependents due to several legal and customary obstacles to ownership of land or access to land, natural resources, capital, credit, technology and other means of production. To overcome these, a number of legislations have been enacted to protect them. The Maternity Benefit Act 1961, Equal Remuneration Act 1976, Child Labour (Prohibition and Regulation) Act 1986, the Building and other Construction Workers (Regulation of Employment and Conditions of Service) Act 1996, are some of the legislations, which seek to protect women.

The principle of gender equality is enshrined in the Indian Constitution in its Preamble, Fundamental Rights, Fundamental Duties and Directive Principles. The Constitution not only grants equality to women, but also empowers the State to adopt measures of positive discrimination in favour of women. The Department of Women & Child Development, being the national machinery for empowering the women in the country, has been made responsible for mainstreaming women in the national development by raising their overall status on par with that of men. The Department, in its nodal capacity, formulates policies, plans and programs, and enacts or recommends legislation affecting women and guides/coordinates/ streamlines the efforts of both governmental and non-governmental organizations working to improve the lot of women in the country. The programs of the Department include: continuing education and training, employment and income generation, welfare and support services and gender sensitization and awareness generation.

The Central Social Welfare Board, which is an apex organization at the national level, acts as an umbrella institution networking through State Social Welfare Boards and through them with thousands of voluntary organizations working for welfare and development of women and children in the country. From time to time, various committees are set up to evaluate the impact of constitutional and statutory provisions and the different schemes for social and economic development of women implemented by the departments of central and state governments and to identify gaps or deficiencies. The international conferences have also strengthened the agenda of women's movement. New challenges are bound to arise in the near future and should be met by the concerted efforts of the women's organizations, legislation, judicial interpretation, and its effective implementation of the policies and programs of the Government by the various departments involved in the welfare of women.

5

Multiplicity of Religons

While I was in New Delhi, my host took me to Puronthawali Gali in Chandni Chowk. Chandni Chowk, opposite Red Fort area, as I saw it, is the busiest commercial centre in Delhi. What I found most impressive is the confluence of all cultures and religions making it the miniature India. It is at this place that I could see people following all religions, whether they were Hindus, Sikhs, Muslims, Jains or even Christians. They co-exist with each other, as if they are people of the same fraternity. A similar synthesis of cultures could be witnessed in Agra and Jaipur when I went there. I was told that almost everywhere in India one can find people following these myriad religions. One can also find people of almost all religions occupying the highest offices and posts. This made me curious to find out information about all the religious groups in India and share it with you.

As I have already stated in my previous chapter on Lands and People, Hindus in India constitute almost 82.41 per cent of the population, Islam 11.67 per cent, Christians 2.32 per cent, Sikhs 1.99 per cent, Buddhists 0.77 per cent, and Jains 0.48 per cent. In addition to all these, there are followers of other religions, in the range of 0.43 per cent. If one goes deep into the matter, all religions do not have any conflicting issue. Each of them believes in fraternity, fellow feelings, social cohesion, and spirit of tolerance. If it is so, I do not know why some people follow the fundamentalist approach and promote ill-feelings and enmity. It is, therefore, better to study the cardinal features of all the major religions in India.

But, at the outset, it may be useful to briefly mention what actually religion denotes. This is particularly essential in this age of extremes where ethnicity, religious strife, and the people killing in the name of language, culture, race and religion have become quite common. It is distressing to see that in the name of religion, untold violence is being perpetrated, though no religion ever divides, rather it always unites. Every religion encourages that there is a world, which is still inhabited by people who believe in freedom: freedom to live, freedom to explore and freedom to experience death peacefully.

The term "religion", in fact, is western in origin. It comes from Latin and originally means the bond between the people and the gods. Religion, according to Swami Chinmayananda, imports the "art of living" by which each one discovers, in himself, the equipoise to stand up to life's situations, meeting efficiently the ever changing world of challenge he has to meet. It has a major role in uniting the people, providing them peace, enabling them to cultivate discipline and developing characters. A religious man will never commit sins in privacy or in darkness because he is aware of the supreme force that witnesses his presence everywhere and in acts. According to Vivekananda, "each soul is potentially divine and to manifest that divinity is the aim of religion".

The religion, in essence, is *dharma* or law, a fine thread that binds all human beings. It lays down the proper norms the followers of the religion have to follow. Compassion and love, for instance, is the quintessence of all religions. What religions do is to try to strengthen these qualities which are inherent in every person right from birth. All religions believe in some sort of life after death. They speculate on the destiny of the disembodied entity called soul. Religions of Semitic origin believe that the soul is eternally consigned to Hell or Heaven depending on its sinful or virtuous performance in this world. All religions claim that the knowledge was transmitted through divine revelation through the *Rishis* or various prophets. However, dogmas and extreme rituals have paved the way to fundamentalist approach and a hiatus between one religion to another. It is, therefore, essential to know and understand the cardinal features of each of the religions in India.

Hinduism

Hindus form an overwhelming majority of Indian population. According to 1991 census, they are 82.41 per cent of the Indian population. Hinduism is based on four *Vedas* and the *Upanishads*, which are a holistic compilation of knowledge, philosophy and ethics. Yet, it is not a religion of the book, but a way of life that has been systematically evolved over the past 5,000 years.

Thus, Hinduism, dating back to 1500 BC, is the oldest living organized religion in the world. It starts with the basic conviction, based on the actual spiritual experiences of *Rishis* or seers that man is essentially divine and this divinity is immanent in all creations, animate or inanimate, in a more or less manifest form. It is the realization of this divine nature in him that invests man with the highest and everlasting joy. That this conviction is not a mere blind belief but a matter of living experience has been borne out by the effulgent lives of spiritual masters right from the ancient *Upanishadic* seers to Ramakrishna Paramahansa and Ramana Maharishi in modern times. This inherent divinity can be made manifest by following certain disciplines in life.

Hinduism believes that the universe is continuously changing. It has its own creative process. The Hindu thought suggests that our life is an apprenticeship to the truth, that around every circle another circle can be drawn.

Hinduism's main theological belief is in one omnipresent Divine Being, named Brahma. Orthodox Hindus have believed in every kind of theism, polytheism and pantheism. They worship any object, which they prefer or virtually none. They follow any standard of morality or almost none. Yet, they are recognized as Hindus. This religion is the complex gradual growth of a very religiously minded people with many different temperaments. It has been diversified, yet unified, by its theoretical belief in one immanent, all-inclusive, all sanctifying World Soul, and by its practical social control through caste. It has developed at least six different types of religions, which have been embodied in successive sets of documents. These together constitute the sacred scriptures of Hinduism. They are all written in the Sanskrit language.

The type of religion, which is found in these earliest documents, is mostly nature-worship. The *Rig Veda* contains prayers addressed to 76 different objects, mostly personalized objects or powers in nature, for example, sun, moon, sky, wind, rain, dawn, earth, air, fire, etc. The most important of the Vedic deities is Indra, regent of the atmosphere and the rain. The desires expressed in the prayers to these early Hindu deities are mostly for long life, sons, cattle, good crops, freedom from disease, success over enemies, and general worldly prosperity.

All the *Vedic* deities are to be regarded as manifestations of some power. Brahma is to be interpreted as the absolute, infinite, eternal, omnipresent, impersonal, indescribable, etc. It may also be designated as the spirit (*atman*), a world soul, into which the individual human spirit is also to be merged.

In practice, Hindus worship a huge pantheon of gods and goddesses. They range from a bewildering array, ranging from anthropomorphic symbols and shapes to exotic, half-human, half-animal forms. Each god has a personal *vahana* (vehicle) and symbols of power. Community worship takes place in temples, especially on festivals. Most of the Hindus perform their daily *puja* either at home or in shrine and each of them has his personal deity. Each of these deities is an embodiment of certain virtues. Hindus worship gods/goddesses to seek their blessings.

Saraswati, for instance, is the goddess of learning and music. She is the consort of Brahma and has a swan as her *vahana*. She is worshipped to gain wisdom and understanding. Ganesha is the elephant-headed son of Siva and is invoked at the start of any auspicious task. Hanuman is the monkey god, well-known for his devotion to Lord Rama and undertaking most difficult tasks involving courage and fortitude. Hindus worship him on every Tuesday with a view to imbibe the qualities Hanuman had. Rama, the epitome of virtue, was Visnu's seventh *avatara* (incarnation) and Krsna is the embodiment of love. Parvati is worshipped in many forms, which collectively represent the Devi (goddess) cult. Durga, riding a tiger with her deadly arsenal of weapons destroying evil, is the fierce persona of the gentle Parvati. Kali, wearing a garland of skulls, rampages through creation, annihilating evil. Along with Durga, she is the patron goddess of many Rajput clans who lived by the sword.

Socially, the Hindus are divided into four castes—the upper caste *Brahmins* (priests), the *Vaishyas* (merchants and traders), and the lowest

Religious Symbols

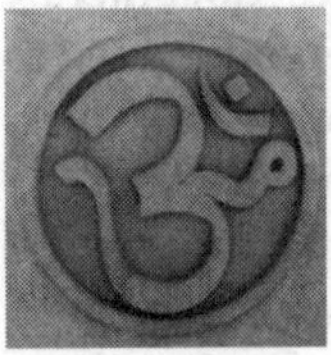

Om, a symbol of primal sacred sound, recited to start all religious ceremonies.

Kamal (lotus), a Vaishnavaite symbol for purity.

Ganesh is worshipped to start any auspicious occasion.

Chakra (wheel), the universal symbol of the wheel of life.

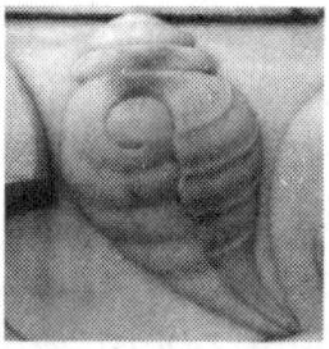

Shankh (conch shell), a Vaishnavaite symbol of the life-giving ocean.

Trishul (trident), a Shaivite symbol of asceticism.

caste, *Sudras* (workers). The caste system envisioned society as an organic whole with each part or caste performing a vital function. The traditional family structure was that of a joint family presided over by its patriarch. This is now fast disappearing in urban areas. Yet, *sanskara,* traditional values, are still instilled into children, and complicated rites mark each stage of orthodox Hindu life. There is also an aspect of Hinduism, which shuns idol-worship, and prefers to concentrate on larger philosophical issues. *Sadhus,* who wear saffron to indicate their retreat from the material world, are its most visible practitioners. They hold a most respected position in Hindu society.

Like all other religions, Hinduism believes in life after death. It strongly supports reincarnation. In fact, this is its most distinguishing feature. This feature of Hinduism greatly reduces the fear of death. The insistence on spiritual experience, time and again, in Hindu scriptures, also sets Hinduism apart. It accepts the basic beliefs of other religions that their faiths are based on divine revelations. Yet Hindus are not content with immortality. They are happy to get rid of birth-death cycle. The aim of every Hindu is to merge his/her soul in the Absolute. It is the union of individual spirit with the Universal Spirit, which is his ultimate theme, i.e. *moksha.* Even for those who have not yet attained *moksha,* but who are free from worldly lifetimes, there is work to do. They have the option to be born for upliftment of souls who are still toiling under *karmic* debts and compulsions. Such beings are called *Jivanmuktas.*

They come here by choice and owe no debt to nature. Hinduism is thus not a religion in the ordinary sense. It is an eco-system, which embraces not only this world but the world beyond as well.

Manusmriti, the law book of Manu, is the most highly revered and influential among several codes of Hindu law. In its 12 chapters, it contains some wise maxims, e.g. respectful obedience to parents and teachers, repentance and confession, fulfilling truth, reverential eating, unresentful patience and endurance of evil. Manu has presented the fourfold caste system in detail.

Among the many scriptures of Hindusm is the one which has been most highly esteemed by Hindus themselves, and also by outsiders. It is the *Bhagvad Gita*. It has been rendered into English by more than a dozen translators. It is a dramatic poem, which starts with a stirring scene at the beginning of a battle. Arjuna raises the question of the propriety of killing people in war. His charioteer allays his conscientious compunctions by a remarkable discourse on the immortality of the soul. The chief speaker in the *Bhagvad Gita* proves to be the deity Krsna in the form of a charioteer. The practical message of the *Gita* may be put in simple language: "Do your duty and trust your God for the rest of your salvation". Salvation, according to *Gita*, is to be obtained chiefly through personal devotion to a personal deity.

Idolatry, as explained earlier, is abundantly manifest throughout Hindu India. It is directed towards all kinds of human and animal representations and even to images of the male and female sexual organs. Popular Hinduism has innumerable temples and shrines, large and small, for the worship of local as well as general deities. The devotions here are chiefly individual, often with offerings, made to the images of the deity and to the attendant priests.

Devotees in large numbers make pilgrimages to various holy rivers, mountains, cities and temples all over India. They observe holy days, fasts and gala celebrations in the lunar and solar cycles. The sowing of seed and the harvesting of crops and other activities in agriculture are connected with religious ceremonies.

Popular Hinduism has been brought intimately into home life through prescribed observance for meals, birth, marriage, death, funeral and offerings for the dead. Though caste is the only feature, which has been present through all the historical features of the religion, yet some modern Hindu reformers are attempting to reject caste. Though reverence for the *Vedas* is the main feature of this religion, yet very few Hindus possess personal acquaintance with their revered scriptures. *Karma* and transmigration are the two other beliefs.

There have been many conscious protests and endeavours for improvement. Mahavir, Gautam Buddha, Tiruvalluvar, Manikka-Vasagar, Ramanuja, Madhva, Ramanand, Nanak, Chaitanya, Kabir, Tulsi Das, Dadur, Ram Mohan Roy and Dr Atmaram Pandurang have attempted to bring in some reforms in Hinduism.

Islam

Do you know that nearly one in five people in the world today constitute a part of the large family of Islam and over fifty countries have Muslim-majority populations, including India? Do you also know that the present population of Muslims in India is around 130 million, more than the total population of Pakistan? Islam is, therefore, reckoned as the major religion in the world and it is essential to know it in detail.

The word 'Islam' is derived from the Arabic word *'salaam'* and has been presented to mean "peace" or "surrender", depending upon the time and place of presentation. Though Hinduism is based on the revelations made to various *Rishis* or seers from time to time, Islam embodies the revelations of Prophet Mohammed. The teachings of Prophet Mohammed are contained in *The Holy Quran*, where Mohammed has emphasized on the unity of God. He asked His followers to have faith in angels who brought message from God. Signs of spiritual genius had been visible to Mohammed even before revelations came to Him. He would retire to the caves of mountain for prayers and meditation. He was fond of solitude. During the time of His revelations, He got a call from angel Gabriel: "O Mohammed, Thou are the Apostle of God and I am Gabriel". Numerically, Islam stands next to Confucianism as the largest non-Christian religion. Again, next to Christianity, it is the fastest growing in the whole family of religions. Among the larger historic religions, Islam, with its 1,300 years of history, is the only one, which originated later than the Christian era. It is the only one now which is an active rival of Christianity in more than one continent.

Arab traders introduced Islam into western India in the 8th century, but it gained prominence in the north only after the 12th century, when it was declared the state religion under the medieval Muslim rulers. At present, Muslims constitute the second largest religious community in India. This is despite the large exodus of Muslims to Pakistan after the traumatic Partition of 1947. Historically, Muslims were able to set up some notable dominions in various countries. But, at present, the largest and most flourishing group of Muslims is in India.

The founder of Islam, Muhammad, was born in Mecca, which is the most important city in Arabia, and had been the center of animism and idolatry. Like the other members of the Koreish tribe to which he belonged, he followed the business of shepherding and trading. He traveled on his mercantile operations to Syria and Palestine, where he mingled with Jews and Christians. An incident in the temple at Mecca, whereby he settled a quarrel between three *sheikhs*, prompted the idea that he might be a great religious leader of his people, who then were sadly distraught by feuds. He was dissatisfied with the existing moral and social conditions. He learned something of monotheism from Jews and Christians. In a moment of mental depression, Muhammad suddenly felt himself appointed to go forth and preach religion of one Absolute God, Creator, Potentate, and Judge of the world. For twelve years, he continued to have visions. His preaching of monotheism and future judgment and his denunciation of idolatry and infanticide won only slight success either in Mecca or in the neighboring city of Taif. With one sole companion, Muhammad fled for his life away from his native city. Hiding in a cave three miles north of Mecca, he experienced a narrow escape from his pursuers. At the age of 52, he set up the rule of Allah on the basis of the six-fold Pledge of Akaba.

He built a mosque for daily prayers and for the weekly congregation to worship on every Friday. He drilled his followers in devotions, religious education, and zealous aggressiveness. To his previous method of preaching he added an entirely new method of military campaigning. He acknowledged that only the help of Allah enabled him to win against the overwhelming foes the battle of Bedr and also the battle of the Ditch. He became powerful and independent as a religious and warring leader. The *qiblah* or "facing" in prayer, which formerly had been toward Jerusalem, he changed toward the Arabian center, Mecca. The fast, which formerly had been observed on the Jewish Day of Atonement, was changed to a new distinctly Muhammadan fast, covering the month of Ramzan. His former policy of general friendliness toward the Jews was changed to persecution and killing. After the death of his first wife he took unto himself an increasing number of wives, eleven in all. He exercised political sovereignty over all Arabia and was determined to abolish idolatry and reduce Judaism and Christianity to a position of dependence. He sent embassies to Greek, Persian, Egyptian, and Abyssinian kings, demanding their acceptance of his faith. He died after a short fever in the arms of Aisha, his favourite wife in his harem. His last words were a prayer.

The Holy Quran is scripture of Islam. It is unique among the religions of the world in that it is a revelation of God to the founder. The main speaker in this is Allah. It has been declared to be a revealed book and its authority cannot be questioned by Muslims. The followers have been asked to have faith in the final resurrection. There was to be a Day of Judgement when everybody was to be punished or rewarded according to his deeds. The followers were required to perform five duties. They were required to recite *kalma* (prayer) and have a living faith in God and the Prophet. They were required to give *zakat* or one-fortieth of their total income in charity. They were to say prayer or *namaz* five times a day. They were to observe *rozas* or fasts during the month of *Ramzan*. They were to go on pilgrimage to Mecca or do *Haj*. They were not to worship any idol. Their mosques were to have no images or portraits. Each mosque was to be an open court surrounded by Colonnades and unadorned, save for *Quranic* texts, a *miharab*, or a niche showing the direction of Mecca, a pulpit and minaret were the *muezzins* to utter the call to the prayers.

The Holy Quran embodies the complete code of conduct for men in life in all spheres of activities, whether social, political, economic or ethical. *The Holy Quran* and the Prophet's sayings together are called the Traditions or *Hadit*.

Monotheism is Muhammad's pre-eminent religious message. The historical origin of Muhammadan monotheism was threefold: partly in Muhammad's own insight into an ultimate unity in the Supreme Being of the universe, partly in his learning this great idea directly from Jewish monotheism, and partly in his conscious reaction against the crude theism of the Syrian Christians whom he met. His main practical message about God was that He would punish the wicked and reward the good people. Allah is frequently lauded as gracious and forgiving toward the persons who submit to His sovereignty.

Muslims can be broadly divided into two sects, the Sunnis and the Shias. Only 10 per cent of the world's one billion Muslims belong to the Shia sect, while the remaining are Sunnis. Both the sects have emerged as parallel groups, witnessing many clashes that have, at times, become violent. Yet, the basis of their belief is the same. Both of them believe that Mohammed is God's last prophet, and that the *Quran* is the only correct account of His words. Both groups also agree about many of Mohammed's sayings, called *Hadiths*, which are considered essential instructions for the believers. But, in other ways, Shias are different from Sunnis. They accept different sacred texts, have a different sense of religious authority and have a long history of mutual antagonism.

The historical divide of Islam into Sunni, or so-called orthodox Islam, and Shia, was caused more by political dispute over successors than doctrinal differences. These differences gradually assumed theological and metaphysical overtones. The division goes back to almost 1400 years, when Mohammed died in 632 AD. The Shiites of the Shia sect (from Shiat Ali, meaning "followers of Ali") felt that Mohammed's son-in-law and cousin, Ali, and his descendants, were the rightful heirs. Ali was later named the fourth Caliph, or leader of Islam, but was murdered after five years by a Muslim dissident while praying in a mosque. However, Sunnis became a larger sect, growing in power after the death of Mohammed. They did not recognize the heirs of Ali as having automatic right to become Caliphs but believed in the Prophet as their sole liberator.

Sunnis do not have a formal clergy, just scholars and jurists, who may offer non-binding opinions. Shias, however, believe that their Supreme Imam is a spiritual guide who holds the authority to interpret law and tradition. They believe that Prophet Mohammed's cousin, Ali, and His descendents are the two *imams*. Traditional Muslim education, based on *The Holy Quran*, is still important by the clergy in *madrasas* (schools to impart Islamic education) near mosques, which are central to the entire community. In India, the Friday public prayers, led by the local *imams* are only open to men and nearly all Muslim places of worship follow strict rules of worship.

In Shiite Islamism, there is a strong theme of martyrdom and suffering, focusing on the death of Ali and Hussain. This is best illustrated during Muharram—the first month of the Muslim year—when each evening, over a period of ten days, the Shias commemorate the Battle of Karbala, with a wailing *Imam* whipping the congregation into a frenzy of tears and chest beating. Shiite women also observe all the mourning customs like breaking bangles, abstaining from the use of ornaments, wearing black clothes, non-participation in social functions etc. Sunnis, on the contrary, carry out a very quiet procession. Shias not only have a separate call to prayer but also perform some part of their prayers differently, like placing their foreheads onto a piece of hardened clay (believed to be from Karbala) and not directly onto the prayer mat when prostrating, unlike the Sunnis, who do so

They also tend to combine prayers, sometimes worshipping three times a day instead of five. While praying, Shias fold and rest their hands on their chests whereas the Sunnis rest them on their abdomens.

But, Sunnis and Shias agree on the core fundamental beliefs of Islam. They are: (1) Beliefs and witness in there being one God and that Muhammad is their messenger; (2) Praying daily, (3) *Zakat*, or spiritual alms-giving, in which all Muslims should donate at least two and a half per cent of their income to needy Muslims, (4) Fasting, which is done throughout the month of Ramazan, (5) Haj or the pilgrimage to Mecca.

Apart from these two main sects, there are other sub-sects in Islam as well, like the Wahhabi, Ahmadiyas, Ahle Hadis and other such schools of thought. Though there is an ongoing strife between Sunnis and Shias in places like Pakistan, there has been significant co-operation between the two groups in Lebanon in recent years.

The Sufi sect of Muslims exhibit still another religious trait. They are characterized by the pantheistic tendency that even ordinary men may almost become divine by a process of asceticism and mysticism. They are located mostly in Persia and India. The most famous Sufi was the Persian mystic Jalal-ud-Din Rumi (1207-1273 A D). Sufism is a less orthodox mystic Islamic order. Its teachings emphasize direct experience of God and Sufis believe that mystical ecstasy can be attained even through music and dance. Sufi saints, like Nizamuddin Auliya, attracted many converts from Hinduism, and the synthesis of the two religious traditions led to a flowering of poetry, music and art.

Every year, Muslims all over the world eagerly await for the month of Ramzan, which is marked by fasting. They observe fast during these days with a view to get close to God and bring God closer to them. It is believed that fasting during Ramzan is about staying away from food and water but it also entails abstaining from hypocrisy, covetousness, lies, dishonesty, back-biting and all other forms of evil. It is said that the person who is fasting is happy when he breaks his fast and when he offers *namaz.* In *Hadith,* Prophet Mohammed said: The fast and *The Quran* are the two intercessors for the servant of Allah on the Day of Resurrection.

The fasting helps in cleaning the body of intoxicants. Doctors in the USSR are said to have successfully treated Schizophrenia and other mental illneses through this process. This implies that there is a scientific reason behind fasting as well.

Muslims also believe that Allah's blessings and mercy are so abundant during this month that anybody who sincerely repents becomes free of sins at the end of the month. For them, it is a glorious chance offered by the Almighty to cleanse and purify themselves from all the accumulated sins. A fasting person also feels close to other human beings and rest of God's creation. He can feel the pangs of agony suffered by a beggar, be sympathetic towards his co-workers, overlook other people's frailties, whims and petty jealousies.

Christianity

The rise of Christianity in the Indian region dates to the late 15th century when Catholic missionaries traveled to India in the wake of Portuguese traders. Around this time, Christian Armenian communities also settled in Munhall India, procuring a license to trade. There is evidence that the Mughal Emperor Akbar invited Jesuit priests to religious discussions held in Fatehpur Sikri. With the advent of East India Company, Protestant missionaries spread across the country, setting up educational institutions and hospitals in the 18th and 19th centuries. Many are still run by dedicated workers. They also involve themselves with reform movements and influence the government to take measures against practices, such as *sati*. Marriages between Indians and the Europeans, who came, led to the birth of the Anglo-Indian community. Indian Christians believe that the apostle, St Thomas, brought the religion to south India in the 1st century AD. Church services have now been Indianized to a large extent by absorbing some dialects, practices and rituals to make it easier for local worshippers to follow them.

Christianity, on the whole, is one of the nine religions, started by a historic leader of great spiritual insight, whose teachings have created a permanent following. Its historic development and influence have been mostly in the west and the peoples of the west have derived their ideals of justice, freedom, opportunity, cooperation, and progress from no other religion than that of Jesus Christ. The Christian scripture is *The Bible*. This book is the primary source of information concerning the founder and the origin of the Christian church. It is the authoritative compendium of the principles of Christianity. It comprises of 39 books of the *Old Testament* and 27 books of the *New Testament*. The distinctively Christian part of the *Bible* is the *New*

Testament, which records the life and teachings of the founder and the thoughts and experiences of his early disciples. Its influence has exceeded that of any volume ever written in human history. By 1922, it had been translated in 550 languages of the world.

The founder of Christianity, Jesus Christ, was the son of Joseph and Mary. He was born in Bethlehem of Judea and was brought up in Nazareth of Galilee. He was a typical Jewish child. His parents complied with characteristics peculiar to Jews and other customs at the time of his birth and while he was growing up. He drew upon the best available instruction and experience of his day.

When Jesus reached the age of 30 he joined the reform movement. At the moment of his baptism, he received a vivid conviction that God, his loving heavenly Father, was calling him. He was determined that he would realize the fulness of sonship of God. The common people looked upon him as a prophet and flocked to hear him. The trained leaders of the Jewish Law saw in him a revolutionary and regarded his teachings as dangerous. They didn't interfere with his ministry at the outset. But when they saw that their authority would be set aside by the way in which he was preaching and teaching and acting, they became his bitter enemies. The people didn't accept him and eventually the priestly authorities at Jerusalem arrested Jesus. He was condemned to death by the Supreme Jewish Court, because he had admitted that he was the Christ, the son of God. Roman governor, who had to confirm the conviction, found no fault in him, yet permitted his crucification.

During his lifetime, Jesus conveyed profound religious lessons, which went to the very heart of each of his hearers, setting forth, as they did, eternal principles of truth. As a preacher, Jesus took every opportunity to declare that the rule of God was at hand. But he emphasized it to be a spiritual kingdom in the heart, achieved through righteousness and friendliness. Most of those who listened to him found him a visionary or an iconoclast.

Jesus healed many sick people and restored to sanity abnormal personalities. These impressive deeds were done regularly out of compassion. His deeds signified the power and help of God. He did them not simply to accredit himself, but as the spontaneous expression of his spirit of love.

On the apprehension of Jesus by the soldiers, all his disciples forsook him and fled. Apparently, some of them gave up all hope, his tomb was sealed and three days later it was found empty. Even his own disciples found it hard to believe that he had risen. But through personal interaction they felt convinced that he was alive again. His last words were a benediction, with an assurance of his perpetual spiritual presence, and with a command to bear witness of him and of his gospel throughout the world.

The assurance of a resurrected and living Christ transformed the defected followers of the crucified Jesus into outspoken witness. The early Christians continued to worship in the temple at Jerusalem as faithful Jews. But they formed a distinct community devoted to Jesus as their Lord. The rulers, however, persecuted them severely, and scattered them widely. Yet, their numbers increased. Paul became the first Christian leader to realize the fuller significance of Jesus and to make Christianity international. His letters to the churches, which he established in Europe and Asia, were the earliest writings in the *New Testament*. They have become permanent expressions of Christian thought and practice.

The first Roman monarch to be converted to Christianity and receive formal baptism was Constantine. He made Christianity the official religion of the empire, and adopted the cross as the official Christian symbol.

During 325 to 1054 A D, Christianity became the official religion of the entire Europe. During 1054 to 1517 A D, supremacy of the Pope was established, even over some of the governments of Western Europe. The church became the most effective agency for aiding the poor and the weak, and for promoting law, order and education. It strived for spiritual unity of all people, which is superior to all political or racial groupings, functioning for the promotion of justice, peace, mercy, cooperation and fraternity. After 1517 onward, a number of reformers, including Martin Luther, led the "Protestant Reformation". Roman Catholics underwent a certain corresponding "counter-reformation" and revival.

God in Christianity, as in Judaism, is the sovereign moral personality of the world. Many verses in the *New Testament* describe his characteristics, e.g all-seeing and all-knowing. However, Jesus made a certain new emphasis in Jewish monotheism when he taught that the Supreme God is supremely living, and that the indispensable practical consequence of love to God is unselfish love to one's neighbour.

Jesus taught that God forgives sins not merely upon condition of personal repentance, but also upon condition of the sinner himself having given forgiveness to all who might have done wrong to him, even to his enemies, because God also gives unfailing good treatment to all. This is unparalleled among all religions of the world. Second, while dying on the cross, Jesus was thoughtful for his enemies and prayed for them. This forgiving attitude has helped to interpret the character of God and Jesus' own filial relation to God's plan for the redemption of the world. Christian's conception of God is that "he is the Father of our Spirits".

Christianity presents the most remarkable combination of evils to be overcome and also of abundant satisfaction to be secured in comprehensive, harmonious salvation.

Sikhism

In New Delhi, I had an opportunity to visit Gurudwara Rakabganj, a Sikh temple. There I found most of the people sporting beard and donning turban over their heads with their unshorn hair folded inside the turban. A few of them, who were clean-shaven, covered their heads. When I asked a few persons, donning turbans, what was their name, I was told that they were Gurucharan Singh, Ajit Singh and so on. The word 'Singh' suffixed to every name was common. In my own country, I have seen a few such persons but they are referred to as "Mr Singh". I had all along been thinking how every such person could be called "Mr Singh" and what "Singh" could mean. I, therefore, became curious to know more about Singhs and their religion.

In Gurudwara Rakabganj, I went to the *sanctum sanctorium*, covering my head with a piece of yellow cloth provided to me at its threshold. Here every visitor intuitively bowed before the scripture. This scripture, I was told, is *Guru Granth Sahib* which embodies the Holy Words of the Sikh Gurus, which should act as torchlight to the Sikh *Panth* (the Sikh way of life). The holy book comprises of compositions of six Sikh Gurus: Guru Nanak, Guru Angad, Guru Amar Das, Guru Ram Das, Guru Rajan and Guru Tegh Bahadur. Since it was the spirit of Guru Nanak, the first Sikh Guru, that traveled from one Guru to the other Guru, the Gurus following Guru Nanak used 'Nanak' at the end of their respective hymns.

Before we know what Sikhism implies, it may be useful to understand the lives and contributions of at least the first and tenth Gurus, who played a significant role in laying down the edifice of Sikhism. Guru Nanak, the first Guru, was born on April 15, 1469 in west Punjab in a Hindu family. At the time of his birth, the family priest prophesied that the boy "will sit under a canopy. Both Hindus and Turks will respect him and his name will be famous on earth and in heaven". The boy was named Nanak Chand. As a child, he displayed traits of character and temperament that were to remain with him throughout his life. He was polite to everyone. He learnt the alphabets quickly and was ahead of other boys in his school. He learnt Persian and Arabic from a *Maulvi* (Muslim teacher). He took his cattle for grazing and showed some miracles. He also composed hymns and fascinated people with his melodious voice by reciting the hymns. He was married and had children. He traveled for 15 years, starting in 1507, and went to a number of countries in addition to various nooks and corners of his own country. His three important precepts are: there is neither Hindu nor Mussalman, one must work and share one's earnings, and active life is superior to contemplative life. He believed in one god and broke the barrier of caste. He laid stress on inward devotion, or pure love and did not believe in the antics of the *yogis* and the sufis of his time.

However, it was Guru Gobind Singh, the tenth Guru, who gave a distinct identity to Sikhism. He was born in 1661 and was the son of the ninth Guru, Guru Tegh Bahadur. His original name was Gobind Rai. As a young boy, he was pained to see the plight of Kashmiri Pandits who suffered because of the atrocities of the Mughal Emperor Aurangzeb. Aurangzeb was ambitious to spread Islam and didn't tolerate if any person refused to convert himself to Islam.

In 1699, on the day of the Baisakhi festival, Gobind Rai asked all his followers to come to Anandpur without having their hair shorn. There he introduced his five faithful followers (*Panj Pyare*) or the Five Beloved Ones after each of them proved that he is ready to sacrifice his life. He took a bowl of steel in which he put clean water and stirred the water with his double-edged dagger. *Batashas* (sugar crystals), offered to him by his wife, were mixed in it. He stirred the water again saying that his dagger will make sure that his Sikhs will be heroes when they go into battle and the sugar crystals will ensure that they always spread sweetness wherever they go. The water now was taken as *amrit* (nectar). He recited hymns from the *Guru Granth Sahib* and baptized the five Sikhs who then baptized the Guru also by drinking the *amrit*. The Guru explained that the five had experienced a rebirth and belonged to the family of the Guru. These five Sikhs, one Jat, one Kshatriya and three outcastes, formed the heart of the *khalsa*, the new order that the Guru founded. The five were given the same powers as the Guru and by doing this the Guru had taken the first step in abolishing the tradition of a living Guru.

The Guru-Sikhs from then on are to wear five symbols of purity. They have become the symbols of the *khalsa*. They are: *kesh* (uncut hair and untrimmed beard), *kara* (a steel bracelet), *kanga* (a small comb), *kachcha* (short breeches like underwear) and *kirpan* (a dagger). The Guru's idea of a true *khalsa* was one who is both a saint and a soldier. Long hair in India has always been associated with saintliness. He introduced a new greeting *"Wahegur-ji-ka-khalsa, Wahegur-ji-ki-Fateh"* (the *khalsa* are chosen by God, victory be to our God). On being given the *amrit* the Guru was also given the surname "Singh" and he became Guru Gobind Singh. Thereafter, every male child born in a Sikh family, after he is baptized, has to add "Singh" after his name. The Sikhs were asked by the Guru not to smoke and take any intoxicant.

Thus, Sikhism is a reformist religion founded by Guru Nanak in the fifteenth century. It is opposed to idol worship, rituals and the caste system. It believes in a formless God. The Sikh community, which forms an inalienable part of Hinduism, but with a separate identity, constitutes almost 1.99 per cent of India's population. Many Sikhs do visit Hindu temples and worship Hindu deities. Similarly, one can find many Hindus going to *gurudwaras*. In some Hindu families, some boys are baptized as Sikhs. The Sikhs essentially follow the teachings of ten *gurus* that are contained in their holy book, *The Adi Granth*, kept at the Golden Temple in Amritsar in north India.

As already explained, it was the religious persecution by the later Mughals that led to the *tenth guru*, Guru Gobind Singh, to re-organize the community in 1699 as a military order, called the *Khalsa* (pure *sikhs*). It was based on the principles of *sangat* (congregation), *simran* (meditation) *kirtan* (singing of hymns), *langar* and *pangat* (sharing and partaking of food in a common kitchen).

Like Islam, Sikhism is also based on the revelation of Sikh *gurus*. The experience of Guru Nanak and the divine words, which he uttered, are embodied in the scripture, *Guru Granth Sahib*. The precise idea about God in Sikhism is available in the opening *shabad* (hymn) of the *Adi Granth: "Ek onkar satnam karta purukh nirabhav niravair akal murat ajuni saibhang gur prasad"*. (This being is one. He is eternal. He is immanent in all things. He is creator of all things. He is immanent in his creation. He is without fear and without enmity. This being is not subject to time. He is beyond birth and death. He is himself responsible for his own manifestation. He is known by the grace of the Guru).

Sikhism is a synthesis of knowledge, action and devotion. A Sikh is necessarily a householder and a man of the world. As a citizen of the world, all his activities are based on *dharma* (righteousness). His body, mind and wealth belong to the *guru*. He is completely a disciplined soldier of the *guru*. For him, the *guru* is *Sachcha Padshah*, the true king whom he follows in action, mind and speech and who leads him both in worldly prosperity and spiritual advancement.

A Sikh is supposed to be an amalgam of *shakti* and *bhakti, miri* and *piri*. At the time of assuming the responsibility of *guruship*, at the age of 11, the young Guru Hargobind wore two swords of *piri* and *miri* over his right and left shoulders, making the Sikhs realize that the *guru* is not only a spiritual guide (*pir*), but he is also a director of the worldly life and defender of the faith. He is *sachcha* as well as *padshah*. The throne that Guru Hargobind established for himself, was associated with *Akal* (the Eternal Being), thus differentiating it from the thrones of *mundane* kings.

A Sikh essentially works for the livelihood and for the release from transmigration and merger in the Lord. His *triratna* (three jewels) are *kirt karo* (work for the livelihood) *nam japo* (remembrance of the name of the lord), and *wand chhakko* (sharing the earnings with the deserving and the needy). At every major *gurudwara*, we find *langar* (community food) being served to every visitor on a daily basis. Visitors are asked to sit together and they are served food.

Every Sikh is required to cultivate the spirit of courage. To live with honour and self-respect have been the guidelines to Sikhs ever since the time of Guru Nanak. The division of human life into two separate compartments, like material and spiritual, amounts to doing injustice to the spirit of *piri-miri*, requiring one to be saint inside and prince outside.

Buddhism

Buddhists are followers of Gautama Buddha who lived and preached the gospel of non-violence and peace. Buddha strongly advocated the equality of human beings.

Gautama Buddha relaxed under a Bodhi tree in Budh Gaya, by the side of a small river. It was on a full moon night that he became enlightened. He realized that the aim of life must be to transcend all sufferings and it can be achieved by treading the path of *Bodhisatva*. *Bodhi* means the understanding or wisdom of the ultimate nature, of reality, and a *sattva* is someone who is motivated by universal compassion. Thus, the *Bodhisatva* ideal is the aspiration to practice infinite compassion with wisdom. However, compassion can be put into practice by one who recognizes every human being as a member of humanity and the human family, regardless of the differences in religion, creed, colour and region. A *Bodisatva* is one who is on the path to Buddhahood and dedicates himself entirely in helping all other sentient for release from suffering.

The four noble truths enunciated in Buddha's philosophy are the truth of suffering, the truth of the origin of suffering, the truth of the cessation of suffering, and the truth of the path leading to cessation. The Buddha's decision to teach the truths in this sequence has great significance. The importance of understanding that what we ordinarily regard as happiness is, in fact, suffering. Suffering is caused by living entity due to body identification with material existence, *maya* (illusion).

When one perceives that he has fallen into an ocean of suffering, he must develop the wish to be liberated from that suffering. For this purpose, he will feel that it is essential to eliminate the origin of suffering. When one looks at the origin of suffering, he will find the delusions and *karmic* actions. He will then be able to perceive that the cycle of existence and its sufferings are produced by his own *karmic* action, which, in turn, are propelled by the delusions, which are routed in the mistaken belief in the solidity, or inherent existence of the self. If we analyze how we think of the self, we will find that we tend to think of it as existing intrinsically, independent of the mind and body. Yet, when we seek to locate it, it eludes us. Buddha felt that no such self exists and that our belief in an independent self is the root cause of all sufferings.

The truth of suffering at the initial stage may not be very obvious, but as we get close to it, it becomes increasingly self-evident. Something false at the initial stage might seem very vivid and firm, but eventually, as we probe it further, it becomes more flimsy and eventually dissolves. Human existence is said to be the best form of existence to practice *dharma* and try to bring an end to this cycle.

Insight into the truth of the impermanence, suffering and impersonality of all corporal and mental phenomena of existence is *Vipassana* meditation. This is the meditation, which leads to insight, used in *Theravada*, and recommended by the Buddha. Meditation is the way to truth. There is no other way to truth. Truth is not something readymade. It is something that one has to discover by becoming somewhere else, but within one's own being. Meditation is nothing but a device to make one aware of one's self.

Life manifests itself in different ways and thus reveals its distinctive character. As each form of life has its own unique qualities, the two concepts of the Ten Worlds and the ten factors alone are not sufficient to perceive life in its entirety. The three realms of existence, which are also expounded in the *Lotus Sutra*, are essential for a full expression of life. They are the realms of five components, the realm of living beings and the realm of environment. In the natural environment, such as air, and, the sea, rivers and the sun's rays, living beings of a particular species assist each other and cooperate with other forms of life in the struggle to survive. As they grow, living beings influence and incorporate his surroundings both spiritually and physically.

The summum bonum of Buddhism is *nirvan*, which is riddance from the cycle of birth and death. Buddha (like Krsna of *Gita*) remembered his previous births. He, who had lived 550 previous births during more than 25,000 years, stresses that attachment to earthly existence confined human beings to the cycle of rebirth. *Nirvana*, like enlightenment, is transcendental experience and hence not expressible in mundane terms. Buddha aptly kept silent on its nature.

It is unfortunate that Buddhism, which spread to other countries of Asia, has itself nearly vanished from the land of its birth. The 14th Dalai Lama, the spiritual leader of the Tibetan Buddhists, now lives in India with his followers in exile and is a widely respected figure.

Buddhism was the first religion in the world to become international. Yet, theoretically, it has often been denied the designation of being a religion. It is a mere system of morality and philosophy founded on a pessimistic theory of life. Gautam Buddha, its founder, did not teach a personal deity, worship and prayer. He taught a moral law in the universe, which was ethically superior to the metaphysical Supreme Being, taught in Hinduism from which he reacted. Subsequently, Buddha himself was deified and the number of Buddhists in the world are now in the range of 137- 500m. But it has virtually died out in the land of its birth.

Gautama was the only heir presumptive of the Hindu king of Sakya clan in the town of Kapilvastu, about a hundred miles of Benaras. He was brought out in luxurious circumstances. When he was at the age of 16, his father built three palaces for the young prince. At 19, he was married to a neighboring princess, but he had no son for ten years.

When Prince Gautama was 29, while he was out on a pleasure trip, he was impressed by four passing sights, viz. a decrepit old man, a loathsomely sick man, a corpse and a calm religious ascetic unperturbed by any suffering. He became distressed at the thought that he himself and all mankind were liable to the miseries of oncoming old age, sickness and death. He became convinced that only resolute self-sacrifice and search would win triumphant peace. Therefore, he renounced his wife, a newborn son, and the inheritance of his father's throne. Cutting off his hair, he assumed the garb of a monk.

Gautama tried bodily asceticism. He sat cross-legged under a bo-tree and analyzed a simple physiological solution of the cause and cure of evil. He arrived at noble eightfold path of right belief, aspiration, speech, action, livelihood, endeavour, thought and concentration. The word which seems most completely to have characterized his critical spiritual experience was "*buddha*', the past particle of the Sanskrit verb "to become enlightened" or "wise". Since then, he was referred to as Gautama Buddha.

Gautama Buddha went to his native country of Magadha in north India and preached his new found gospel of salvation by psychological, self-disciplinary, ethical culture, saying that an earnest person needs only to exercise a wise manipulation of his own state of consciousness, without any of the conventional appliances of religion, such as deity, worship, ceremony, dogma, priesthood, or supernatural connections. Buddha inveighed particularly the current Hindu conceptions of an alleged metaphysical supreme being and the value of prayer and the sacredness of the Vedic scriptures.

Buddha sent his 60 disciples to spread his simple message of salvation. He died at the age of 80, very decrepit in body but invincible in spirit. During his lifetime, he never taught any divine object of worship.

There have been two main branches in Buddhism. The flowers of the "Lesser Vehicle" Hinayana Buddhism in southern Asia have sought to remain true to his own teaching, viz. that he was only a teacher of a way of escape from misery and that speculative questions are profitless for religion. The northern branch, which has carried Buddhism extensively to China and Japan developed certain theological doctrines which constitute the Mahayana "Greater Vehicle". It sees in Buddha not simply a teacher who passed into *nirvana* at his death, but a veritable divine saviour. Thus, Buddha has been deified.

The practical message of Buddha is in marked contrast with the dreamy speculations of philosophic Hinduism concerning an ineffable Supreme Being. It is in marked contrast with the paid priest, the ritual sacrifices and the many religious ceremonies of Hindus.

Jainism

Jainism, like Buddhism and Sikhism, may be regarded as an offshoot of Hinduism. All these religions have risen on the Indian soil as a reaction against excessive Vedic rituals, but neither of them could free itself from the essentials of Hinduism. Jains form a very small segment of the Indian population. They account for 0.48 per cent of the Indian population, ranking Jain community as the sixth largest religious group in the country. They are spread over all parts of India and have contributed much to the economic, political, cultural, social, literal, art, architectural and spiritual fields. It has, therefore, a distinct place in the religious and human society.

In fact, Jainism was established in various provinces of India much before Mahavira and Buddha began their missionary activities. During their period, Magadha, Kausala, Kapilavastu, Vaishali, Pava, Mithila, Varanasi, Simhabhumi, Kausambi, Avanti were prominent Jaina centres. After Mahavira's *parinirvana*, Jainism was patronized by the Sisunagas, Nandas, Kharavela, Mauriyas, Guptas and others who provided all possible facilities to develop its literature and cultural activities. The southern part of India was also a great centre of Jainism. Numerous Jaina temples and sculptures throughout the ages were erected by kings and many facilities were provided for literary services throughout India.

Jainism is one of the more ancient religions, which came into existence as a result of the most non-violent approach and humanitarian viewpoint towards all creatures. It believes that all particles of earth, water, fire, wind and plants are possessed of life. Unlike Buddhists, Jains believe that a substance is dynamic (*parinami*) in character. Ritual, according to this religion, is not a means of emancipation. The only means of escaping from the misery of *samsaras*, the cycle of birth and death, is the path of moral, mental and spiritual development based on complete non-violence and truth.

Jains are divided into *Svetambaras* (dressed in white) and *Digambaras* (who shun clothing). It is said that about a hundred years after Mahavira's *parinirvana*, a terrible famine in the northern region took place for twelve years. Therefore, Bhadrabahu sent a part of the *sangha* (Order) to southern India, particularly Karnataka, where Jains were very powerful under the leadership of Visakhacarya, the Maurya Emperor Chandragupta who followed severe conduct of Mahavira in toto. Another group of the church went to the Sindhu region under the businessship of 'Sthulabhadra who found the need to relax the traditional practices. Both the groups came back to Magadha as soon as the famine came to an end. The former, who stuck strictly to the regulation of nudity and prescribed the methods of begging and eating food came to be known as '*Digambara*' (the sky-robed). The latter, who continued to live under famine conditions and changed their ways, became known as '*Svetambara*' (the white-robed).

The Jains have their own scriptures called *Agamas* or *Srutas*, which are believed to be directly derived from the Tirthankaras. This religion promotes man's self-awareness, his understanding of the nature of self or life and clarifies the content of problems that has been traditionally philosophical. Jaina philosophy is based on the nature of reality, which is considered through non-absolutism (*Anekantavada*). The reality or substance, in its opinion, posseses innumerable attributes which cannot be perceived by an ordinary person. According to this view, reality possesses infinite characteristics, which cannot be perceived and is known at once by any ordinary person. Reality or substance in Jainism is distinguished from *Dravya* which means that which exists and possess three fundamental characteristics, viz. origin (*utpada*), destruction (*vyaya*) and permanence (*dharauvya*).

According to Jaina philosphy, soul is eternal and beginingless. *Karma* in Jaina philosophy emphasizes that one has its pivotal stand for deciding the fruits of one's activities on an individual basis. The God cannot exercise His power as a middleman. One will have to bear the result of one's own deeds. The vibration (*yoga*) and the passion (*kasaya*) of soul attract *karmic* matter and transform it into *karmic* body. Yoga is the action of mind, speech and body due to desire, aversion and cognition. The relation of *karma* is a cause that makes it a subject to the cycle of birth and death.

Jainism preaches ideals for attaining spirituality. Its religious aspects enjoin discipline for social upliftment and philosophy justifies them for exemplary behaviour. For spiritual realization, right faith (*samyagdarsana*), right knowledge (*samyagjnana*) right conduct (*samyagcaritra*) constitute path of spiritual salvation, termed as triple jewel (*ratnatraya*).

Jain scripture prescribes a code of conducts for a spiritual aspirant. It is called *sanacaro* (right conduct), which is formulated in consonance with the spiritual vigilance for a mendicant. He stays in temples of woods with total renunciation and proper conduct. He must observe fully all the twelve vows prescribed to the householder. After observing the eleventh *pratima* he accepts initiation from the teacher and becomes a mendicant by pulling the hair out from his head with his own hands. He proceeds to arrest the *karmic* matter by controlling passions, careful movement, observing virtues, engaging himself in contemplation and concurring the sufferings by endurance and conduct. For curbing the threefold activity of body, speech and mind, an ascetic takes every care in walking, speaking, eating, lifting and lying down and depositing waste products for avoiding injury to organisms.

In Jainism, moral restraints are considered to be quite significant. Whenever moral restraints are ignored and spiritual observances are put centrestage, religion loses its meaning. In Jainism, restraints means self control. It requires self or personal management to awaken one's innate potentialities, develop oneself and guard against unwarranted obstacles. In the Jain scriptures, restraints are divided into 17 types, including control our senses and thoughts. For a harmonious and peaceful life, one should practice all types of restraints, regardless of whether they are easy or difficult. The degree of control would naturally differ from person to person.

Non-violoence, truth, non-stealing, restraint and non-possession are the five great vows observed by Jain monks. The second vow—truth—is colossal and eternal. It is the greatest pursuit of life. Lord Mahavira said, "Search truth yourself."

The search for truth involves two things: the search for truth and the search for the self. The truth we search cannot be put to use by anyone else. Only the one sho searches for truth can put it to use and enjoy the supreme bliss obtained through self-realization. Man has highly developed brain and centres of supersensual knowledge. That is why he alone is capable of searching the truth.

Jainism does not prescribe invocation, propitiation, offerings, prayers and the like. But in popular practice, a devotee expresses his or her devotional attachment to idols, which symbolize the glorification of the spiritual state and the attributes manifested in the idol. A Jaina devotee worships the Jaina image in two ways. First is the abstract worship (*bhavapuja*) which needs neither idol nor ritual. Second is formal worship (*dravyapuja*) which needs the idol and some ritual performance. The mendicants usually perform the abstract worship. It is also performed by those who do not have the sufficient facilities to accomplish formal worship. There is a certain method prescribed for formal worship. After taking a bath and wearing clean clothes, the devotee goes to the temple and recites *namokaramantra* (the *mahamantra*) with devotional songs and hymn, puts down a few grains of rice, bows and goes around a circamambulatory path three times, and repeats *arihanta-siddha* etc. Then, on a rosary of 108 beads, he starts performing *astadravyapuja* which is an eight-fold worship. Among other Jaina rituals, idol installation includes *Jinabimbapratistha* or *Pancakalyanakapratistha* with devotional songs and hymns which initiates the image for worship in a Jaina temple. It is performed with a great ceremony under the leadership of a learned priest through the depiction of the five auspicious events of a *Tirthankara's* life, namely, conception, birth, renunciation, enlightenment and *nirvana*.

There are some social ceremonies like *samskaras*, which are, somehow, connected with spiritual and with physical purity. They are of three types: First, 53 *kriyas* (rites), which cover the entire life of a person from conception to death (*garbhanvayakriyas*), Second, 48 rites, which are related to new converts and their spiritual developments (*diksanvayakriyas*). Third, 7 rites, which are meant for

Jain nuns cover their mouths to avoid swallowing of insects, thereby showing concern for all living beings.

personality development of meritorious souls (*kartranvyayakriyas*).

Jaina community celebrates some festivals. *Paryusana* or *dasalaksana parva* is held during the rainy season for eight or ten days in Jaina temples where the sermons on the *dasadharmas* which are the ten virtues of soul, described in the *Tattvarthsutra* and *Kalpasutra* scriptures, are regularly read to an audience. At its end, *Ksamavaniparva* or *Samvatsariparva* is celebrated, which is the day of the universal forgiveness, when every Jaina asks for forgiveness from everyone else, and he himself forgives others for wrongs done towards him during the past year. Other festivals are social in nature. They are: *raksabandhana, soda sakaranvrata, aksayatrtiya, srutapancami, dipavali, mahaviranirvana jayanti, siddhacakravidhana, astanhikaparva, nandisvaravidhana*, etc.

Zoroastrianism

Of all the living non-biblical systems of religion the one which has had the closest connection with the *Bible* is Zoroastrianism. This religion is not mentioned by name in the *Bible*. But kings of Persia, who were Zoroastrians, are mentioned in eight books of the *Old Testament*. Parsis are followers of Zoroasterinism, whose original home was in Pars or Persia. They came from Persia in the seventh century. It has nevertheless played a significant role in Indian industry and is known for its philanthropy.

Prior to the emergence of a world-wide outlook and aim in the course of biblical history, Zoroaster was the first among the founders of the world's living religions who taught a religion which should be voluntarily and universally adopted. A form of confession of the Zoroastrian faith, which stands in the earliest of its canonical scriptures, and which is still repeated as part of the daily liturgy of its worship, asserts the belief that Zoroastrianism is permanently superior over all the religions of the world.

Unfortunately, during the last 400 years, Zoroastrians have lost their founder's vision and purpose. Numerically, the adherents of

Zoroastrians, while including some brilliantly able and noble source, now constitute the smallest community among the 11 organized historic religions of the world. They number slightly more than 100,000. Most of them are located in India, particularly in Mumbai. They are descendants of unyielding devotees of their faith in Zoroaster, who escaped from the sword of Arab conquerors devastating Persia in the seventh century AD.

Zoroaster has been revered as the most adorable personage in history. But there has been much uncertainty and variety of opinions concerning the actuality and date of his existence. Prophecies of this great Saviour had been made 3,000 years beforehand. The Glory of God (*Ahura Mazda*) was transmitted to "that girl who became the mother of Zoroaster". Marvels connected with this very unusual young unmarried woman were inexplicable to her family, except as a piece of witchcraft. It has been stated that at birth, Zoroaster laughed. As a young boy, he was unusually wise in conversation. At the age of 15, he selected the sacred girdle as a symbol of his devotion to a life of religion. He was very kind and helpful to the poor as well as to animals. At the age of 20, without the consent of his father and mother he wandered forth and gave himself to religion. When his father sought a wife for him, he expressed a desire to see and approve of her, contrary to the prevailing custom.

At the age of 30, Zoroaster was called in the presence of Ahura Mazda to be purified and appointed to the work of a prophet. The deity, Ahura Mazda, is represented as having selected Zoroaster on account of his pre-eminent responsiveness and fitness. During the next ten years, he had interactions with Ahura Mazda and felt convinced that the deity selected him. He resolved to preach a universal progressive religion and convert even the wicked. He condemned the filthy, deceiving intoxicant. He preached the religion of an all-seeing God and was a vehement preacher of the truths first revealed to him divinely, and a denouncer of his opponents. Once, during winter, he was refused shelter in a certain house. He was tempted by the lying evil spirit to renounce the religion of Mazda and to obtain temporal sovereignty, but prayer and worship repelled the insidious attack. He was rejected both by his own peers and by the nobles. He pleaded with God for friendly support.

Zoroaster was successful in converting the king Vistaspa. He also converted king's brother, son, a counselor, and the grand vizier. The figure rose further. But after a certain delayed success with conversions in the court of Persia, Zoroaster turned to a policy of military propaganda in the interests of his nation and his religion, and conducted warfare against neighbouring nations. He married the daughter of the king's counselor. The king himself propagated the new faith. Zoroaster is said to have expired at the age of 77.

The sacred scripture of Zoroastrianism is *Avesta*, which perhaps means "knowledge", which is parallel with the *Veda* of Hinduism. The language is Avestan, cognate with Sanskrit. Persia was immediately reanimated by the new religion. Its armies conquered the powerful western neighbour, Babylonia (539 B C), developed the great empire which Darius ruled, and pushed onward into Europe until stopped at the battle of Salamis. Persia came under the rule of foreigners, at first Alexander's Greek successors, and then the Partians. Zoroastrianism in this period showed a marked tendency to sun-worship and polytheism connected with the religion of Mithra. The Arabs, another small nation, electrified by a new religion, Islam, conquered Persia, and drove out the Zoroastrians. The modern Parsis are scattered in successful business all over the world, but the majority of them are in Mumbai, as explained earlier. In philanthropic gifts they hold the highest per capita record of any religious community in the world.

6

Festivals and Ceremonies

On March 17 and 18, 2003, when I was in New Delhi, I found all offices and shops closed. I could see only few vehicles on the road. But what was quite amazing and new to me was a group of men and women, both young and old, with their faces fully smeared in colours. I saw some people throwing colours on each other, on their faces and heads. Some children were seen sprinkling water with *pichkaris* (a brass syringe which squirts water in a spray or even in a straight line) on the passersby and then enjoying. I was told that it is the Holi festival being celebrated by Hindus. I, therefore, became curious to know about the festivals of India, not only of Hindus but also of other religious groups in India.

Holi

The festival of Holi, I was told, is celebrated in north India when the winter months give way to summer, the crops have been cut, threshed, and stored or sold away. The farmers and their families are then free to enjoy. The festival is seen in its full intensity in Mathura and Vrindavan, the two towns near Agra, where the Hindu God, Lord Krsna spent his childhood and youth. He loved festivity, and the hamlets of Vrindavan, Gokul and Barsana are full of fun and frolic for almost a week. Krsna played Holi with so much gusto that even today the songs sung during Holi are full of the pranks that he played on the Gopis and the Gopis played on him. Krsna played Holi with a *pichkari*. *Gulal* made up of numerous colours, such as pink, magenta, red, yellow and green, along with *abeer* (small crystals or paper-like chips of mica) is bought. The *gulals*, heaped up in cone shapes, put on gunny bags, were displayed and sold in numerous shops. Soluble colours, available in colouring water, were also available in different hues and were being sold well.

There is no *puja* associated with Holi, except putting a little colour on the faces of the gods, at the beginning of the festival. However, on the evening of March 17, I found bonfires being lit in streets. I was told that Holi is 'burnt' on the eve of the final day of the festival. Usually, it is a community celebration and bonfires are lit on crossroads. People do *puja* and bring green sheaves of gram known as *'boot'* to be roasted black with shells on. Wheat sheaves are also roasted likewise. They are then taken out of shells and eaten right there. One gets one's face quite black and one's hands also are made black, but it is very enjoyable nonetheless, and the stuff is quite tasty.

I was told that bonfires date back to the days of Hiranyakashyap, when he ordered his son, Prahlad, the great *bhakt* (devotee) of Lord Narayan, to be burnt alive, because Hiranyakashyap was an *asur* (demon) and hated Lord Narayan. He asked his sister Holika, to wear the set of clothes she possessed which could not catch fire. She was asked to hold Prahlad on her lap tightly, so that he could not escape while in flames. Holika quietly transferred the clothes onto Prahlad and got burnt herself, thus saving Prahlad to grow up and be the greatest *bhakt* of Lord Visnu. The bonfire is reminiscent of this event and shows how Lord Visnu protected his own *bhakt* (devotee).

The next day of the bonfire is the real day of Holi, played for half day. This day is called the *parva* (festival). People visit each other's houses, carrying colour and water, drenching each other as they visit different places, hug and entertain each other. It is a complete holiday everywhere and there is hardly any public vehicle on roads. Boys and girls are seen at some places giving mud baths to their friends. Children are seen chasing each other with mugs full of water or taking hold of a hosepipe attached to a tap and squirt water all around. Those who do not like their faces smeared with colour or drenched in coloured water are pleased when a *teeka* (mark of colour) is put on the forehead by their friends and relatives. The idea is to sustain friendship, forgetting the enmity or ill feelings of the past.

Moharram

Muslims in India have their own festivals and ceremonies. In March itself, they have Moharram to commemorate the death of Immam

Husain, the grandson of Prophet Mohammed, and his associates in the desert of Karbala. A number of rituals and congregations have grown around it. In Delhi, public *majlises* (congregations) are held at Darga Panja Sharif in Kashmere Gate and at the Immamia Hall on Panchquin Road. While both of them are Shia institutions, the Sunnis hold public *majlisis* at Imambara Nizami in Nizamuddin and at Jama Masjid. The *majlises* are held for 12 days.

The *majlise* is primarily a congregation where the incidents of Karbala are recalled with expression of grief and sorrow. The stages in the *majlis* are *sozkhali, merieakhani* religious discourse, *matam* with *noha ziarat* and *tabarrink.* Sinking of short poems in Urdu is called *soz.* They are composed in praise of Prophet Mohammed and his descendents. *Salaam* or salutation generally follows singing of *soz.* The former consists of 6-9 verses and the latter of 5-10 verses. *Sozkhani* is generally done by 2-5 persons—one person leads the song and the others help him to maintain the *swara* or note. It generally lasts from 15-30 minutes, depending upon the number of poems to be sung. The normal practice is that *saz* as well as one *salaam* are sung. This is followed by *merciakhami* or singing of *degies.* In the context of Moharram, the *mecia* narrates the martyrdom of Imam Husain as well as the events relating to the tragedy at Karbala. The *mecia* is recited in a rhythm and like *sozkhani* no musical instruments are used in *merciakhani* either. The religious discourse follows next. It consists of two parts, one consisting of discussion on different theological issues of Islam and the other recalling the events of Karbala. The discourse is given by the speaker called *Zakir* and like professional *soz* and *mercia* singers. During the discourse, he frequently bids the mourners to send their *salwats* or invocations to God for peace to the soul of the Prophet and his descendants. By this, the mourners earn religious merit, called *sawals.* After the discourse, the mourners stand up for observing *matam,* which lasts for about 20 minutes by beating their breasts to the accompaniment of *nohas* of *dirges.* The latter are lamentations composed in the form of poems having 4-8 couplets. They are sung in the *majlise* as well as *tazia* processions. The leader recites a line of the *nohas,* which is repeated by the mourners, beating their breasts at the same time. This is followed by *zariat,* i.e pilgrimage from a distance, while incanting *zariat.* The mourners keep standing, facing west, and point out with index finger the direction of Mecca. *Tabarruk*(food or drink) is next distributed, after which the *majlis* disburses.

Mahasivratri

Mahasivratri is the Hindu festival to worship Lord Siva. Hindus worship three main deities, viz. Brahma, Visnu and Siva. Since the creation of this universe, this trio is said to have distributed the duties among themselves. Brahma is the creator of this world, Visnu the preserver and Siva the destroyer of evil forces. Gradually, Brahma ceased to be worshipped while Visnu and Siva continued as deities. Magh Vad 14, according to Hindu calendar, is the day of worship of Siva at night and is known as Mahasivratri. The fourteenth day of the dark half of each month is called Sivratri but that of Magh is Mahasivratri or the greatest of Shivratris, which is celebrated by Shaivites all over India.

It is said in the *Puranas* that on the night of Magh Vad 14, Lord Siva had created his idol in the form of a *linga* to show His might to Brahma and Visnu who were fighting *inter se* for superiority. Both of them approached Siva for a decision. Lord Siva at once assumed the form of a *linga* and asked both of them to find out the upper and lower ends. The *linga* was spread over all the three worlds of *swarga, prithvi* and *patal*—heaven, earth and nether region. Brahma and Visnu failed and returned to Mahadev and praised him and acknowledged his superiority among the trio. Since then Siva is worshipped in the form of *linga* throughout India. Lord Siva then created twelve such idols called *jyotirlingas* in different parts of India to worship him. They are in Somnath in Maharashtra, Mallikarjun in Andhra Pradesh, Mahakaleshwar at Ujjain, Omkareshwar on the bank of Narmada, Vaijnath in Bihar, Bhimashankar in Dakini forest, Rameshwaram in the south, Nagnath in Daruka forest, Viswanath in Varanasi, Tryambakeshwar at Trimbak, Kedareshwar in the Himalayas, Ghusruneshwar or Ghushmeshwar Verula. These places are known as Sivpuris.

The day is observed as a public holiday and the festival is celebrated in every Hindu home. People observe fast on this day, worship Lord Siva and keep awake throughout, worshipping the deity with *bilva* leaves and *dhatura* flowers. It can be undertaken at home or in temple. At midnight, the deity is worshipped in temples when the idol is bathed with *panchamrit*, a mixture of milk, *ghee*, curd, honey and sugar, and then again with holy waters of the Ganga or some other river or sea and worshipped according to 16 rites with the chanting of *mantras* etc. Temples are illuminated.

It is a post-harvest festival occurring at the conclusion of the *rabi* season, when there is no work in the field. The day is also important for Hindus who are Arya Samajists and do not worship idols. Swami Dayanand, the founder of Arya Samaj, got divine inspiration to begin his search of truth on the night of Mahasivratri at his native place, Tankara in Morvi *taluka* of Rajkot district. He belonged to devout followers of Saiva. They celebrated the festival at night but Dayanand, whose original name was Mulshankar, got disillusioned when he found at night a rat taking away the offerings. He felt that the god who cannot protect himself need not be worshipped. He realized that there is no god in the idol.

He left home and went to the Himalayas in search of a preceptor. Everywhere he found *sadhus* (saints) taking undue advantage of the faith of devotees exploiting in the name of idol worship. Therefore, he himself practiced penance for years and, as a result of divine revelation, was inspired to fight idol worship and root out evil and vicious practices prevailing at that time. He then propagated the true doctrines of Vedic religion. He started his mission from Punjab in north India where the Arya Samaj founded by him has a wide following. Arya Samajists worship *agni* (fire) instead of idol.

Ramzan

The month of Ramzan is an annual reminder to the Muslims all over the world that *Quran* was revealed to Prophet Muhammad during this month. Ramzan is during the ninth month of the Islamic calendar. The celebration of the revelation of the Holy Book is not observed in the usual way. It is marked by abstinence and being grateful to the Almighty. Fasting in this month is acknowledgement of the divine blessings, as *Quran* is believed to be

Muslims offering *namaaz* at Jama Masjid in Delhi after breaking their fast.

a reward to His servants from God.

The fast of Ramzan lasts for the whole month, begining from sun rise and ending at sun set. Fasting in Islam means to refrain and abstain from food and drink as well as certain other things from dawn till sun set. Fasting becomes a mandatory for all with the sighting of the new moon of Ramzan. With the new moon of *Shawwal,* the fast comes to an end. The following day, *Id* is celebrated. The aim of fasting is also to raise man above the material world and bring him close to the spritual world. This process is referred to as *tazkia* (purification) in the *Quran*.

Through fasting man makes himself worthy of being thankful to God. He obeys the command of God and thus gains a keen awareness of the supremacy of God. Having gone through a month's fasting, he creates the ability in himself to lead a life of piety as ordained in the *Quran.* When *Quran* is read in the month of Ramzan, it creates an atmosphere which reminds the followers of Islam of the time when the divine light from heaven falls upon the earth.

Prophet Muhammad used to sit alone in the cave of Hira near Mecca, to pray and meditate, asking the creator of the Heavens and earth for answers to the questions thal surged through his mind. What's man's true role in life? What does the Lord require of us? From where does man come, and where he will go after death? The Prophet sought answers to these questions while meditating.

At one night, while the Prophet was sitting alone in the cave, the Archangel Gabriel appeared before him in human form and taught him the initial verses of the *Quran.* In this way, the Holy Book began to be revealed by Allah to the Prophet Muhammad through the angel. It took 23 long years to complete the revelations of the Holy Book. Being the true words of Allah in human language it is eternal book of instruction for all mankind.

However, Islam doesn't advocate withdrawing from this material world for a world of seclusion that is free from the objects of temptation. The way of Islam is to live in this world but without allowing one's heart to be attached to this world. Therefore, from Islamic point of view, one has to strive to become a spiritual person while leading one's life in this material world itself. Likewise, the purification of the soul is not just for the sake of purification, it is directly linked with the concept of reward in life to come after our physical existence.

In the *Hadith*, Ramzan is called the "month of patience". This month is meant to serve as a training course to enable an individual to lead a successful life by keeping his negative feelings under control, as negative feelings are the ones that present the greatest obstacles to human progress. By observing a fast, he is brought to a life of moral restraint.

The Quran introduces the Creator and explains the relationship between the Creator and His creations. A major portion of the *Quran* deals with the stories of the prophets, such as Adam, Noah, Abraham, Joseph, Moses, Jesus and many more. These stories enshrine a moral code of conduct for believers of all times. A sizable portion of the Holy Book talks about the hereafter, which mainly covers the graphic description of the delights of Paradise and the agony of Hell. Historical events, faith and religion, religious commandments, devine promoters, prayers and matters of civil law are also dealt with. It provides correct and understandable answers to all the central questions which arise in an inquisitive mind. It serves as a guiding light, inspring and leading the devout on the right path. It tells mankind how to conduct himself so that in his eternal life he may gain entry into Paradise which is the ultimate goal. Fasting in Ramzan is the path to it.

Id-uz-Zuha

Id-uz-Zuha, or Id-ud-Duha, the Muslim festival popularly known as *Bakri Id* or *Id-e-Baqr*, is a Thanks giving Day to god by means of sacrificing to Him some animal like a goat, sheep, camel or bull. It is on the 10th of the month of *zithijja*, the twelfth month of the Muslim year, which is considered propitious for pilgrimage to Mecca. The practice of sacrificing an animal to God dates back to the time of Prophet Ibraham (Abraham), who lived long before Prophet Mohammed. Ibrahim, who had no son, prayed to God for a son when he had attained a very old age. God blessed him with a son. The son was named Isaac, who was quite dear to his father. When Isaac was quite a young boy, his father had a dream for three consecutive nights that it is God's desire that the boy be sacrificed to God. Both the father and the son were devout worshippers of God. When the father told his son about his dream, the son insisted that God's wishes have to be fulfilled. Both of them went to jungle and as Ibrahim was flinging a knife across the throat of Isaac with closed eyes, uttering *Bismillah Allaho Akbar* (in the name of Allah, God is Great), a heavenly voice congratulated him for carrying out God's mandate. When Ibrahim opened his eyes, he found his son alive. Instead, he saw a sheep lying sacrificed.

All the Muslims commemorate this occasion as Bakri Id. Whether they are in Mecca for pilgrimage or anywhere else in the world, the Muslims sacrifice a goat, sheep or any other animal to God on this day. At Mecca, the sacrifice is offered in the valley of Mina near Mecca. It was in Mina that Ibrahim had offered his son as his sacrifice. Before offering the sacrifice, all Muslims go to the mosque and offer *namaz* (prayer) of *Id*. Thereafter, two sermons are read from the pulpit to all the worshippers. The *Id* prayers are offered sometime after the usual morning prayers. A partial fast is observed on that day from early morning till the *Id* prayers are offered and worshippers return home and sacrifice the animal earmarked for the purpose, which has been well fed and taken care of during the preceding period. The animal offered for sacrifice must be free from all bodily defects, and in case of a small animal like a goat or a sheep, must not be less than one year or more than five years of age. Two or more persons cannot sacrifice one and the same goat or sheep. But the cost of a big animal, like a bull or a camel, can be shared by seven persons and they can jointly sacrifice one big animal on behalf of all of them. At the time of sacrificing the animal, an Arabic verse in the *Quran* is recited, which means, "Verily, I turn my face to that being who has created the heavens and the earth and I am his obedient follower and not one of the ungrateful. Verily, my prayers, my sacrifice, my life and death belong to God, the Lord of both the Worlds, who has no partner. This is what I have been bidden and I am the first of those who have resigned themselves to God".

The flesh of the animal sacrificed is distributed among friends, relatives and the poor. The person sacrificing it for use by himself and his family members retains its small portion. According to *The Quran*, neither the flesh nor the blood of an animal thus sacrificed to Him reaches Him but the piety and the virtue alone reaches Him.

Budda Purnima

Buddh Purnima is the full moon day of Baisakh (April/May) and is considered most auspicious by Buddhist tradition. It is a declared holiday in central government offices and is celebrated to keep the Buddhist tradition alive. Buddha, his wife, Yashodhara, his disciple Ananda, his charioteer Channa, and his horse Kantaka, are believed to have all been born on the same day and at the same hour. The Boddhi tree at Gaya, under which Buddha got the enlightenment,

too sprouted at the same moment. Buddha Purnima was the occasion of his enlightenment and later of his *nirvana* (death and deliverance from rebirth). The day is a pious homage to Lord Buddha. Buddhism flourished in India under the royal patronage of Ashoka. With the passage of time, the number of his adherents has dwindled. On this day, the pilgrims visit Lumbine (Nepal), the birthplace of Buddha, and Bodhgaya (Bihar).

Ram Navmi

What are the other festivals being celebrated in India by Hindus? I asked my host. I was told that Holi festival is followed by Ram Navami in the month of April. Ram Navami happens to be the birthday of Lord Rama, the seventh incarnation of Lord Visnu. Lord Rama was born to rid the world of demons, headed by Ravana, who was creating havoc. It is stated that when Ravana was destroying *dharma* on earth and in *devlok* (the place where gods live), *devtas* (gods) ran to Lord Brahma. At the instance of Brahma, Lord Visnu appeared on this earth as the incarnation of Lord Rama. The activities of Lord Rama are embodied in the Hindu scripture, *The Ramayana*. Lord Rama was the perfect man and, in the words of Swami Vivekananda, he was 'the ideal son, the ideal husband, the ideal father and, above all, the ideal king. He was a man who grew into perfection as he faced the turmoil of life. His own life as well as that of his consort, Sita, have become role model for the people. By adhering to these ideals, one can get guidance as to the right or wrong of a situation when one is confronted with a dilemma in human relationship.

Puja for Ram Navmi is simple and is done in the morning. Some people observe fast and eat only in the afternoon. *Bhajans* (devotional songs) are organized in praise of Ram, Sita and Lakshman, and *prasad* (offerings) is distributed. Many Hindus observe fast for eight days, taking, of course, water, tea, coffee, milk and fruit. *Kanya puja* takes place on the ninth and concluding day when their feet is washed, *teeka* (red mark) is applied on their forehead and they are given some sweet etc.

Baisakhi

Baisakhi, which is generally on April 13, is a festival of north India. Just before Baisakhi, the first crop of the year, the Rabi crop, has been harvested and sold. Therefore, the farmers have ample money and are free from worry to enjoy collectively and thank the Almighty for His benevolence. The morning starts with people taking bath in the nearby rivers or tanks. Dressed in festive attire, people go to temples and *gurudwaras* (sikh temples) with *mithai* (sweet) and money. The day is considered very auspicious to conduct any business or undertake activities. Colourful *melas* (fairs) are organized on the banks of rivers and tanks where people congregate. People take newborn baby to temple or *gurudwara* and the first drink of water is given to the child with a rose petal. Of course, if the baby is a few days old, one is not supposed to deny water to a baby for long.

For the Sikhs, Baisakhi has religious sanctity. It was on this day that Guru Gobind Singh initiated the *Panch Piyara* (the five loved ones). He decorated the *Khalsa*, pure Sikh (*khalsa-sajaya*) at Anandpur Sahib, near Chandigarh, and gave these five persons (all from the scheduled castes, and from different provinces of India, e.g. from Punjab, from Uttar Pradesh, from Andhra Pradesh and from Bihar) the first sermon on being a true Sikh. He made them promise not to cut their hair or beard, to always keep a comb, always wear an iron bangle on one arm, always wear an underwear, and always carry *kirpan* (a small sword) so as to be ever-ready for battle.

One of the most sacred pilgrimage centers for the Punjabis, especially for the Sikhs, is Amritsar, where the Golden Temple is situated. The temple is known as Harmindar Saheb. It has a huge tank all round the temple and anyone bathing in it is believed to be purified, thus washing his or her sins. On this day, water is brought from all the sacred rivers of India and poured into this *sarovar* (mini-ocean). It is also the first day of the solar calendar. Therefore, Hindus in north India give charity to inculcate in themselves the spirit of benevolence to the less fortunate people. This festival also has its social impact. By bringing people at one place, sparing time from their otherwise busy schedule, the festival serves to strengthen social relationship and fellow feelings.

Mahavir Jayanti

Mahavir Jayanti, the birthday of Lord Mahavira, is a public holiday in India. It is a festival of Jains. People visit temple of Mahavir or any Jain temple on this day. Besides religious ceremonies at shrines, processions and *prabhat feris* (morning processions) are taken out through major places at times with the idol of Mahavir seated in chariot, when people have an opportunity to have a glimpse of their deity and pay their obeisance. Meetings are organized wherein discourses about Mahavira's life and teachings are given.

Lord Mahavir was born as Vardhman in 599 B C in Videh (Bihar). His father Siddharth was a Kshatriya King. Both he and his wife, Trishala, were devout followers of Lord. He had 14 significant dreams, which indicated his future greatness. After Mahavira's birth, the family gained wealth, fame and merit. The boy was, therefore, named Vardhman. He rejoiced in making sacrifice for others and displayed exceptional abilities in studies. He respected the wishes of his parents and married Yashodha at the age of 13. Yashodha gave birth to daughter, Priyadarshini. He renounced the world in search of the path of salvation. His parents died when he was 28 years old. After two years, he succeeded in obtaining the permission of his elder brother and others to take *diksha* (alm) and adopt the ascetic way of life. His next 12 years were spent in penance and deep meditation. He endured hardships, restrained the impulses for the purification of the soul and remained unperturbed even in the most provocative circumstances.

Mahavir now understood the eternal truth, earned omniscience and attained the highest knowledge and intuition called *keval jnan* on *Vaishakh Sud* under a tree, near the village Jrumbhikagrama on the bank of river Rujupali. Thus, at the age of 42, Mahavir became a *jina* and *arhat*, a *kevalin*, omniscent, all seeing and all-knowing. He then started his career as a teacher explaining to the people the way of salvation as he visited a number of places, finally attaining *nirvan* in 527 BC at Pavapuri. Lord Mahavira is believed to be a contemporary of Buddha, and one of the greatest teachers of mankind. He preached five great vows by adding *brahmacharya* (chastity) to the fourfold self-restraints already prescribed by Lord Parshvanatha, viz. *ahimsa* (non-violence), *satya* (truth), *asteya* (abstinence from stealing), and *aprigraha* (non-attachment to worldly things).

Mahavir further preached that beatitude could't be attained through mundane happiness but through mortification of flesh. He exhorted his disciples to develop their power of reasoning and argument. He keenly watched the conduct and progress of disciples to ensure exemplary behaviour on their part.

Good Friday

Good Friday, in Holy Week, being the actual day of Christ's death, is known as Good Friday. For Christians, it is the most solemn day of the whole year. It is a public holiday.

Most Christian churches hold a special service in the morning. Many churches also hold another service lasting from 12 noon to 3 pm. These were the dark hours during which Christ was hanging on the cross until he died. During this time, it is a common custom for the people to think specially about the 'Seven Words', the seven sayings which Jesus Christ uttered at various times after he had been nailed to the cross. As Good Friday is a solemn day, some Christians in Gujarat in India observe fast for the whole day. In Roman Catholic Churches, the death of Christ on the cross is commemorated by the singing of 'Passion' (the story of the crucification and death of Christ) and by the unveiling and veneration of the cross.

Christians also gather together for special meetings in the evenings on every day during the whole Holy Week. Special sermons are delivered at these meetings, and many congregations invite a preacher from some other place to come and give a series of sermons, night after night.

Janamashtami

Janamashtami is a Hindu festival. It is not only celebrated in India but also in the western countries where Krsna sect has been established.

When the ruling classes had created terror in *Kali Yug* (there are four *yugas* or epochs according to Hindu mythology: *Satya Yuga, Treta Yuga, Dwapar Yug* and *Kali Yug*) in response to requests from saints and sages, Lord Visnu emerged on this earth as an incarnation of Krsna. He was born as a son of Devki, the wife of Vasudev. Devki was the sister of King Kans of Mathura, a tyrant, who had dethroned and imprisoned his father, Ugrasen.

On being warned through an oracle that the eighth son of Devki would be the destroyer of King Kans, he put in jail his sister Devki and her husband Vasudev. King Kans killed the first six infants of Devki and the seventh embryo was shifted to the womb of Rohini, the second wife of Vasudev, living at Gokul. Rohini gave birth to a son at Gokul, who was named Balram. Kans had asked the prison guards to be strictly vigilant and inform him immediately about the birth of a child at its first crying.

Before taking birth as the eighth child of Devki, Lord Visnu appeared before Devki and Vasudev in a premonition and said, "I shall be born as your child as promised in your previous birth". He advised them to take the new born child to Gokul and put it near Yashoda, the wife of Nand, and bring back the daughter born to her. After the birth of Krsna at midnight, through a miracle, all the guards fell asleep and the doors were unlocked. Vasudev took the child in a basket on his head and slipped out, crossed the flood of Yamuna, and reached the house of Nand in Gokul where everybody was sound asleep. He placed the child near Yasodha and brought back her daughter.

When King Kans came to know of this new-born baby, he instantly rushed to the jail. He snatched the child from the hands of Devki and dashed the child on the stone when she sprang from his hand into the sky warning him that the destroyer of Kans hadalready been born. Kans, in his anxiety, ordered a thorough search of the child. In Gokul, the birth of the boy was widely celebrated. As days passed, Kans tried in vain to kill the child through his demons whom the child Krsna killed one by one. When he was 12, Kans invited Krsna to Mathura for wrestling bout with the intention of getting Krsna killed. Krsna and Balram not only killed the wrestlers but also Kans and released his parents, restoring the throne of Mathura to Ugrasen.

Krsna and his brother Balram studied four *Vedas*, six *shastras* and politics. They learnt 64 arts in 64 days. In the battle of the *Mahabharata*, Krsna joined the Pandavas as Arjun's charioteer under a vow not to take up arms while his army of one *akshavahini* was sent to fight for the Kauravas. In the beginning of the battle, Arjun became nervous after looking in the battlefield his elders, brothers, cousins, relatives and dear ones, with whom he had to fight. He refused to fight even at the cost of his life. Krsna then advised him to follow the path of duty. This advice in *Gita* shows the way of self-realization and self-development. It gives peace of mind and shows the path of action. It destroys ignorance and guides one to salvation.

For thousands of years, *Gita* has been the most sacred book showing the path of duty not only to Hindus but also to mankind as a whole. It is the essence of *Vedas*. Hearing the advice of Krsna, as embodied in *Gita*, duty without attachment and without any concern for the result of actions, the dejection of Arjun vanished. He realized his duty, the path of action, and was ready to fight. In the great battle of *Mahabaratha* that ensued, the Pandavas were victorious over the Kauravas.

The significance of Krsna's life and his message in *Gita* is recalled and illustrated on Janmashtami. His message of love, equality of all beings and sympathy for the lowest strata of society has its enduring effect and has to be remembered for the generations. He is worshipped not only as the perfect human being but also as a complete incarnation of God.

Krsna's birth is celebrated in every Vaishnavite temple and in orthodox household. Krsna is worshipped in his infant form. The idol is anointed with sandal and saffron paste, dressed in costly garments and placed in a decorated cradle, and swung by the devotees. Some people do observe fast. This day, as Janamashtami, is celebrated with great enthusiasm in Mathura, Brindavan and Gokul. At all such places, colourful *raslilas* (dramas enacting the life and activities of Krsna) are also performed. However, at some places in India, Krsna is worshipped in his youth.

The festival is celebrated with great pomp and show in temples and homes. It is Lord Krsna who later gave us the life-enduring message of the great epic, *Bhagavad Gita*. Most families observe fast on this day, but one meal can be taken. In the afternoon, the *prasad* is prepared for distribution in the evening. The *prasad* consists of the same eatables that a new mother used to be given after childbirth, and is still given in traditional homes. Fruits like banana, guava and apple, cut in pieces or slices, can be added to the *prasad*. Krsna is the main deity of the day.

Independence Day

Independence Day on August 15 is the day when India became independent in 1947 after it was ruled by the Britishers for over 200 years. The day is now observed as a national holiday.

It was on the midnight of August 14, 1947 that the transfer of power to popular ministers at the national and state level elevated India to Dominion status with a Constituent Assembly of its own, which would frame its future Constitution. The country was partitioned into India and Pakistan and there was a large-scale killings and migration of people from one country to the other. Since that day, national flag is hoisted on the ramparts of Red Fort with the Prime Minister's address to the nation. The day also begins with the official functions of flag hoisting at the state, district and *taluka* headquarters. The national flag is flown on top of public and private buildings, and cultural programmes are organized.

Raksha Bandhan

Raksha Bandhan in August is the most sentimental festival once again bringing to focus the pious relationship of brother and the sister. It symbolizes the most sacred relationship of life, without any ulterior motive or demand of any kind, when the sister ties a *rakhi* (a sacred thread) on the right wrist of his brother to seek protection from him. He, in return, would acknowledge this relationship by accepting it with grace and love. With this *rakhi*, she bestows deep affection and blessings on her brothers so as to guard them against all harms. Gifts of money and/or other presents in kind are given to sisters on this occasion as a symbolic gesture.

On this day, all ladies are found dressed up well, moving to the houses of their brothers with *rakhis* and some sweet. Those who are not able to go because of distance, make an arrangement to send all this by post or by courier so that their brothers are once again reminded of their obligations towards their sisters. A *rakhi* has to be tied onto or placed before the chief deity of the family. The sister applies *teeka* before she ties the *rakhi*. The *teeka* is applied by the thumb on the forehead, along with *roli* (red sacred thread) and then a little rice is stuck onto the red mark on the forehead. This is done by dipping the third finger of the right hand in the liquid. It is believed in every Hindu home that every person should have a *rakhi* tied, even by an adopted sister, to have his good wishes at every stage in the performance of his work. There are numerous stories to illustrate how the festival originated. During olden times, kings used to seek the best wishes of their sisters before going to war and thus they could win.

This festival of bonding is celebrated with fervour all over India. As we go through social and political churnings, agonise over the increasing incidence of broken relationships, whether of family, community or political entities, this is a good time to take a breather and ask ourselves: Can the delicate strands of the *rakhi* help dissolve the country's endemic problem of communal discord? Considering the fact that *rakhi*—also known as *Raksha Bandhan*—has eclectic appeal, it is worthwhile to try and transform what is essentially a Hindu custom into a more universal one, making it a meeting point of mutual trust and love for people of all faiths and persuasions.

There are several myths and legends about the genesis of this unusual festival of bonding. One belief attributes the tradition of sisters tying the sacred thread round the wrist of brothers as a symbol of protection, to the story about Indra and his consort, Indrani. On *Shravan Poornima* (full moon day) Indrani tied silk *rakhi* (known as *raksha* or protection) on Indra's wrist when he was ready to go to battle on behalf of the *Devas*, with Demon King Daitya Raja. Indra vanquished the demon and came back home victorious. The victory is attributed in large part to the protective bond of love and faith, symbolized by the sacred thread or *rakhi*.

Over the years, *rakhi* has served to cement Hindu-Muslim bonds. Emperor Humayun rushed to the rescue of a Rajput princess who had become his '*rakhi* sister'. The enemy was the Sultanate of Gujarat. In this way, here was a case where the *rakhi* motivated Muslim succour for a Hindu kingdom against another fellow Muslim. The wife of an invading army general tied a *rakhi* around the wrist of the Indian King Porus, seeking assurance that her husband would not be killed. When Porus rushed to strike the invader to kill him, it is said that it was the *rakhi* on his wrist, which stopped him from delivering the final blow, thus saving the life of his mighty adversary, Alexander the Great.

Gurus are known to celebrate Raksha Bandhan with their disciples as a way of forging the *guru-shishya* relationship and confirming love, brotherhood and trust. Taking this concept a step further, devotees pray for God's eternal protection and love, to deliver themselves of worldly bondage, while striving towards achieving salvation through bonding with the Almighty.

These traditions have continued even at present to forge love and affection. Kiran Bedi, while she was Inspector-General of Prisons in Tihar Jail in Delhi, encouraged the celebration of this festival, demonstrating that it could be used as a subtle vehicle for generating positive social vibrations. Undertrials and convicted criminals were made to feel the bond of human relationship when volunteers celebrated Raksha Bandhan with them, distributing sweets and wishing them well. Thus, in a wider social context, *rakhi* epitomizes the resolve to protect an individual or even a whole community. Extending the festival to include all sections of society, we can take collective pride in a common altruistic heritage and bring people of all hues together.

Kumbh Mela

The Kumbh takes place every 12 years at different times at Haridwar, Prayag, Ujjain and Nasik in India, the places where *amrit*—the elixir of life that emerged from the churning of the ocean—splashed out of the pitcher and fell on earth. In the ensuing tussle between the *devas* and *asuras* to take possession of it, a fierce war was fought which lasted 12 days. During this period, the Moon did not let the *amrit* fall from the *kumbh* (pitcher), the Sun did not let the pitcher crack or break. Jupiter protected it from demons and Saturn saved it from the rapacious Jayant. These four planets responsible for saving the *amrit-kumbh* are an integral part of this festival. The Kumbh at Nasik begins when the Sun and Jupiter are in the Leo sign, on a full moon day. Similarly, the timing of

Sadhus in saffron cloths and with ash-smeared bodies.

the Kumbh *melas* at Prayag, Haridwar and Ujjain are related to specific planetary configurations.

Astrologers have deduced by working backwards that the *Mahabharata* war broke out on November 18, 3060 B C and lasted 18 days up to December 6. Bhishma, who was blessed with a boon to choose the time of his death, waited up to January 14 for the Sun to enter the tropic of Capricorn before shaking off his mortal coils.

The earliest record of the Kumbh Mela is Chinese traveller Hieun Tsang's account of it (629-45 A D). During Samudragupta's reign, the Kumbh Mela was a major event. According to Hieun Tsang, up to 250,000 people assembled on the occasion and Harshavardhan donated all his belongings at the Kumbh. The two Kumbh Melas at Prayag and Nasik evoked great interest worldwide. According to Hindu mythology, seven brothers from Prayag went to different parts of the world and established seven Prayags. Prague is believed to be one of them, according to the indigenous history of the Slovaks.

The Kumbh Mela basically symbolizes the community's emotional unity just as the pitcher (*kumbh*) containing the elixir of life (*amrit*) symbolizes the importance of love and amity. It also symbolizes the religio-cultural ethos of the people of India and reflects their close relationship with water. In fact, the Hindu way of life is largely aqua-centric. Water is an integral part of all rituals. Rivers and mountains in India are venerated as mothers and fathers. Indian mythology attaches sufficient importance to *snan* or bath, which is an essential component of the daily ritual of personal cleanliness. A bath is mandatory for participation in any important religious occasion or festival. But the physical bath is incomplete in itself as it is only the outer manifestation of its real meaning, i.e. to bathe in the ocean of knowledge. Thus, *kumbh melas* are symbolic rituals that remind us that knowledge is an important way of attaining enlightenment.

Knowledge is essential for improving one's self and ultimately attaining salvation. Though there is no concept of salvation in the *Vedas* we get a clear concept of the emancipation of the soul and beatitude in the *Upanishads*. With the passage of time, *snan* lost its real import and slowly became nothing more than a mechanical ritual. Self-styled spiritual leaders advocated taking a bath at the confluence of the Ganga, Yamuna and invisible Saraswati during the Kumbh to achieve salvation. *Siddha tantrics, Nathpanthis* and poets like Kabir, however, stressed that the physical bath itself was immaterial. What was far more important was inner cleansing.

Phool-Walon-ki-Sair

Phool-Walon-ki-Sair (Festival of Flowers) is held at the temple of goddess Yog Maya in Mehrauli, New Delhi, every year in the month of September. This temple is situated near Kutab Minar. According to a legend, it was built during the time of Yudhistar, and is dedicated to Yog Maya, the sister of Lord Krsna. The shrine is believed to have been built by Syed Mal, a noble in the time of Akbar. The temple and 21 other associated buildings stand within the walled enclosure of 400 feet. Syed Mal also built most of these buildings. It is about 42 feet high from its marble covered floor to the top of the pinnacle. A doorway, with a marble frame, gives access to a room 17 feet square. A sacred stone, covered with cloth, is placed on a marble well 2 feet white and a foot deep. Over this stone are suspended from the ceiling a few *pankhas* (traditional fans) which are presented to the shrine on the occasion of Sair-e-Gul Faroshal Fair. Two stone tigers are kept in an iron cage (5 feet square and 10 feet high) about 8 feet in front of the temple.

Yog Maya is a goddess of austerity and white flowers. Sweets are acceptable to her. Her devotees must eschew wine and meat. On every Tuesday, there is a *mela* (fair) in the temple grounds. But the major event is the Sair-e-Gul Faroshan, the flower sellers' fair. It is one of Delhi's oldest and most picturesque festivals and has received the state patronage. After parading through the narrow streets of the town the processionists, carrying large fans, embroided with fresh flowers, arrive at the temple to pay homage to the goddess of purities.

Ganesh Chaturthi

Ganesh Chaturthi is celebrated to mark the birth of Lord Ganesha, the foremost God of the Hindu pantheon. Ganesh is the god with the elephant head and second son of Siva and Parvati, though in south India he is regarded as the first son. He was born in Kashi in the home of his maternal grandparents, Himachal and Maina, while Lord Siva had gone to Mount Kailash for *tapasya* (meditation). Parvati had not informed Shankar Bhagwan (Siva) about the birth of their second son. She did not even tell her son the identity of his father. Siva also did not seem to know that a child was born to Parvati, who, after his birth, threw Ganesh in the Ganga in sheer anger, but Ganga saved him and gave him back alive to Parvati. Since then he is known to be a *devta* with two mothers.

Without knowing Siva, Ganesh grew up into a lovely little boy. One day, when Parvati went for a bath, little Ganesh was asked to stand at the entrance of the *baori* and would not let anyone enter while she was bathing. At that very moment, Siva came back from his *tapasya* and not finding out where his wife was, made straight for the *baori* and decided to go down to the water. Ganesh stopped Siva right in front of him. This annoyed Siva very much and he ordered Ganesh to step aside. Ganesh did not budge. In his anger, Siva chopped off Ganesh's head. The noise and commotion brought Parvati out of her bath and she was very angry with her husband. Siva was horrified to learn that he had chopped off the head of his own son. He then promised Parvati that he would put the head of the first living thing that came his way on the shoulders of his son. He came across an elephant and put elephant's head on Ganesh, thus making him alive. When Parvati was more angry, Siva promised that in future Ganesh will be worshipped by all people before any activity or auspicious occasion is initiated. From then onward, no *puja* can be performed without first worshipping Ganesh. Ganesh is reputed to be highly intelligent and is the giver of *buddhi* (wisdom) and knowledge. *Buddhi* is even shown as his consort although he was married to two damsels, Ridhi and Siddhi, which means success and prosperity.

Children are initiated into study by praying to Ganesh. In Maharashtra, when children start going to school, their first lesson is on Ganesh Chaturthi. Although Saraswati is the goddess of learning, she is worshipped after Ganesh. Ganesh was chosen by Narad to be the stenographer to write down *The Mahabharata* for posterity, while Vyas related the tale of his grandsons to him. He chose his broken tusk to write. He told Vyas that he would only write if Vyasji gave the dictation continuously and did not stop or hesitate and waste time. His mother Bhagwati (Parvati) asked Ganesh to use his *buddhi* while writing also and explain certain points so that the generations to come would understand the great epic, as it was meant to be understood.

Ganesh is the remover of all obstacles. According to a legend, all the gods and *devtas* were married and those that were not were getting ready offers because of their positions and good looks. No one was, however, ready to marry his daughter to Ganesh although he was the first among all the gods and *devtas*. His elephantine look dismayed everyone and no one was ready to give his daughter to him in marriage. Therefore, Ganesh decided to create problems for the other gods and *devtas* who had the audacity to make fun of him. He asked all the rats to go and make burrows in the path of all those getting married and make it impossible for them to tread the path, thus creating much confusion in the way so that no one could move without falling into one pothole or another. All the gods then rushed off to Brahma and asked him to do something. Brahma went to Ganesh and asked him to stop creating chaos. Ganesh was adamant and declared that until he got married, he would not let anyone else get married either. Brahma, in consultation with his wife, Saraswati, then created two lovely maidens, Riddhi and Siddhi (success and prosperity) and gave them in marriage to Ganesh. He did the *kanyadan* along with his wife. He and Saraswati thereby became the father-in-law and mother-in-law of Ganesh. Ganesh then stopped the rats from creating havoc. He gave the rats the honour of becoming his *vahan*, the vehicle, on which he rides. He thus won the name of Vigneshwara or Vighnaraja, the Lord of obstacles. He always has a rat under him in all his idols and pictures.

Ganesh is usually shown with four hands, each one has a special symbolic object in it. One has an *ankush* (a goad), the second has a *trishul* (a three-pronged weapon) or an axe made from his own broken tooth, the third has a lotus flower, and the fourth has a rosary. He has many faces and is sometime shown with two hands in a dance pose (*abhaya* and *varda mudra*). *Gajamukh* (elephant face), *Baraganapati* and *Tarunaganapati* depict him as a child and a young man. Vinayak has the four arms in which he holds his symbols. In this stance, he sometimes holds a pot of *moodak* in one hand instead of the rosary or holds it in his trunk and retains the rosary. In his form as *Herambeganapati* he has five heads and ten hands, three eyes in each face and rides on a lion. The extra eye in each face is between his eyebrows. As Viranvighnesa, he exhibits a martial spirit with several weapons held in his ten hands. *Shaktiganapati* is shown with his *shakti* or his consorts Riddhi and Siddhi (success and prosperity) or *buddhi* (wisdom) or even Lakshmi sitting on his thigh. Worship of this aspect of Ganesh is supposed to grant us wishes very quickly. Then there is the Natyaganapati, a beautiful form, showing him in a graceful dance pose. Ganesh is supposed to have taken this stance when the Creator bowed to him and he was so happy that he started to dance and thus earned the title of the master of the arts of music and dance.

Varasiddhi Vinayak is the aspect worshipped during Ganesh Chaturthi. He is shown standing on a demon, named Vighnasura, whom he destroyed. The *swastika* is accepted as the graphic symbol of Ganesh and is therefore found at every auspicious place or occasion. Lakshmi, the consort of *Visnu,* is always placed along with Ganesh. Because we love Lakshmi (wealth) and do not wish to annoy her, to be on the safe side we worship her along with Ganesh. Since she cannot precede him, she sits next to him. She is always placed to the right of him as she is like a mother to him.

Ganesh Chaturthi is celebrated all over India, but the people of Maharashtra have made Lord Ganesh their patron. Lokmanya Tilak realized that community celebrations would bring people together and he started the Ganesh Chaturthi celebrations in a big way, making it into a community affair. Thus, Ganesh became the beloved of the people of Maharashtra. The Maharashtrians celebrate this festival like the Bengalis do Durga Puja and the Oriyas undertake *Rath Yatra*.

Since the festival is a community affair, everyone in the locality contributes towards the making of the idol, the upkeep of the *pandal*, as well as the expenses of keeping a *pandit* and the cost of the offerings of *prasad* every day. The devotees gather in groups and sing songs in praise of Lord Ganesh. Singing is done mostly in the evenings, while during the morning and the daytime, individuals and families come and offer *prasad*.

Ganesh is worshipped in *Maharashtra* in his mature form. His idols are not dressed with actual clothes, but clothes are painted in red. The torso has an *angavastra,* jewellery covers the neck and reaches right up to the stomach, and the lower part has a yellow or red *dhoti*. Ganesh's stomach protrudes as he loves good food. He always wears a *tiara* or a crown on his head and a belt round his stomach to keep the garments from slipping off. The belt is in the form of a snake, which he inherited from his father, Lord Siva, who has serpents hanging all over him. The trunk of Ganesh can point either to the right or left.

The very pious people keep fasts, or *vrats*. In Rajasthan, many households right outside their entrances, install the image of Ganesh, bathed in red *kumkum* with a garland of red flowers. A small *thaal* with *haldi* and *kumkum* is also placed at the entrance so that people who come to visit take a pinch of each and put it on their foreheads and throat. A *kilo* of *laddoos* are usually kept in the house and after offering them to Ganesh they are offered as *prasad* to whoever visits. The annual celebration comes to an end on Anant Choudas when all the idols used for the community and private celebrations go for *visarjan* (consigned to water) in the sea in Maharashtra or the nearest river or tank in other towns of India.

There is a procession of all the local devotees as they take the idols with great fanfare to the waterfront. In Maharashtra, people take the idols, shouting *Ganapati Bappa Maurya, Pudchya Varsha Luvkarya*. There are fireworks all the way and the procession stops now and then for people to have their last *darshan* of the year. Please also see p. 200.

Onam

Onam is celebrated mostly among Hindus in Kerala for five days in August or September in memory of King Mahabali, who was the grandson of Prahlad and son of Valchana. Mahabali's was the golden age in Kerala. The people believe that Mahabali comes to Kerala to see his people once in a year because of a boon granted to him by Lord Visnu in his Vaman *avtar* (incarnation). Onam falls two days before Anant Choudas, when the immersion ceremony of Lord Ganesh is being celebrated in Maharashtra and some other states of India.

It is a national festival in Kerala and is celebrated with great fervour irrespective of caste or creed. It is, of course, a harvest festival but every one remembers the King Mahabali who brought great peace to this land. The story of Mahabali or Bali is told in the *Bhagwat Purana*. Bali was a noble, generous, righteous and powerful king who ruled with justice, wisdom and generosity. Although he was an *asur*, no *devta* was as noble, in thought or action, as he was. He never refused boon to anyone who asked for it. He did the Viswajit *Yagna* under the guidance of Guru Sukre, the *guru* of all *asurs*. This bestowed on him the strength of the three worlds. No one could stand against Bali. The people loved him and he glowed like a jewel. He looked so handsome that Indra, the king of the *devtas*, who was always afraid that his throne would be taken by someone and who became too noble, got very jealous.

Mahabali decided to perform the Ashvamedha Yagna on the banks of the river Narbada to become a powerful king in the three worlds.

He was proceeding with the rituals when he saw a great glow coming towards the *yagshala.* He found a small boy, glowing like the sun, with a *kamandal* in one hand and an umbrella in the other, coming towards them. Bali knew that it was not an ordinary child and in all humility asked him to sit down. He asked him to demand anything he desired as his glory and sanctify the *yagshala*. The child demanded three paces of the ground, measured by his own foot. Bali thought that three paces of a child's foot was not enough and told the child to ask for something more. The child, Vaman, insisted on three paces. Vaman took the first step and became Lord Narayan. With one pace he took the world and with the second he took the heavens. Then there was no land left and Narayan became Vaman again and asked where he should take the third step. Bali asked him to step on his head as he would be blessed by the feet of Narayan. So, he was sent to *satalok* (*patal lok*) with one foot on his head, but was blessed with the words that even after losing everything on this earth he would gain eternal wisdom and the personal love and care of Lord Narayan.

Bali asked for one favour, that he be allowed to visit his people on earth once in a year. It is believed that he comes to his people on Onam. The people rejoice to know that he is with them and want to show him that they are as happy as they were when he was their ruler so as not to cause him pain and unhappiness.

On this day, the houses in Kerala are usually kept clean. The celebration for Onam starts with decorating the gate or the main door as well as the inside of the house. Branches full of coconut, banana leaves, along with coconut decorate the corners and walls of the houses. There is no deity associated with Onam and there is no special *puja*. The first day of the Onam is known as *Attam*. On this day, the formal functions start with the ladies waking up early in the morning, taking a bath and dressing in clean clothes. They wear jewellery, generally of gold. Children also get up very early, pluck flowers to decorate their homes. Everyday, the flower decorations are renewed. The old one is not scraped but water is sprinkled on top and a thin layer of cowdung added and a new design is carefully patterned on it. This is done right up to the main day of Onam and every day everyone dances around it. Community *attam* is becoming popular now. Common grounds are used for singing and dancing around beautiful flower decorations which are guarded day and night. For ten to fifteen days, something or the other in the name of social or cultural activity takes place in homes and at the state level. On the third day of

Onam, feasts are arranged by families at lunch time and everyone is invited in one home or another. The food is vegetarian. Food in Kerala is served on banana leaves.

The government celebrates Onam with boat races and pageants. On this day, the government takes out floats as it does on Republic Day, with each competitor vying with the other for the prize. Elephants from nearby temples are decorated and paraded on the main road as they are considered auspicious. The parade goes to the main roads and the Governor takes the salute. There may be some illuminations in shops, but houses are not illuminated at night, as this is a daytime festival.

Shraadhs

Hindus set aside 16 days in a year to invite those, who have departed, to be a part of the family when, in their honour, feast befitting the sanctity of their abode in the heavens, is given. These days are known as *Shraadhs, Pitrapaksh* or *Kanaagath*. The *tith*. or the date, according to the Hindu calendar of death, is considered as the *shraadh* of that particular person. These *shraadhs* fall somewhere in August or September. They have *Purnima, Parva, Dooj, Teej, Chauth, Panchami, Chat, Saptami, Ashtami, Navami, Dashmi, Ekadashi, Dwadashi, Treodashi, Chaturdashi,* and *Amavas*. One can find out from the *jantri* (almanac) or from the priest, the corresponding dates according to the English calendar and note them down against the name of each individual who is to be honoured. Individually, on the *tith* of each person, the ceremony can be performed. There may be a common date for two or three persons.

On the appointed date, a *pandit* or *panditani* (male or female priest), as the case may be, is invited as a special guest, and he/she personifies the departed soul. Such persons are supposed to be away from monetary and other worldly desires. The *shraadh* ceremony is not to be performed in the *puja* room. The chosen place is cleaned properly and sponged with water. No one is to be allowed to wear any footwear inside this room. A low table or *chowki* is placed against the wall on which the photograph(s) of the departed person(s) is/are made to stand. *Agarbatti* (incense) is lighted near the photograph(s) and a small *thaali*, containing *roli* and rice is kept nearby. *Panditji* is made to sit comfortably. According to the custom, the eldest male member does the *shraadh*. Lady of the house makes all the arrangements. The woman along with her husband does the *turpun* (offering of water) for both sides of the family. One *turpun* is also done for Bhishma Pitamah, who died without getting married and had no children. To honour him, and to remember him, is the duty of every Indian, for he lived for the betterment of the people, without caring for himself. Any childhood friend is also remembered. In fact, at Badrinath, each one has to make 22 rice balls in memory of at least three generations on both sides of the husband's family, and three generations on both sides of the wife's family.

The kitchen is also cleaned properly, and the person cooking should bathe early and wear clean clothes. On this day, no onion, garlic or turmeric (*haldi*) is used. All vegetables are allowed. The vegetable, *mithai* or fruit most liked by the person, who is being honoured, should be served to *Panditji*, who applies *teeka* on the photograph and garlands it. Then he applies *teeka* on the foreheads of those who are doing the *shraadh*. He chants the *mantras* and asks the gods, Navgrahas, and the departed soul to come and grace the occasion. If *Panditji* is not available, then one may close one's eyes in remembrance of the person whose *shraadh* is being performed and pray for his/her soul. Water is offered to the departed soul by pouring it onto the right hand and letting it fall into the saucepan amidst the chanting of Sanskrit *slokas*. This is known as *turpun*. From the cooked food, four shares are apportioned on four different banana leaves. Each part consists of half a *puri* with a bit of other eatables. One is for the cow, one for the dog and one for the ants. This concept embraces the idea of all living beings being partners in this world, and shareholders in the realm of man. *Panditji* then eats whatever he wants. He has to be looked after very well.

It may be difficult to set individual dates for each person to be so honoured. Hence, on *amavas*, the last day of the *shraadhs*, or on the *tith* of the most revered member of the family, the ceremony can be performed at one time for all the departed souls. Even if one has forgotten to do it on the actual *tith*, or one is unable to do it on the particular date, because of one reason or the other, *amavas* is the day when one can perform the *shraadh*. If, however, there is no way of conducting the ceremony, then one can send all things to the *mandir* or temple. It can also be uncooked food like potatoes, green vegetables, white radish, curd, lemon, ginger, wheat along with oil, sweet and money. This can be done for every one individually or together on *amavas*.

Shraadh should not be taken as a sad day or occasion. It is a day of remembrance for the whole family. Hindus do not undertake any auspicious activity during these days. Sisters and brothers are invited along with their families on such a day. However, during the year of a death, no *shraad* is observed during the *shraad* period for the particular person who expired, but every month Pandit or Panditani, as the case may be, is fed. This is a private affair of immediate family. *Havan* is performed on the *tith* of the eleventh month, when the extended family members are also invited. A *shraadh* lunch is also organized for everyone. For any individual, whose date of death has not been determined, i.e. in case of war etc., the *tith* is observed as it is on the day the news is received.

Durga Puja

Among Hindus, Mother Goddess, is regarded as *shakti*—the power of Brahma, Visnu and Mahesh. She takes the form of their consorts, without whom none of the gods can achieve anything. She is worshipped all over India with the same ardour under different names and manifestations. The most benign face of the Goddess is Durga, the fearsome Goddess with ten arms, who rides a tiger and defeats invincible buffalo-headed demon, Mahishasura. Durga Puja, therefore, is performed for nine days during the moonlight fortnight, known as *Navaratris*. This is immediately before Dussehra.

During these days, huge *pandals* (tents) are erected and are beautifully decorated with images of Durga Ma in her varied moods. In each locality, almost everyone contributes towards the event and every evening *kirtans* and *bhajans* are sung in every *pandal*. The images of the goddess are beautifully decorated so as to develop a feeling of faith and good way among all the children and adults alike.

Little girls are regarded as a form of Durga (*devi ka roop*), as they are supposed to be pure and innocent. Little boys are regarded as the '*roop of langooras*', supposed to be the servers of the Devi in her celestial abode. They are invited for lunch on *ashtami* (eighth day). Feast is served to them. No item in the feast should contain onion. Sometime garments or the length of material (cloth) are given to both the girls and the boys. Some even prefer to give a utensil. In inviting the children one symbolically invites the goddess herself. Before serving the food to the little ones, the elders perform the *puja*, wash the feet of the children and welcome them by serving with their own hands. When the children finish eating, the elders touch their feet and seek blessings from them.

Durga *puja* is celebrated in Bengal during September and October. On the sixth day or *sashthi*, the images of Durga, along with her four children, Lakshmi, Saraswati, Ganesh and Kartikeya, as it is believed to be in Bengal, are installed in the various *puja pandals* erected for the festival in the state and outside it. For Bengalis, the advent of the Goddess Durga assumes a special significance. It is believed that the mother goddess along with her children visits during these four days from her icy abode in Kailash in the Himalayas, where she lives with her consort Siva. According to a legend, every year she comes in a special transport, a boat, because there are floods in the eastern parts of India.

Durga *puja* has become as much essential even as it is a religious one. Women observe fast for the welfare of their family. Especially those who are Vaishnavites take vegetarian food during these days. The worshippers of Kali, or those known as Shaktas, however, eat meat. On Mahanavami, wheat is eaten as part of great feasting. The last day coincides with Dussehra. Idols are taken away in large processions for immersion in water. Before this, married women of all age groups visit the nearby *pandal* to apply vermilion (*sindoor*) to the parting of each other's hair. The women and the priest apply *sindoor* on the forehead of the goddess. A mother-in-law gives an iron bangle interlaced with gold or silver (for decoration) to a new bride as the first gift, a token of *suhag*, which the daughter-in-law wears throughout her life. The younger members do *pronam* (touching the feet) to the elders while the men embrace each other. Please also see p. 204.

Gandhi Jayanti

Gandhi Jayanti on October 2, commemorates the birthday of Mahatma Gandhi, Father of the Nation. It is a national holiday in India.

Mahatma Gandhi is respected both for his saintly qualities and able leadership in the national struggle for freedom. The festival assumed great popularity during pre-independence days and many activities relating to social and economic welfare of the people were undertaken in connection with the celebration on this day. They included continuous spinning for 24 hours. The spinning wheel was

looked upon by Mahatma Gandhi as the symbol of the country's independence. It signified self-purification, self-help and self-reliance. It was also an expression of one's desire to help the poor, *daridranarayan*, through the revival of cottage industries. The program of cleaning the public streets, tanks, Harijan localities and other places was also undertaken for the purpose of inculcating among the people an awareness about cleanliness, dignity of labour and removal of untouchability. Various other constructive programs were also initiated or executed on this day.

The day stands for national unity and integration, self-dedication and complete negation of ill-will. It is a festival for introspection and sublimation of the soul, cultivating respect for all religions and pursuit of the various ideals Mahatma Gandhi laid down for the nation.

The day begins in Delhi by the visit of the President of India and the Prime Minister and others to Raj Ghat, the final resting-place of Mahatma Gandhi. They lay wreaths on the *samadhi*. This is followed by meeting at various places to recall the contributions of Mahatma Gandhi. Functions are also held at Sabarmati Ashram and Harijan Sewak Sangh, specially known for the contributions of Father of the Nation.

Dussehra

Dussehra is celebrated to mark the legend of Lord Rama, the Hindu deity. The celebration is for ten days when *Ramlilas* (the activities of lord Rama) are organized. These dramatize episodes from the *Ramayana* reminds the generations the life and deeds of Rama, including his exile, accompanied by his brother Laxman and wife Sita, Sita's abduction by the Demon King Ravana of Lanka and the epic battle for her rescue and the role played by the monkey god, Hanuman. Huge effigies of Ravana, his brother and son, Meghnad and Kumbhkaran are stuffed with fireworks to be set on fire on the last day, Vijaya Dashami. Please also see p. 194.

Diwali

Diwali is the most significant festival for the people of almost all religions of India, especially the Hindus and Jains. Just as Christmas is no longer the monopoly of Christians, it is celebrated by other communities as well with equal zest. Thus, Diwali is not restricted to Hindus but is also enjoyed by everyone. It marks Rama's return to the capital city, Ayodhya, after being exiled for 14 years by his step-mother, Kaikai who, in fact, wanted her own son, Bharata, to be installed to throne. The entire town was lit with lamps to greet Rama, Laxman and Sita.

For Jains, Mahavir became enlightened on this day. Though, according to one version of *The Ramayana,* Diwali marks the return of Rama to his native Ayodhya following his victory over demon King Ravana, in many southern versions, it commemorates Krsna's slaying of the demon Narakasura. The idealised masculinity of Maryadapurushotam Rama, with stress on a strict moral and righteous conduct, stands in striking contrast to the playful amoral *lila* (activities) of child-god Krsna .

Diwali also heralds the Hindu New Year when old accounts in business are closed. Hindus believe that Laxmi, the Goddess of Wealth, visits her devotees on that night. To welcome her, they clean all their houses, get them white washed and have their doors painted. The festival also serves another purpose. The houses become dirty because of the preceding monsoon season. Now they need to be cleaned.

Sweets are exchanged among relatives and friends on this day. People light up their houses, set off crackers, gamble and have good time. It is the most beautiful of all the festivals. There is no rowdism as it happens on Holi festival. Dussehra is more a public spectacle ending in the burning of mammoth effigies of Ravana, Meghdoot and Kumbhakarna than something to be celebrated at home. Diwali is essentially a get-together of friends and family members. In this way, the festival helps in bringing social cohesion among members of the society. On Diwali, markets and streets are profusely decorated and there is a large scale of firework till midnight.

Diwali comes exactly 20 days after Dussehra on new moon. It is believed that Laxmi, the Goddess of Wealth visits the houses at mid night. People keep their house well-lit and worship her at night. This is done on an individual basis. *Puja* starts at dusk when *diyas* (earthen lamps) or candles are lit and there is complete illumination. Fire works are brought out and the children join in the fun and frolic by setting fire to the crackers.

From the year 2003, Diwali has also been included in the White House calendar of celebrations. On October 25, 2003, the Indian American community lighted a big brass lamp in the White House in front of the images of the Lord Ganesa and Goddess Lakshmi.

People living away from their families are no longer deprived of the sense of togetherness on this day. The new technology has facilitated remote family *pujas,* and e-crackers. Digital Diwali albums and festive ring tones have brought in never before excitements. They kindle the festive fervor. With a handy photoshop applications one can instantly share one's Diwali memories with any one and everywhere. But what one neeeds is simply the gadgets for a remote family Diwali *puja.* Exchange of ring tones and warm tidings through chat on the Internet with our dearest ones at far off places, using webcom, cell phones, that can take photos and perform remote family Diwali *puja* through video chat, again sustains festive fervor and cohesion among the family members.

Chhath Puja

Chhath Puja is a 3-day festival on the fourth day after Diwali. In fact, *chhath* derives its name from the day it is held, i.e. the sixth day after Diwali, according to the lunar calendar. Diwali is on *amavasya* (moonless night) and *chhath* is calculated accordingly. It even stretches over a number of days because the devotees go through increasing stages of ritual purity.

Though Sun worship is not an integral part of Hinduism anymore, as it vanished in the early *Vedic* period, its origin can be linked to the revival of Sun worship in Bihar, where it has continued over a period of time. This seems to have been initiated when some *Brahmins* from Rajasthan traveled across the country, reintroducing the practice. Construction of the Sun Temple in Konark, Orissa, is reminiscent of the early Sun worship. It is a meditative activity which culminates on the fifth day's sunset and the sixth day's sunrise. Basically, the devotee does a *namaskar* (salutation) to the Sun as it sets and rises around the critical *chhath* night. This Vedic traditional style of worship has continued not only in Bihar, in some parts of Uttar Pradesh but also in other parts of the world where Biharis are concentrated. It is celebrated on a very large scale to offer *prasad* to the Goddess Sarita, a form of Sun—Dusk and Dawn. The *chhath* is also known as *Dala Chhath* and *Brat Bihari*. This is one of the five-day long religious vow in which sanctity and celibacy are maintained. Food is vegetarian and even the onions and garlic are shunned. New utensils are purchased and cooking is done on wood.

Several myths have become associated with *chhath*. It is said that one has to do it at least two years in a row to fulfil one's material wishes. Bihari women, decked in traditional, vermilion-bordered yellow saris, are even seen conducting the *puja* on the banks of New York's Hudson River as well as in other cities of the world on any river bank or pond.

Chhath is an agrarian festival. People worship the Sun after the monsoon and before the winter when the sunlight is needed to dry the ground to plant the next crop of wheat. It is indeed a festival of fertility on water cosmology. Freshly-cut sugarcane figures in the offerings made to the Sun. The devotees start enjoying their first sugarcane only after the *puja* is over. Thus, *chhath* is a type of thanksgiving for agricultural Bihar. The distinctive *prasad d*uring *chhath* is *thekua*—a mix of wheat, Joggery and milk which is deep-fried in *ghee*.

The devotees observe 3-day fast and then pour the *arghya*—offering of water and milk to the Sun God at the dawn and dusk. They stay awake during the night and adjacent either to the river or a pond or some other water body. In the absence of river or a pond, some innovative enthusiasts even make temporary pools to store water in them and perform *puja*.

The *puja* is performed at the local river, as the holy dip is considered as an integral part of ritual purification. In Bihar, one can see a sea of humanity converging to the riverbed in buses, trucks, *rickshaws*, cycles and even on foot. For Brahmins, Thakurs, Kurmis or for people from any other caste, distinction becomes meaningless as devotees worship cheek-by-jowl and even share their offerings. Engineering and medical colleges are seen in Bihar setting up *pandals* to distribute *prasad*. Throughout the night, cultural programs are organized that include folk music, dance and *bhajans* (devotional songs) in Maithili, Magadhi and Bhojpuri. *Utsav Bhoj* (festival food) is also arranged for those who stay during the night at the *ghats* (river banks).

Bhaiya Dooj

Bhaiya Dooj, two days after Diwali, is a family festival in honour of brothers. It again brings together the brothers and sisters and marks the sustenance of affection between the two. On this day, sisters apply *tilak* on the forehead of their brothers and offer them sweet as token of their best wishes. The brothers, in turn, offer their sisters some token money. Thus, like Raksha Bandhan, this festival also reminds them of the pious relationship of brothers and sisters.

Govardhan Puja

Govardhan Puja, or Annakut in both Rajasthan and Mathura commemorates the day when Krsna lifted Mount Gowardhan on his little finger to protect the area from a deluge sent by the irate Indra, the god of rain.

Karva Chauth

Karva Chauth in October or November is the day when complete fast is observed by the married Hindu ladies in north India for the wellbeing of their husbands, who are supposed to be their protector after they leave their parental home. In olden days, widows became a burden to their households and they were encouraged to burn themselves on the funeral pyre of their husbands. This tradition was glorified by attributing great virtue to the woman concerned. She was brainwashed to volunteer herself for pyre and become *sati*. Therefore, it became important for her to pray for the long life of her husband.

On this day, the married women are not to take anything from morning till night and end it after worshipping the moon. But nowadays, those who do not have enough stamina have started taking liquid after *puja* in the evening but food is to be taken after worshipping the moon. No food or water is to be taken after Sun rise. They can, however, have the food before sunrise. These food items are generally provided by the mother-in-laws a day prior to the actual fast. Among the educated women nowadays, it has become a symbol of sentiments for their husbands. Great festivities are attached to this festival. On this day, the women are dressed in fine clothes. They are not supposed to do any household work, or any stitching or knitting. They approach *mehndiwallahs* (professionals making designs with henna) and *chooriwallahs* (bangle sellers) to get their palm and feet decorated with henna and get their arms filled with bangles.

The first *puja* takes place at about 4 or 5 pm. All the married women join together at one place to perform this *puja*. They together worship Parvati. The *baya* for each individual is kept on a *thaali* over the *karva* which has a little bottle and seven items. A story is narrated to all the women by an elder member of the family and a ceremony, known as *manasna*, follows, which means to give away and never take back. *Roly tika* is applied on the forehead of Gaur Mata. All the women doing the *puja* also apply *roly tika* on their foreheads and hair parting, known as *maang*.

Traditionally, the moon is worshipped to end the fast. This is done on an individual level. Each woman offers water to the moon by holding the lamp in her left hand. With her right hand she pours water on the ground seven times. This is done with the chanting of *mantras*. This chant is repeated seven times. She then ends her fast by taking little water and some sweet. The family dinner is served. Rice and *dal* are cooked on this day.

Guru Nanak Jayanti

Guru Nanak Jayanti, some time in November, is celebrated to mark the birthday of first Sikh *guru*, Guru Nanak. Guru Nanak happened to be the founder of Sikhism, which is one of the eleven major religions of India. Sikhism is found almost exclusively in the land of India and that too in the province of Punjab. Yet, in less than 200 years after its foundation, it extended itself across the north India and southward to Ceylon. Sikhs form a martial community. Most of the provincial Governors of India have bodyguards who are stalwart Sikhs. They are also used for police petrols in the streets of Penang and Singapore, Hong Kong and Shanghai and other Far Eastern countries. But 95 per cent of all Sikhs in the world are concentrated in northwest India in the same region where the religion originated.

Nanak was born in a little village known as Talwandi, about thirty miles southwest of Lahore (now in Pakistan). Talwandi has been renamed as Nanakpura in honour of the great *guru*. His parents were common villagers. His father was Hindu and was an employee of a Mohammedan feudal lord. His mother was a pious and devoted lady.

At the age of seven, Nanak was admitted in school. There, the boy exhorted the Hindu teacher to know the true name of God rather than study all the *Vedas*. At the age of nine, he started learning Persian. At a time when he was being invested with the sacred thread of Hinduism, this religious minded boy gave instructions to the officiating priest concerning the spiritual significance.

There are many legends to show Nanak's aversion to ordinary invocations, his preference to the life of quiet meditation and religious devotions as well as his supernatural power. Because of Nanak's indifference to physical or commercial activities, his relatives and friends were in despair. A government post was secured for him, but he remained pensive and unhappy. He retired to the desert and passed his time under trees in religious contemplation. He gave money to holy men, which his father had entrusted to him for some purchases. His father punished him, but Nanak was unrepentant.

Nanak took Mardana, a Mohammedan, and went around singing and teaching One True God to the people. They traveled widely over north India. After twelve years, they returned home in Punjab. In Ceylon, Nanak preached to the King and the Queen. He also visited the extreme northwest of India, Srinagar in Kashmir, Mount Sumeru among the Himalayas, and Peshawar on the frontier. He described himself as a Mohammedan pilgrim, and was perhaps the first Hindu to make pilgrimage (*Haj*) to Mecca. There his simple preaching of the universality of God produced a miraculous effect in front of the sacred Kaaba stone.

When Nanak was imprisoned unjustly, he preached to the Mohammedan officer, who then released him. When he was attacked by a band of robbers, he gave them spiritual instructions and told them that their sins would be wiped out if they abandoned their evil career. Through his humble preaching he converted a notorious villain to confess and give all his possessions to the poor. He denounced Hindu ascetic practices and converted many Hindus by his reinterpretation of Hinduism. Similarly, he reinterpreted Islam.

The most frequent title for Nanak has been "*Guru*", meaning "religious teacher". He has also been referred to as "chief" or "king" or "Nanak Shah" and endearingly as "father", "Baba Nanak". During the latter part of his life he was revered as saint and even as a divine savior. His teachings are contained in *Guru Grandh Saheb*, which was compiled in 1604 by the fifth *Guru*. Nanak's first utterance, when he felt the divine call, *Ek Onkar*, constitutes the first two sentences in the sacred scripture. The chief designation for the deity in Sikhism is "*Sat Nam*", meaning "true name". These two words are the first words in the text of the sacred scriptures. They recur at the beginning of each hymn. The Sikh religion teaches that salvation consists in knowing God and in obtaining God, or in being absorbed into God. The main method of worship in Sikhism is meditation on God, particularly in the form of a repetition of the "*Sat Nam*".

After the death of the tenth Guru in 1708, the supreme loyalty of the Sikhs was transferred from the personal *guru* to the book, *Guru Granth Saheb*. Thus, the birth day of Guru Nanak is celebrated by visiting *gurudwaras* to pay obeisance to scripture of the Sikhs, recall the advice of the Sikh Guru and follow his teachings.

Id-ul-Fitr

Id-ul-Fitr, the Muslim festival, popularly known as Ramzan, is celebrated on the first day of *Shawaal*, the tenth month of the Hijri year, since the time of Prophet Mohammed. According to English calendar, it is around November.

Fitr means breaking the fast or refraining from fasting, while *Id* means happiness. The festival thus marks the end of the fasts kept during the preceding month of Ramzan. Muslims regard this month as one of the great bounties from God. The texts of previous scriptures were revealed by God to various prophets who preceded Prophet Mohammed, viz. Ibrahim (Abraham), Moosa (Moses), Dawood (David) and Isa (Jesus) in Ramzan. *The Quran*, revealed by God to Prophet Mohammed also began to be revealed in the month of Ramzan.

Muslims practice self-denial throughout this month by abstaining from eating, drinking, smoking, chewing, snuffing or smelling anything whatsoever throughout the day, i.e. from before the dawn till sunset. In addition to the usual prayers offered five times a day, i.e. in the morning before sunrise, soon after the moon, in the afternoon, just after sunset and at night, about two hours after sunset, special additional prayers are recited by them every night during Ramzan. Mosques are illuminated with intense devotion to Allah, the Almighty God, during the entire month. It is believed that there is one night hidden among the Ramzan nights, which is known as the night of power, *Shab-e-Qadr* or *Laylat-ul-Qadr* when prayers and devotion to God earn religious merit equal to one thousand times that during any other night God showers His mercy and blessings on all who pray to Him during that night. No one knows which particular night in Ramzan is *Shab-e-Qadr* but the general belief is that the 27th night following the 26th fast in Ramzan is the night of power and is spent in prayers.

In Delhi, and so it should be at other places, as soon as the month of Ramzan is over and the crescent on the western horizon heralds the advent of the day of Id-ul-Fitr, the Muslims celebrate it as the day of thanksgiving to God for having enabled them to successfully perform the austerities. They wear new clothes, eat sweet dishes, greet one another and rejoice in a mood of relaxation after the self-denial practiced in Ramzan. Each Muslim gives to the poor 3 kgs of wheat or 6 kgs of barley or its value in cash or any other kind. This charity is prescribed for every Muslim and also for all the members of his family. It is called *sadaqah*, which is usually given before going to the special prayer of *Id*. Some sweet thing, usually sweet milk, with dry dates and *shev* cooked in it, is taken before going for the *Id* prayers. The special additional prayer is offered some time after the usual Morning Prayer.

After the *Id* prayers and when sermons are over, those present shake hands, and some embrace each other. They also congratulate each other on the occurrence of *Id*. After returning home, the parents give money to their children. They visit the friends and relatives who are treated with sweet or greeting cards are exchanged. Thus, the day is spent in feasting, praying and receiving wishes and making presents. All the Muslims, whether Sunnis or Shiahs, celebrate this festival.

Christmas

Christmas on December 25 is celebrated as the birthday of Christ. It is a public holiday in India. The religious observance of this day includes the customary decoration of the inside of church buildings with coloured flags, lanterns and lights. A popular form of decoration, both in church buildings and in private homes, is a bright star. It commemorates the unusual star which appeared in the sky at the time of the birth of Christ, and which was seen by the 'wise men' from the Eastern countries who went to Bethlehem to give precious gifts to the child Jesus soon after his birth.

A special feature of the Christmas day is the singing of Christmas carols (songs about the birth of Christ). It is customary that Christmas parties go till night. People visit the homes of their friends and relatives to sing such carols. It is done especially on Christmas eve. Roman Catholics and Protestants alike share the common tradition of singing Christmas carols, i.e special songs celebrating the coming of the Saviour to the world in the form of a child. This tradition has come from Europe and these carols are sung in western tunes.

Special services are organized in all churches in the morning. In these services, the hymns, prayers, *Bible* readings and sermons are countered on the life of Christ's birth. It has also become customary in some churches to bring 'white gifts' and hand it over to the minister for the support of the church's work. In some churches, people get their children baptized on this day, thus making them members of the church.

It is traditionally a time of great rejoicing for all Christians. People wear new clothes, decorate their homes, and exchange sweets and gifts. Greetings are also exchanged through greeting cards. The popular legend of Santa Claus (an old man with a white beard, dressed in a red cloak and hat) has been introduced in India from Europe and America. In accordance with this tradition, Christians often try to help the poor at Christmas time by giving them food, clothing or money. Christian families also set up Christmas trees, hanging on them coloured lights, candles and parcels of gifts which are to be given on Christmas day. Short dramas portraying the story about the birth of Jesus Christ, as per *The Bible*, are also enacted by the children.

Since the birth of Christ is believed to have occurred at midnight, daily service of the Mass is not offered in the morning as usual, but at midnight between December 24 and 25. The midnight Mass is often celebrated in the open air for the benefit of the hundreds of villagers who come for the occasion from all the villages around. The church compound is gaily decorated with lights, green-leaves and flowers. Before the midnight Mass, the crowd enjoys a religious drama, staged each year by the people of one of the villages. Carols are sung from December 25 till January 6 in churches, at homes and at Christmas parties.

Every Catholic home also puts up a crib inside the house and an illuminated star in a prominent place outside. The crib is a representation of the sense of the nativity or the birth of the Christ. The child Jesus, lying in a manger between his mother Mary and Joseph, and an angel from heaven appearing to the shepherds, and hosts of angels singing the Christmas message to the world—Glory of God is the highest and on earth peace to men of Goodwill is also displayed—are shown.

Pongal

Pongal, which is close to Lohri festival in north India, is observed in south India. It is a harvest festival and comes after the winter harvest. It combines thanksgiving to the God of the harvesting with the day of feasting followed by a day allotted to the veneration of cattle. The festival is an expression of the joy of the farmer when he is able to stock food grain in his granary. He takes care of his bulls and spends money in sports with his best bull. Jallikatu, the spot of bulls, is a joyful manner of testing and sorting brave bulls. The farmers would take their cows to the best bulls.

The festival is celebrated with full vigour in south India with songs and dances. After the harvest has been gathered, it gives the farmer the inclination to express his joy, which he does with folk songs and dances.

Lohri

Lohri, the festival of Punjab, invariably falls on January 13, a day before *Sankrant*, the holy month according to Hindus. It is essentially a festival of the agriculturists. In January, the weather in Punjab is very cold and people light bonfire in the precincts of their houses to feel warm. The people gather around a bonfire at night and enjoy dancing and merry-making. Dancers perform *bhangra* (Punjabi dance) and other dances around the bonfire. They offer *chirva, meva, revri* and *gajak* to the fire in the form of *puja*. The fire becomes the deity of

the day. It has its own sanctity. Everyone is supposed to do *parikrama* around the fire. After offerings to the fire, *prasad* is offered to all those present.

On this festive occasion, young women intricate *mehndi* patterns to decorate their hands and feet. They buy the most colourful bangles and *bindis*. Their garments are grand, especially the *chunni*, which is very heavy with *zari* and *gota, salma* and *sitaras*. *Sindoor* is applied in the parting of the hair. Again, the first Lohri celebrated by a new bride represents a grand occasion. The mother-in-law presents heavy garments and jewellery to the new bride. The first Lohri of a new-born is equally important. There is a family get-together and feast. The festival is celebrated with traditional dances and bonfire. To conclude, it is a great fun festival when people find time to eat and dance together while they relax on the winter day when they otherwise dare not come out. But on this day they have an opportunity to relax in the open around the bonfire.

Teej

Teej is basically a festival of Rajasthan and Gujarat in the month of July or August when dandia dances are arranged by professionals and performed in courtyards at home and in public places. The colourful *dandas*, moving in rhythmic beats, with each swing of the hands and feet, hitting either at one's own *danda* held in the other hand or at the one held by the other dancers attract our attention. Such a dance needs sufficient practice. Swings are also set up in the open courtyards. Girls, with henna on their hands and feet, run about joyously. The parents generally present new clothes to their daughters. Similarly, the children also feel happy to get new clothes from their parents. This custom of giving new clothes and jewellery by the parents, from time to time, to their married daughters has the impact of strengthening social relationship and making the in-laws aware that the women have the backing of parents or brothers. Parents also present *baya* to their married daughters in the same way as they do on *karva chauth*.

Republic Day

Republic Day on January 26 is the national festival in India. It was on this day in 1950 that the Constitution of Independent India was adopted by the Constituent Assembly, formed on attaining Independence in August 1947. It was on this day that the country became a sovereign democratic republic, called India or Bharat. This event is commemorated by the celebration of Republic Day every year.

It was on this day in 1930 that the Indian leaders had observed the Purna Swaraj Day (complete independence day) after the Indian National Congress, presided over by the late Jawaharlal Nehru, had passed a resolution declaring independence as its goal. On this day, a declaration in terms of the resolution was read out in public meetings all over the land as a pledge to work ceaselessly for *Purna Swarajya* or complete independence. The celebrations generally started with *prabhat pheris* (morning processions) followed by flag salutations.

In the independent India, it has been declared as a national holiday. In the morning, at the capitals of states and every district and *taluka* headquarters, national flag hoisting ceremonies are performed followed by a parade of the armed forces and the police. The national flag is flown on public and private buildings.

Each state is also represented on this occasion at the Republic Day parade in New Delhi. The President of India takes salute. Cultural programs are also organized. The President of the Republic of India also declares national awards, in recognition of services rendered in several walks of public life. The festival affords an opportunity to the citizens to rededicate their lives to the welfare of the country and give vent to their feelings of patriotism.

A Kaleidoscopic View of the Indian Marriages

A Christian bride on her way to church.

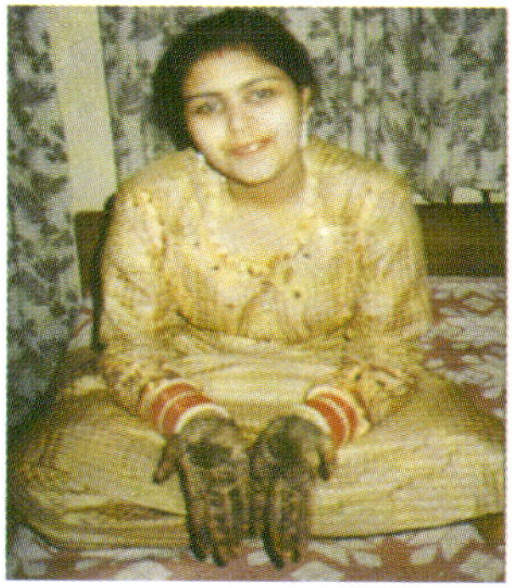

A bride with patterns of *mehndi* on her palms and ivory bangles before joining her groom.

The couple taking a vow around the sacred fire to remain faithful to each other.

Another groom all set to meet and bring his bride.

The groom riding on mare and accompanied with his parents, friends and relatives on his way to bride's house for marriage.

Yet, another groom with his *sarbala* sitting in chariot in marriage procession.

Underlying Concept of Hindu Marriage

It is again interesting to know that among Hindus too the practices are not identical. They vary from region to region and from one language group to another. India is a vast country, consisting of a number of religious and language groups. Even among the Hindus, spread over in various states, what is almost identical is the enunciation of three *shlokas* from among the 72 recited during the Hindu marriage ceremony. In one, the bride and the groom say: "May all the gods join our hearts, may our relationship be blessed with mutual love and respect". In another, the bride's father says: "I give you this girl, born and brought up in my family, before all the gods as witnesses, for the purpose of perpetuation of your family and the salvation of your ancestors". In the third, the bride says: "I invoke the lord of the fire to bless me as I leave my father's family and enter my husband's family. May my husband enjoy a long life, may my relatives be blessed with good wishes, may the lord of fire protect and perpetuate my love for you".

Most of the 72 *shlokas* are an invocation to protect the girl, to obtain for her feelings of love, respect and generosity in her husband's home. The husband's acceptance of his bride in the *shlokas*, as well as the subsequent rituals, are all meant to cement this feeling of bond between the couple, indeed the two families. The primary feeling on the part of the bride, in Hindu marriage, is one of *samarpan* or surrender to her new home. On the part of the groom, it is one of *sweekar* or acceptance in the true spirit of love. This may sound like gender bias to most women, but Hindu scriptures say that for both man and woman, life remains incomplete if she/he remains alone. It is only by union, complementing one's partner and living out married life through its various ups and downs, that the meaning of life becomes complete.

According to Hindu philosophy, without a wife, the life of a man is incomplete and meaningless. The portrayal of *Ardhanareeshwara* (the half male, half female form of Lord Siva) indicates the incompleteness of either sex without the other. The wife is an equal partner in all respects. It is also reflected in the *shloka* uttered by the father of the bride, as he hands over his daughter to her husband: "To you, I hand over my daughter, who shall be the instrument for you to realize your four *purashaarthas*, or the purpose of your being born on this earth. It is the aspect of man's 'completeness' that the Hindu marriage ritual, primarily the *shlokas*, seeks to strengthen.

The code of Hindu marriage holds that each person comes to earth for the purpose of serving out certain *karmas* (duties), which are reflected in his/her horoscope. A marriage arranged through matching horoscopes, it is believed, brings together two people of similar *karmas*, who will be able to serve their own *karmas* as well as help their partners serve theirs. However, each region in India, over the years, brought in some changes to suit the social needs of the time. It is, therefore, better to know what are the major practices in each one of the regions, but before this it is better to explore some more information about some practices prevalent in India.

Arranging a Marriage

Arranging marriage in India in almost every religion and language group is the responsibility of parents and other relatives of both the bride and the groom. Marriage alliances essentially entail some redistribution of wealth as well as building and restructuring the social realignment which, of course, result in the biological reproduction of family. The entire marriage ceremony lasts for few days. It involves invitation to friends and relatives, arranging the function, purchase of items for gifts, which the bride has to take with her to her new home, etc. This is the reason why there is no greater event in a family than a wedding, dramatically evoking every possible social obligation, kinship bond, traditional value, impatient sentiment, and economic resource. The ceremony is so vast that a number of professional organizations have been set up to accomplish this task in a meticulous way.

Age of Marriage

Keeping all this in view, some parents in India begin marriage arrangement on the birth of a child, but most wait till the child grows up. In the past, the age of marriage was quite young, and in a few small groups, especially in Rajasthan, children under the age of 5 are even now united in marriage. In rural communities, pre-puberty marriage for girls was traditionally the rule. In the late 20th century, the age of marriage is rising in villages almost to the level set in cities. Legislation making minimum 18 years for girls and 21 years for boys has been made mandatory. But such laws have little effect on actual marriage practices in remote villages. Legislation doesn't seem to be adequate to change the mindset. Nearly 20 per cent of the females still get married before 18 years of age. The proportion is higher in rural areas.

The Hindu Marriage Act was amended in 1976 vesting rights in a girl to repudiate child marriage, irrespective of whether the marriage was consummated or not. But there is no provision for invalidation of marriages below the permissible age, if they do take place. In the case of *Munshi Ram v Emperor,* AIR 1936, Allahabad, the Court held that the Child Marriage Act only aimed at the restraint of such marriages, the validity of which was beyond the scope of the Act, once performed. This position seems to hold ground in *P Venkataramana v The State,* AIR 1977, AP 43. The 1978 amendment to the Child Marriage Restraint Act has not addressed this issue. According to Hindu Marriage Act, a girl can opt out of marriage and get divorce if she was below 15 years of age at the time of marriage and repudiate the marriage between 15 and 18 years. Punishment for marriages in violation of permissible age limit are relatively minor, i.e. 15 days' imprisonment or fine of Rs.1000.00. If a male contracts such a marriage over 21 years of age the punishment is 3 months' imprisonment and fine.

Finding a Suitable Match

Finding the perfect partner for one's child is indeed a challenging task for the parents. They have to locate potential brides and grooms of appropriate social, economic, educational and professional status. Urban dwellers use classified matrimonial advertisements in newspapers. The advertisements usually mention the religion, caste and educational background, stressing female beauty and male's earning capacity, sometime hinting on the sign of dowry. In rural areas, matches between strangers are usually arranged without the couple meeting each other. Generally, parents and other relatives come to an understanding. In cities, however, photographs are exchanged among the educated classes and, at times, the couple is allowed to meet each other. A number of marriage bureaus have also come up to bring the two parties together and to discuss and finalise the matrimonial arrangement.

The parents always advise their children that arranging marriage for them is their prerogative, but an increasing number of young people are finding their own spouses. Such love marriages are deemed to be slightly scandalous alternative to properly arranged marriages. Some young people convince their parents to arrange their marriage to people with whom they have fallen in love. In upper classes, such semi-arranged marriages are increasingly taking place between young couples, who are from different castes but are educationally or professionally on the same level. However, if there is any vast difference in love marriages, say between Hindus and Muslims, parents would generally not agree and there are some family disputes.

Marriage Rituals & Regional Differences

After arrangement for marriage has been made, a number of wedding rituals take place. As already stated, each religious group, region and caste has a slightly different set of rites. The bride's family normally hosts most of the ceremonies and bear the expenses of such an arrangement, including accommodation, feasting, decoration and gifts for the groom's party. All such arrangements are made with a view to enhance the status of bride's family. The groom's party usually hires a band and brings gifts for the bride. But, their expenses are far less than that of the bride's family.

In all, Indian weddings are noisy and colorful affairs. The musical escort of the bridegroom riding on a mare with brass band dressed in colorful uniforms makes it a splendit and panoramic marriage procession. Sometime the groom comes riding a gaudy, gilt-plated chariot, accompanied by an entourage of young relatives dancing to popular tunes from Hindi films. Mostly the groom is accompanied by a young boy wearing a string of flowers over his face. The whole spectacle is a modern-day re-enactment of the pomp and pageantry associated with royal wedding processions in the past.

What are the distinct rites associated with the various religious and language groups? I tried to explore this information and would like to share it with the readers.

India is divided into two large regions with regard to Hindu kinship and marriage practices, the north and the south. Various ethnic and tribal groups of the central mountainous north, and eastern regions follow a variety of other practices. The Indo-Aryan families in the north seek marriage alliances with people to whom they are not already linked by ties of blood. The families look for alliances beyond their kinship. In the Dravidian-speaking south, a family seeks to strengthen the existing kin ties through marriage, preferably with blood relatives. In the north, every kinship term clearly indicates whether the person referred to is a blood relation. All blood relatives are forbidden as marriage mates to a person or a person's children. As for matrimonial relations in South India, there is no clear-cut distinction between the family of birth and the family of marriage. As marriage alliances in South India commonly involve a continuing exchange of daughters among a few families, for the married couple all relatives are ultimately blood kin.

On the Indo-Gangetic plain, Indian marriages are conducted outside the village. It is felt that daughters should not be given to villages where daughters of the family or even of the natal village have previously been given. In most of the regions, marriages in the families of brothers and sisters are shunned. The emphasis is on creating wider alliances. In most of north India, the Hindu bride goes to live with strangers in a home, which is quite alien to her. There she is sequestered and veiled. Her natal family is often geographically far away. In central India, the basic north Indian pattern prevails, with some modifications. For instance, in Madhya Pradesh, marriages within a village are not uncommon. Marriages between caste fellows in neighboring villages are frequent. In South India, marriages are preferred between cousins, especially cross cousins, i.e the children of a brother and sister, and even between uncle and nieces. The principle involved is that of return, the family that gives a daughter expects one in return, if not now, then in the next generation. The effect of such marriages is to bind people in relatively small, tight-knit kin groups. A bride moves to her in-law's home, the home of her grandmother, and is often comfortable among these familiar faces. But, nowadays, many South Indian marriages are contracted outside such close kingroups when no suitable match is available among the close relatives, or when other options appear more advantageous.

Bengali Wedding

The Hindus, whose mother tongue is Bengali and are mainly concentrated in Bengal and Tripura, initiate the wedding ceremony by offering *puja* (prayer) to their ancestors. It is performed a day before the marriage and is attended by all the family members. On the day of wedding, 10 married women from the house of bride/groom accompany the bride/groom to a nearby pond in the morning to individually bathe the bride/groom. Food is offered to them. The meal consists of *machar laija bhaja* (fried fish) followed by *jan dhala bhaja* (rice cooked in water), curd and *chiruya*. In the evening, relatives or friends paint and decorate the *piris*, which are brought to the bride's house a day before the wedding or the wedding day. Conch shells are blown. *Tattvas* or gifts are exchanged between the families of the bride and the groom. A relative of the groom arrives at the bride's house with the *gae halud tattva* (gifts). They include at least six sarees, cosmetics, fish, assorted sweets, curd, betel leaves, etc. Incense is lit to welcome them and conch shells are blown. The bearers are given sweets and money. Yet, other ceremonies associated with Bengali wedding are *adhivas tattavas* or gifts from the bride's house, *cubi patta* or a ceremony to rever Saint Kuber, *snan* on the day of wedding when a few married women apply turmeric and oil on the hair and body of the bride/groom. After bathing, the bride and the groom must wear the new set of clothes that have been presented to them by their in-laws. It is followed by *sankha porana* when the bride is required to wear conch shell bangles that have been dipped in turmeric water. The bride adorns herself in all her bridal finery. Her hair is tied into a bun and covered with a veil. The *mukut* (crown) is placed on her head and secured in place by pinning it to the veil. After her bridal makeover, a design of the *mukut* is traced on her face using the *chandan* (sandalwood) paste.

The groom and his relatives arrive at the bride's house to the ringing of bell, blowing of conch shells etc. The groom is offered sweet etc and water is sprinkled on the doorsteps into the house to mark the auspicious movement. Both the mother of the bride and of the groom do not attend the ceremony. It is believed that this will protect the people from the 'evil eye'. A priest conducts the wedding ceremony. The bride and the groom exchange garlands while the priest chants *mantras*. Her paternal or maternal uncle gives the bride away. This part of the ceremony is called *sampradhan.*

The next morning, the groom adorns the forehead of his bride with vermilion. He does this by looking it to a mirror. The newly-weds visit the *mandapam* and worship the Sun God in the presence of the priest. This is followed by *bidai* (farewell) ceremony, which marks the departure of the bride and the groom.

Catholic Wedding

Both the bride and the groom must fill in a form declaring details of their lives. They take an oath of the *Holy Bible* that they have not withheld any information and that they are aware of the duties within a Christian marriage. They must produce their baptism certificate. In case of a mixed marriage, only the Christian partner is required to produce the baptism certificate. In the bridal shower party, often the friends shower gifts upon the bride. The bride hosts a luncheon party. This is a token of her appreciation for their support she had enjoyed from her friends. With a view to bring together the families of the bride and bridegroom before the wedding, sometime a joint party is hosted.

On the day of the wedding, the groom sends a car to pick up the bride and waits for her outside the Church. When the bride arrives, the Best Man, chosen in a party, welcomes her with a kiss on either cheek and with a bouquet of flowers. The couple walks down the aisle with the wedding procession in tow. The priest begins the ceremony by welcoming them into the church and offering them the good wishes. The wedding mass begins with hymns and selected readings from *The Bible*. The priest delivers the Homily, an interesting lecture, with an emphasis on the sanctity of marriage. The priest asks them if they have come on their own free will and give themselves to the other in marriage. Then the couple is asked to join right hands and declare the consent before God and His Church. The priest blesses the wedding rings so that the couple that wears them will have deep faith in each other, do the Lord's will and always live together in peace, goodwill and love. The bride and the groom exchange rings with a promise of unconditional love and fidelity. The couple and their close relatives come up to the podium and read previously selected passages from *The Bible*. A prayer is offered. The couple brings offering like *The Bible*, a miniature house modeled out of thermocol, candles and flowers. Each offering has significance. The flowers represent the beauty and fragrance of God's creation. The priest gives the couple consecrated bread and wine, which represent the body and the blood of Jesus Christ. The wine is given only on special occasion like marriages. The congregation jointly recites the Biblical prayer. The priest prays for the couple. The bride and the groom offer a thanksgiving prayer to God and ask for His blessings. The priest and the couple sign the Church register that serves as a valid legal document of marriage. A copy of the document is sent to the Registrar of Marriages. The marriage procession, led by the bride and the groom, walks down the aisle and steps out of the church.

Gujarati Wedding

The overwhelming majority of the population in the Gujarat state is of Hindus. Their mother tongue is Gujarati language. They are particular to select bride/groom after matching the horoscopes of the prospective couple. The initial ceremony even takes place on any auspicious day after consulting their priest. Both the families then pray to Lord Ganesha, the Hindu God, who is believed to remove all the obstacles. This *puja* is performed at the bride's house. The other rituals involve the groom arriving at the house of the bride to seek the blessings of the mother-in-law. He must bow his head and clutch his nose. This gesture symbolizes his humility and understanding of the tremendous sacrifice that his prospective wife is about to make. The groom's prospective mother-in-law blesses him and performs a small ritual to ward off the evil eye.

The wedding rituals are performed in front of a sacred fire and are conducted by the priest. The rituals begin with the *kanyadaan* when brede's parents, who abstain from eating to make themselves pure in body and mind for the occasion, give the bride. The bride's father washes the feet of the groom with the belief that the groom is none other than the Hindu God Visnu to whom he is handing over his rightful consort, the Goddess Laxmi, in the form of his daughter.

In the *Hasta Milap* ceremony to follow, the groom's scarf or shawl is tied to the bride's saree. This knot and the joined hands of the couple symbolizes the union of two souls brought together in holy matrimonial. The priest chants *mantras* to invoke the blessings of Goddess Laxmi and Goddess Parvati for the *saubhagyavrata* of wife. The family and relatives bless the couple by showering grains of rice and rose petels on them. This is followed by seven steps or rounds around the sacred fire, as the priest chants *mantras* and asks the groom also to recite *mantras*, which express his heart's desire and seeks the loving support of his wife. In the seven rounds, which the couple takes around the sacred fire, both the bride and the groom have to recite some *mantras* at each step. In these hymns, the groom requests his wife to take good care of the house, cook wholesome and healthy meals for the family, be thrifty with money, be an understanding and supporting partner to him etc. The bride promises to fulfil these requests.

The reception is normally held immediately after the wedding. It is an opportunity for the relatives, friends and well wishers to bless the newly weds, enjoy a sumptuous meal with them and give them gifts. In the next ceremony that follows, which is known as *Vidai* (farewell), the bride is given a tearful farewell by her parents, siblings, relatives and friends. It is a sad moment as she leaves in a specially decorated car for her new home.

The bride's first step into her new home is considered auspicious. She is the *ghar nu Laxmi* or the Goddess Laxmi, who will bring wealth and good fortune to her home. The mother-in-law places a vessel filled to the brim with rice, at the threshold of the house. The bride must knock the vessel down gently with her right foot, spilling some of the rice over the floor. The rice is a symbol of wealth and by following the ritual she conveys her full understanding of her duties and responsibilities towards her new home.

Kashmiri Wedding

Hindus belonging to Kashmir strictly follow the traditional rituals. They believe in the matching of horoscope before opting for matrimonial alliances. An auspicious day is chosen for almost every ceremony, even for the traditional cleaning of the house before the wedding. The floors of the Kashmiri mud houses are cleaned and treated with a mixture of cow dung mud and water. All the female members attend this ceremony. The traditional meal is cooked. *Wanwun* or music sessions are held every evening at the houses of the bride and the groom.

A week before the wedding the *maanzirrat* ceremony takes place. Doors of the houses of the prospective bride and the groom are decorated. In the evening, the prospective bride follows an elaborate bathing ritual, when her maternal aunt washes her feet. After the bath, her eldest aunt decorates her hands and feet with *maanz* (henna). *Maanz* is also distributed among the relatives and neighbors. *Devgon* ceremony is observed separately by the girl's family and the boy's family at the respective houses. Before participating in the rituals, the relatives of the bride and the groom observe a fast. The priest in front of a sacred fire conducts the ceremony. Her family gives the bride ornaments and utensils. The boy/girl is bathed with a mixture of water, rice, milk and curd. Flowers are also showered over the boy/girl. During the day, *Duribat* ceremony takes place when maternal relatives of the bride/groom attend. Gifts are exchanged and a traditional vegetarian lunch is served.

On the day of the wedding, the relatives assist the bride and the groom in elaborate wedding gear. The groom's paternal uncle helps him to tie the turban. A gold thread is used to tie a peacock feather to the turban. Before marriage procession leaves for the bride's house, the groom must stand on a decorative pattern made of rice flour and colours. He is given sugar lumps to eat, conch shell is sounded to announce his departure, and two rice pots, containing some money, are given away as alms to the poor.

When the marriage procession arrives, all the relatives of the bride greet the procession warmly. The groom and the bride, escorted by her maternal uncle, stand on the *vyog* (a decorated pattern made of rice flour and colours). The eldest female member of the family feeds *nabad* (sugar lumps) to the bride and the groom. Both are then kissed on the forehead. Two rice pots are given away to the poor. The couple is led by the family priest to the door where they have to perform a small ceremony called *dwar* (door) *puja*, before leading them to the *lagan mandap*.

The priest in front of a sacred fire performs the actual wedding ceremony. One of the rituals, *aathwas*, requires the couple to cross their arms and hold each other's hand covered with a cloth. According to Kashmiri folklore, the first to be able to pull out the engagement ring of the other will be the one to play a dominating role in the relationship. A *mananmal*, golden thread, is tied to their foreheads. The left foot of the bride is placed on a *kajwat* or grinding stone. Stepping on seven one-rupee coins makes the first *phera* or round around the sacred fire. They have to take seven *pheras* or rounds. The bride and the groom feed each other some rice at the end of the ceremony.

This is followed by *vidai* ceremony, when the newly-weds must stand on the *vyog* while the eldest female member of the bride's family offers them *nabad* thrice and kisses them on the forehead. The bride is seated in a *doli* or palanquin. Her relatives and friends bid her good-bye as she sets off for her new home.

Kannada Wedding

Kannada is the language of Karnataka in south India. Among the pre-wedding rituals among Hindus residing in this part of India, *Dev Karya* is traditionally performed on the day of arrival of the groom's family in the village. All the goods that are to be exchanged or used in the marriage are placed in front of Lord Ganesha to seek His blessings. On the same day, *haldi* (turmeric) is applied to the bride as well as the groom in their respective houses. *Uddin Murth*, a type of grain, is ground. This is considered to be sacred. On the day of the marriage, the first ritual is *mandap puja* to make the hall appropriate for an event or sacred for the purpose of marriage. The bride's father brings the groom to the *mandap* who is worshipped in a ceremony called the *Var*

Puja. The bride's parents honour him by washing his feet and offer him a silk *dothi* and *pitambar*, which are to be worn by him. When the bride is brought in the *mandap* no one is supposed to see her face. Her sister shields her face with a fan of peacock feathers. The bride and groom stand on either side of a white cloth, which separates them. The bride and groom exchange garlands with the chanting of *mantras.* The groom's sister holds a *kalash* of holy water that contains the *coconut, betel leaves* and *kombu gindi.*

It is followed by *dhare herdu* ceremony symbolizing the handing over of daughter to the groom. The groom holds the bride's hand with a coconut and betel leaves while the bride's parents sprinkle the holy water on the hands of the couple. Thereafter, *mangalsutra* is tied around the bride's neck. In the *saptapadi* ceremony that follows, the couple takes seven rounds of the sacred fire. Next is *graha pravesh,* bride's entry to her new house and her kicking of a *kalash* full of rice with her right foot at the threshold of the house. The groom decides a name for his bride, which he inscribes with a ring on a plate containing rice. On the second day, the bride's family comes to take the newly wed couple to their house.

Malayalee Wedding

A traditional Malayalee wedding among Hindus starts with the exchange and matching of horoscopes by the parents of the boy and the girl. Auspicious date is chosen in consultation with astrologers. *Nischayam* or the engagement ceremony is fixed by the elders to announce this to the friends and relatives. The prospective bride and the groom are not present on this occasion. A day before the wedding, a traditional dinner is arranged at the bride's residence. She is seated facing the east, and has a traditional five-course meal with her family.

Malayalee wedding is very short. The bride may wear the traditional saree of her choice. She is adorned with flowers and jewelry. The groom, clad in a *dhoti* and *angavasthram,* arrives at the bride's ancestral home, where the marriage ceremony takes place in a north-western room. The bride's youngest brother washes the groom's feet and welcomes him. The groom then gives him the off white or coloured saree that has to be worn by the bride for the nuptials.

The groom's father gives *taali* or *mangalsutram* on a yellow thread to his son and asks him to tie it around the neck of the bride. Garland or *jayamala* is exchanged. The groom hands over a saree of his choice to his prospective bride which she is expected to wear during her departure to her new home. The bride's father gives his daughter's hand to the groom putting a betel leaf. This symbolises *kanyadaanam*. The Veli follows this or the nuptial ceremony is performed around the *agni* (fire). The bride and the groom take three rounds of the sacred fire. In *sparsham,* symbolizing the meeting of minds, the groom sits in front of the bride and tilts his head backwards to touch her forehead. After this, the girl offers *laja* (puffed rice) to the fire to the chant of various *mantras.* Her palms are placed in her husband's hands and she performs the *havan* (sacred fire). The groom lifts the bride's foot and places it on the *ammi* (grinding stone) signifying breaking the ties from her old family. The groom then moves the bride's foot forward seven times with his hand, symbolizing her entry into his family.

Immediately after the wedding, a sumptuous meal is served. It consists of various vegetarian dishes. The couple leaves for the groom's house.

Marathi Wedding

Before the actual wedding ceremony, Marathi custom requires *sakhar puja* or engagement, *simant puja* when groom's family members are worshipped on arrival in the bride's village, and *ghana bharne,* when married women of the house grind grains in a vessel, and *turmeric* paste is applied all over the groom's body. Some of this paste applied is taken to the bride.

On the auspicious day of the marriage, the bride's maternal uncle comes to take her to the *mandap,* where a partition of cloth, *antarpaat,* is put up. After chanting the relevant *shlokas* this *antarpaat* is removed. At the time of removing the *antarpaat* the people present shower the couple with *akshata* (unbroken rice), symbolizing the blessing from those who are present. The couple exchange garlands as in most other Hindu marriages. They take seven rounds around the sacred fire. This ceremony is known as *saptapadi.*

The bride and the groom are considered as the Goddess Laxmi and Lord Narayan and are worshipped accordingly. After this ceremony, the bride is formally handed over by her parents to the groom by placing 21 lit *diyas* (earthen lamps) in cane dish. The dish is initially placed on the bride's head and later taken around to the groom's family. The bride's father places the dish over the heads of groom's family members to accept his daughter and make her as part of the family. This is called *Jhal Phirawane.*

In the *Suun Mukh Baghne* ceremony that follows, the groom's mother looks (*baghne*) at her daughter-in-law's face. The mother-in-law takes both her son and her daughter-in-law in her lap. Later, she looks at her daughter-in-law's face in the mirror. She also combs her hair. This ritual is probably reminiscent of the olden days when the bride and the groom were mere children, but it still continues. The wedding culminates in a reception. Lunch is arranged generally in the afternoon. The couple takes round of the *mandap* where the guests are having lunch. The couple and their parents take lunch together after everybody has finished his meal.

Marwari Wedding

Marwadi wedding among Hindus, belonging to Rajasthan of north India, is slightly a variance of other Hindu marriages. It starts with the engagement ceremony at the groom's house where ladies do not accompany the menfolk for the *tilak*. The bride's brother apply *tilak* to the groom's forehead to make the alliance official. A sword, other presents, clothes, fruits, sweets etc are given to the groom. It follows a Ganapati *sthapna* (installation of Lord Ganesha's portrait) and *griha shanti* (prayer for peace in the house) ceremony. The *pithi dastoor* takes place at the bride's house when the bride dresses in an orange outfit and is brought under a silken canopy which is held with the help of swords at the four corners by four ladies who must belong to the same clan as the bride. She is brought among the ladies, who apply the paste to them. A similar ceremony takes place at the groom's house as well. There the women singers sing auspicious pre-wedding songs while the ceremony is in progress.

The maternal uncle has an important role to play in a Marwadi wedding. The bride's and the groom's maternal uncles help their sisters by participating in a lavish display of expenditure. The groom is dressed in saffron robes like an ascetic and performs a *havan* before wearing *janeyu* (sacred thread). The significance of saffron robes is that the groom now has two choices before him, either to renounce the world and become an ascetic, or to accept the institution of marriage and its responsibility. After the *havan* is completed and the thread is given, the groom has to make a mock attempt to run from the chains of marriage while the maternal uncle must catch him and convince his nephew to accept marriage.

On the day of actual wedding, or, may be, a day prior to it the *palla dastoor* is brought in by a few of the groom's relatives to the bride's house. It consists of clothes, jewelry and gifts from the groom, which the bride has to wear during the wedding ceremony. The traditional wedding dress is generally red in colour, but it could also be orange, gold yellow, or pink. In certain clans, a bright parrot green is also worn. The jewelry consists of the *rakhri* (circular peace of jewelry for the forehead), *danglers* for the ears, the *timaniyaan* (a choker studded with uncut diamonds), the *chooda* (a set of ivory and gold bangles), the *bajuband* or gold and stone-studded armlets, gold anklets and the *bichhiya* or gold toe-rings for the feet, and *nath* or the stone-studded nose-ring.

A Rajput *baraat* (marriage procession) consists entirely of male members. The groom is usually dressed in a gold *achkan*, with an orange turban and a *choodidar pyjama* with *jootis*. The *baraat* (marriage procession)members also must wear *achkans* or *sharewanis* and *safas* (colourful *turbans*). All members, including the groom, who rides an elephant or a mare, carry swords. On arrival, the groom is taken inside the ladies' section, where the bride's mother with the traditional *aarti*, receives him. He is then taken to the *mandap* for the wedding ceremony. The groom accompanies, at this stage, only one married relative. The wedding ceremony is similar to a Hindu wedding. The bride must, at all times, through the wedding ceremony, keep her face covered by a long veil. While the wedding is in process, the bride's male family members entertain the *baraat*. Only the women members attend the wedding ceremony.

At the time of the *bidai* (departure), a coconut is placed under the wheel of the car before the bride lifts her veil for the husband. At this stage, the groom usually gives a piece of jewelry to his bride. The *baraat* returns with the newly weds in a ceremony known as *grihapravesh*. The bride still wears the veil when she is formally introduced to all the family members of the groom who bless her and give her gifts. The veil is then finally removed.

Muslim Wedding

On the eve of the wedding ceremony or a couple of days before it, the process starts with *mehndi* ceremony. The female relatives of the girl anoint her with turmeric paste to bring out the glow in her complexion. A relative or a professional applies *mehndi* (henna) on the hands and feet of the bride while the women sing traditional songs. The bride wears sober clothes. According to the custom, she must not step out of the house for the next few days until her marriage. The bride's cousins sometimes apply a dot of *mehndi* on the palm of the groom.

On the wedding day, the groom arrives at the wedding venue with his *baraat*. A band of musicians strike up some traditional notes to announce their arrival. This is followed by *nikaah* or wedding ceremony, conducted at the home of the bride or the groom, or at any other convenient place. A *maulvi* (priest), in the presence of close family members and relatives, conducts the ceremony. In orthodox Muslim communities, the men and women are seated separately, the *walis* (the fathers of the bride and the groom) play an important role in the ceremony. The *maulvi* reads selected verses from *The Quran* and the *nikaah* is complete after the *Ijab-e-qubul* (the proposal and acceptance). The boy's side proposes and the girl's side conveys acceptance. The mutual consent of the bride and the groom is of paramount importance for the marriage to be legal. On the day of the *nikaah*, the elder members of the two families decide the amount of *mehar* (nuptial gift). The *mehar* is a compulsory amount of money given by the groom's family to the bride. Marriage contract is registered in the form of a *nikaahnaama*. It contains a set of terms and conditions that must be respected by both the parties. It also gives the bride the right to divorce her husband. For the contract to be legal, it must be signed by the groom, the bride, the *walis* and the *maulvi*. The groom receives blessings from the older women who offers them *salaam* (salute). The guests pray for the newly-weds and dinner is hosted. The women and men dine separately. After the dinner the newly-weds sit together covering their heads while they read prayers under the direction of the *maulvi. The Quran* is placed between the couple and they are allowed to see each other only through mirrors.

In *ruksat* (departure) ceremony that follows, the bride's family bids tearful farewell to the girl before she departs for her husband's house. On arrival at the groom's house, the groom's mother holds *The Quran* above the head of her new daughter-in-law as she enters her new home.

Under the Muslim Personal Law (Shariat) Application of 1937, a minor girl can't enter into a contract and marriage despite her consent. A 14-year old Muslim girl from Assam was married to a major boy. For the boy, it was his second marriage. His first wife couldn't conceive, but the second wife became pregnant when she was minor. The case of the minor girl became the cause for concern among the police, NGOs and state authorities. She was produced before a judicial magistrate and was kept in a women's house.

Parsi Wedding

Parsi community is mostly concentrated in Mumbai and their marriage rituals are different. Before the actual wedding, *madhavsaro* ceremony takes place almost four days before the *lagan* when the families of the bride and the groom each plant a young tree in a pot amidst recitation of prayers by the family priest. This pot is placed at the entrance of their homes. This is generally a mango plant and is treated as a symbol of fertility. The soil, in which the tree is planted, is mixed with chips of three types of metals, usually gold, silver etc., *paan* (betel leaf), *supari* (betel nut), *haldi* (turmeric) and dry dates. The plant is watered every morning till the eighth day after the wedding and then planted elsewhere.

After one day of the *madhavsaro* ceremony, gifts are exchanged. The groom's family visits the bride's home to present her with all the gifts like cloth and jewelry. This is known as *adarni.* The bride herself may also go over to the groom's home for the tradition, but the groom cannot do the same. The relatives, neighbours and friends are treated to a traditional meal of *sev* and *dahi*, boiled eggs and bananas.

The day before the wedding is the *supra nu murat* which is similar to Hindu *mehndi-haldi* ceremony. Four married women are given supra each, containing *paan, supari, haldi,* dates and piece of coconut. While singing ritual songs, these *supras* are exchanged seven times among the women cross-wise, lengthwise and breadthwise. A fifth lady sits in the middle with a *khalbatto* and dry turmeric. After the fourth woman finishes passing the *supras*, all the five join hands to beat the turmeric along with some milk in the pestle and this paste is applied by the groom and bride while blessings are showered on them.

On the day of the *lagan*, wedding, chalk or *rangoli* is used at every staircase, doorway and even the gates of the wedding venue or *baug* are decorated with large colourful designs. The Zorastrians consider the period immediately after sunset or very early in the morning auspicious for marriage. Most weddings generally take place at about 6.40 pm. In the actual marriage ceremony, the bride and the groom go through the *nahan* ritual, when it involves the purification of the body and the soul wherein the family *dastur* symbolically bathes and purifies the man or woman. After the *nahan* ritual, the bride and the groom cannot touch any person outside the family or caste. The bride then dresses in her *madhavate*, the white, ornate wedding saree given by her parents, while the groom wears the traditional Parsi *dagli* and *feta*, a white *kurta* like garment and a black cap.

The Parsi *lagan* takes place either at a *baug* or at an *agiary* (the fire temple). A stage is set for the couple. Before they step on it, the groom first, a ritual called *achumithu* is performed. The bride's mother takes a tray with a raw egg, *supari*, rice, coconut, dates and water. To begin the ceremony with her to be son-in-law, first she takes the coconut and circles it around the groom's head seven times before breaking it on the floor to his right. The bride then steps onto the stage for her future mother-in-law to perform the same ritual.

In the *araantar* ceremony to follow, the couple is made to sit facing each other with a cloth held between them so that they should not be able to see each other. Each of them is given rice. With a length of thread, the priest circles the couple on opposite side of the curtain seven times. As the seventh round ends, the couple showers each other with the rice from over the curtain. It is believed that whoever throws the rice first may dominate the other partner.

Chero bandhvanu ceremony that succeeds represents the seven strands of string binding them. *Divas* or lighted lamps are kept on tables on either side. The marriage prayers or *aashirwaad* (blessing) and showering of rice and rose petals by the priests begin. This goes on for almost one hour after which the bride and the groom exchange wedding rings. The priests now wish the couple, the *var* and *bairi* and fire from the *agiary* is brought to them to pay their respects. Once the couple is officially married, now starts the fun and frolic. The groom's sister-in-law starts extracting money from her new brother-in-law. This ritual is known as *haath borvanu.* The groom is made to put his hand into a glass of water, which he cannot remove until he pays some money. Then in *pag dhovanu*, the groom is threatened with milk on his shoes unless he pays. In the ritual *chero chorvanu* that follows, the sister-in-law again, on payment, removes the seven strands of string binding the couple. The couple then pays a visit to the fire temple.

The Parsi weddings are renowned for the enormous reception with food, drink and music flowing freely throughout the night. Sumptuous dinner is hosted and the wedding day ends when the bride's family escorts the couple home and *achumichu* is performed once again by the groom's mother for the couple together.

Punjabi Wedding

The Punjabi wedding in north India starts with *roka* ceremony when the boy and the girl make commitment to each other to marry. This takes place at the house of the bride-to-be, in the presence of family and relatives. This is followed by *sagan* and *chunni chadana*. Both these ceremonies are generally combined. The father of the bride-to-be applies *tilak* on the forehead of the groom-to-be. The bride is dressed in clothes and jewelry, presented to her by her would be in-laws. She is also presented a red *chunni* by the sister/sister-in-law of her prospective husband. The prospective bride and groom exchange rings.

The families of the bride and the groom hold *sangeet* (music) session, which is generally religious in nature. Friends and close family members are invited. It is followed by *mehandi* ceremony when the prospective mother-in-law sends henna to the bride-to-be. Henna is applied either by a relative, friend or a professional to the bride-to-be and her friends. On this occasion, delicious meal is served to those who are present.

The maternal uncle of the bride plays an important role. He has to observe fast until *chuda* ceremony. The priest performs *havan* (sacred fire). After the *puja*, all those who are present to signify their blessings and good wishes to the prospective bride touch the *chuda* (a set of red and cream ivory bangles). The *chuda* is slipped on her wrist. An iron bangle (for good luck) with shells and beads, and *a mauli*, which the priest ties around her wrist, follow this. Flower petals are showered on the girl after the ceremony and *prasad* is distributed among all. The girl's maternal uncle and aunt, friends and cousins tie *kaliras* (silver, gold plated traditional ornaments that are tied to the *chuda*). The prospective bride must pat one of her unwed female friends or cousins with her *kaliras*. According to the popular belief, the one who is patted thus will be the next one to marry.

In *ghara ghardoli* and *vatna* ceremonies that follow, the ritual demands that the prospective bride should stay at home in her old clothes till her wedding. She must sit in the vicinity of four lit *diyas* (earthen lamps) or oil lamps so that the glow from them is reflected on her face. A sibling and the sibling's spouse usually fill a pitcher of water from a nearby temple to be added to the bath and old garments are given away to a poor person. Before her bath, *vatna* or *uptan* (a paste of powdered turmeric and mustard oil) is applied on her body by female relatives and friends. Both the *ghara ghardoli* and the *vatna* ceremonies are also performed for the groom at his house. Here the pitcher of water is brought for his bath by his *bhabi* (elder brother's wife).

The bride is dressed nicely at her own house by her friends and relatives. The groom, in his own house, also dresses in a formal attire, which may be traditional or western. A young nephew or cousin also dons in similar attire. He is called the *sarbala* (caretaker of the groom) and accompanies him on his mare, chariot or car. *Puja* is performed after the groom dons his wedding attire. His relatives bless *sehra* or turban as well as the silver *mukut* or crown that goes on top of the turban. All those present on the occasion bless the groom and give gifts to him. The groom's *bhabhi* lines his eyes with *surma* (kohl). After this, the groom's sister and cousins feed and doctorate his mare. If the groom chooses to use a car or a chariot for the occasion, it is decorated. The nearest relatives use cash for the *varna*, a ceremony that is supposed to ward off the evil eye. The cash is given to the poor.

When the marriage party reaches the bride's place, it is welcomed with *milni* ceremony (hugging of nearest relatives on one-to-one basis) and exchange of garlands. The girl's relatives give *shagoon* (some money) to the groom's close relatives, beginning with his grandfather, father, uncles and brothers. It is given to honour the relatives.

The bride and the groom exchange garlands, the bride taking the first initiative. The *mahurat* or auspicious time for the wedding ceremony is usually set after dinner. The priest first performs a *puja* for the groom. The groom chants a few *mantras*. At this time, the girl's young relatives grab the groom's shoes and hide it away to be returned after the ceremony after extracting some money. *Kalecharis* (rings of silver or gold) are given to the bride's sisters by the groom. The priest performs another *puja* with the couple and their parents. Her father, in a ceremony called *kanyadaan*, gives the bride. This is followed by the *pheras*, going round the sacred fire with bride's saree tied to the groom's turban with the help of the red *chunni* used in the *ghara ghardoli* ceremony. At the end of the ceremony, the newly weds touch the feet of the groom's parents and elders present to take their blessings. The bride changes her clothes and wears what her in-laws have presented, while her relatives apply *tilak* on the groom's forehead.

In *vidaai* ceremony, marking the departure of the bride from her parental house, the bride throws *phulian* (puffed rice) over her head. She conveys her good wishes to her parents through this gesture. A beautifully decorated *palanquin* or car takes her new home. She is usually accompanied by her brother. Her relatives throw coins in the wake of this procession. On her arrival in her new home, she is welcomed in a ceremony called the *pani* bharna. The groom's mother performs the traditional *aarti* with a pitcher of water. She makes seven attempts to bring the water from the pitcher. With her right foot, she must kick the *sarson ka tel* (mustard oil) that is put on the sides of the entrance door before she enters the house. Along with her husband, she must offer *puja* in their room. Then they must touch the feet of the entrance door before she enters the house. She has to offer *puja* with her husband. Both of them have to touch the feet of the entrance. According to a tradition, the newly weds visit the bride's parents on the day after the wedding. The bride's brother normally fetches them. The bride's parents host a lunch to mark the occasion.

Sikh Wedding or Anand Karaj

Sikhs, who form a different community among Hindus, worship *Guru Granth Saheb*, their scripture enunciating the commands of the Sikh Gurus. Therefore, for any auspicious occasion they have first to go to *gurudwara* (Sikh temple) to seek blessings. The engagement ceremony is also performed by *bhaiji* (Sikh priest) from the *gurudwara* who first reads a hymn by Guru Nanak, offering the groom a date. He also applies *tilak* on groom's forehead, thus marking the engagement. Following the *tilak* ceremony, the groom's father sends gifts of sweet, coconut, rice, clothes, ornaments and henna to the bride.

Then starts *Anand Karaj* (wedding ceremony). Few days before the marriage, bride and groom are in *maiya* confinement for a few days and they are not allowed to leave their respective homes or change their clothes till marriage. An auspicious red thread is tied to the right wrist of the groom and the left wrist of the bride. Auspicious items, such as cowrie shells, and iron key chain, pearls and a small silken bundle, containing sugar, are suspended from the *gana* worn by the bride.

A couple of days prior to the wedding, *vatna*, a scented powder, consisting of barley flour, turmeric and mustard oil, is applied to their bodies to be followed by a ritual bath. On the eve of the wedding, known as *mehndi ki raat*, henna is applied on the hands and feet of the bride. The morning of the wedding is marked by the *gharoli* ceremony at the groom's house. The groom's sister-in-law, accompanied by other female relatives, go to a nearby well or *Gurudwara* to fill an earthen pitcher or *gharoli* with water which is later used to bathe the groom. The groom is made to sit on a stool for bath and four girls hold a cloth over his head.

The girl's maternal uncle takes the bride for the *choora* ceremony. She is made to wear a set of red and white ivory bangles that has been dipped in *kachchi lassi* or buttermilk. *Kaleeren*, ornaments with dangle golden metal plates are tied to the bride's wrist by her close female relatives. The bride now dresses up for the main ceremony. Among Sikhs, marriage generally takes place on Sunday during the day.

At the groom's house, *sehera* or floral veil is tied to the boy's forehead and garlands of currency notes adorn his neck. The groom mounts a decorated mare while his sisters-in-law put *collyriun* in his eyes. On reaching the bride's house, the *milni* ceremony is held with the seniors of both the families embracing each other. *Shabads* (the holy words) are sung and the *ardaas* (invocation to the Sikh Gurus) recited. As the marriage procession enters the Gurudwara, breakfast is served to the guests.

The bride and the groom sit together to attend to the recitation of *Guru Grandh Saheb*. The groom drapes a *chunni* given by the bride's father, one end of which is held by the bride. It is usually pink, red or orange. The groom puts it around his neck while the other end is held by the bride throughout the ceremony. The *bhaiji* of the *gurudwara* recites hymns from the *Guru Grandh Saheb*, which are then sung and the bride and groom encircle the *Guru Grandh Saheb*. The groom walks ahead of the bride with sword in his hand. When one round is over, both take their seats, go and wait for the second hymn. During the fourth and final hymns, flowers are showered on the newly wed couple. A hymn enunciating responsibilities towards each other as husband and wife as well as towards their elders is recited to them. Relatives and friends garland the newly wed couple and the marriage ceremony concludes with a grand feast.

The bride wears new clothes that are presented to her by the groom's family. As she departs from her parents' house she throws back the grains of rice, thereby wishing prosperity to the family she leaves behind.

Sindhi Wedding

After the approval of both the families, the first formal ceremony takes place when the girl/boy is given *mishri* (sugar candy) and coconut to signify that he/she is one and belongs to the other family. This is called *kuchcha shagun* or *Kachchi mishri.* The formal engagement ceremony or the *pakki mishri* takes place a week before the wedding. The boy and the girl exchange rings and there is a get together of family members and close friends. Ten days before the wedding a *satsang* (community worship) in the name of Sindhi God, Jhulelal, is organized. This is called *berana.* It signifies the start of the ceremony for the forthcoming wedding.

Before the wedding day, *mehendi* ceremony is organized where the girl's hands and feet are adorned with pretty *mehendi* patterns, while women play music. Folk songs are also sung on this day. The girl and the boy are asked to wear their old clothes, which are torn and discarded once the ceremony is over. These clothes are then wrapped into a bag and are thrown into the sea/river. In another ceremony known as *santh,* seven married women put oil on the girl's head. It is performed the night before the wedding. The bride is then asked to break the cover of an earthen pot placed before her.

The groom hosts bachelor party and the bride also gives her girl friends a party. The *saagri* or showering of the bride with flowers is performed in the same evening when groom's married sisters, cousins and small children go to the bride's place with the jewelry made of mogra. The sisters dress the bride in a silk saree and adorn her with the flower jewelry. At night, the groom visits the bride's house where he is welcomed with garlands. A feast is held for the family.

Ghari puja is carried out in the respective homes of the prospective couple. The priest performs the prayers with rice, coconut, wheat grains, oil, betel nuts, turmeric and a number of other spices. Married ladies grind wheat on a small old-fashioned grinder, symbolizing that the home will always be prosperous. The groom offers a handful of grains to the priest indicating that he will always give charity to all those who are less fortunate. The mothers of both the bride and the groom dress up in their bridal finery. Carrying an earthen pot of water on their heads, they walk to the threshold of their homes. The sons-in-law of the respective families cut the water with a knife to ward off any evil spirit. Their friends and relatives adorn the parents with garlands of flowers and money. The bride and the groom wear old clothes that are torn off by their friends and family members amidst merriment, illustrating the end of their old life.

The wedding day begins with a series of traditional rituals. The first is the thread ceremony. Oil and *haldi* is applied to the groom's hair and body. From then on he cannot move out of the house. His brother-in-law sits next to him with a knife, symbolic of a protector. Similarly, the bride too goes for a *haldi* and oil massage ritual at her place. *Haldi* is meant to work as a cleanser and purifier. The bride too is not allowed to leave the house after this ceremony.

After the bride puts up her wedding dress, her sisters and female relatives escort the groom to the bride's house. At the threshold, the groom places his right foot on the top of the bride's foot, signifying that he should have the dominating strength in their conjugal life. After the groom enters the house, the bride's parents rinse his feet with milk and water. It is believed that the groom is an embodiment of Lord Visnu on this wedding day. In *hathialo* ceremony, the corner of the bride's saree is tied to a scarf, which is worn by the groom. The right hands of the couple are tied with a thread that has been blessed with religious incantation. The tying of hands signify an eternal bond that will join them for a walk. The couple then prays to the God to give them strength and bless their union.

The priest, in the presence of the family and friends, performs the wedding ceremony. The bride and the groom are seated in front of the holy fire and the priest recites various religious sayings from the holy scriptures. According to Hindu religion, fire is considered the sustainer of life. It is believed that Gods and Goddesses sit around this auspicious fire. The priest directs various family members to give offerings into the holy fire. The couple walks around the fire four time exchanging vows of duty and love, fidelity, respect and a fruitful union. The groom places the bride's hand on his forehead, to denote that he accepts her as his wife, through thick and thin. The couple's heads are held together implying that although they are separate individuals, from this day onward they are one in body, mind and spirit.

In *kanyadaan* ceremony, the bride's parents entrust their daughter in the safe keeping of the groom and his family. After friends and family have greeted the couple, they leave for the groom's house.

Tamil Wedding

Tamil is the language of Tamil Nadu in south India. In *panda kaal muhurtham*, one day before the wedding, the blessing of the family deity is sought to proceed with the wedding preparations in a smooth way. The family of the bride and the groom pray to the deity, who is symbolically represented by a bamboo pole. When the groom and his family arrive at the wedding hall in the morning one day before the wedding, they are welcomed with tray containing offering of flowers, *paan supari,* fruits and *mishri.* Rose water is sprinkled on the groom. The bride's brother applies a *tilak* of sandalwood paste and *kumkum* on his forehead and he is garlanded. The bride's mother offers the groom's parents a sweet dish prepared from condensed milk. A senior female member of the bride's family performs *aarti* and welcomes him. It is also customary to break a coconut on the ground as it is believed to ward off the evil spirit.

Vratham is performed a day before the wedding by the family of the bride as well as that of the groom. They recite Vedic hymns in the presence of a priest (*vaadyar*) and seek the blessings of a family deity. They also invoke the blessings of all their ancestors and pray for their intervention in removing those obstacles that threaten to disrupt the wedding. Before the wedding, the family of the bride performs *pallika thellichal* when clay pots are filled with nine varieties of grain, and married women from both the sides sprinkle water, while traditional songs are sung. The next day, when the grains sprout, these pots are immersed in a pond so that the fish in a pond feed on the grains and bless the newly weds abundantly. In *naandi* ceremony that follows, few *brahmins* (priests) are honoured with gifts and seeds. The brahmins are invited to represent the souls of the ancestors of the bride and the groom.

In *jaanavaasam* ceremony, the groom gets into a decorated car and is escorted to the wedding venue by a large joyous procession of family and friends, accompanied by professional musicians playing traditional wedding music. At times, there are fireworks to celebrate the occasion. The girl's brother welcomes the groom by garlanding him. In *nicchiyadharatham* ceremony that follows, the bride's parents perform *Ganesha puja* in the presence of the officiating priest. The groom's side gives the bride a new saree. A *tilak* of *chandan* and *kumkum* is applied on her forehead, while the *pallu* (one end) of her saree is filled with *fruits, paan, supari,* turmeric, *kumkum* and coconut. A garland of flowers is tied around her waist. *Aarti* is also performed for her.

The priest formally reads out the wedding invitation. Details on three generations of the lineage of the boy and the girl and other information on the *muhurtham* and venue are announced. An elaborate dinner follows all this.

The wedding rituals consist of *mangala snaanam,* the purifying bath that the bride and the groom must have in their respective homes on the dawn of their wedding day. Before the bath, they are anointed with oil and a *tilak* of *haldi-kumkum*. After this, the groom pretends to leave for Kashi, a pilgrimage centre to devote himself to God and lead a life of an ascetic. He carries a walking stick and other meager essentials with him to imply that he is not interested in becoming a householder. The girl's father intervenes and requests him to accept his daughter as his life partner and fulfill his responsibilities as a householder. The groom relents and returns to the *pandaal* where the bride receives him.

There is an exchange of garlands thrice. The couple is made to sit together on a swing. The married women from the families give spoonful of milk and banana pieces. They circle rice balls around the couple in circular motions, clockwise and anti-clockwise, and fling them away. This practice is believed to prevent evil forces from disrupting the wedding ceremony. Again, the womenfolk go around the couple four times, holding in their hands a lamp or container of water. Songs called *onjal paattu* must be sung during these rites. It is followed by *kanyadaanam* when the bride's father welcomes the groom and the latter steps into the *mandapam*. The wedding is conducted around the sacred fire. The bride's mother applies *kajal* in the groom's eyes. The bride's father washes his son-in-law's feet. Through this gesture, the father conveys that the boy is an incarnation of Lord Visnu and believes that he will support and take good care of his daughter. The bride sits on her father's lap with coconut in her hand. The father and the bride offer the coconut to the groom while the bride's mother pours water over the coconut, thus symbolizing the 'giving away of their daughter'. The groom's parents gift to the bride a 9-yard saree to be worn for the auspicious occasion of tying the *mangalsutra*.

After changing the saree the bride again enters the *mandapam*. A sack of paddy is placed on the floor. The bride's father is seated on this as the bride sits on her father's lap. The sack of paddy symbolizes good fortune and abundance in terms of material and spiritual wealth. The yoke of a farmer's plough is touched to the bride's forehead. This gesture carries the hope that the couple will always walk together to pull the plough of life. The priest and relatives bless the *mangalsutra* or sacred thread and hand it to the groom, who ties it around the neck of his bride with two knots. Groom's sister ties the third knot much to the rejoicing of everyone. The three knots symbolize the marriage of the mind, spirit and body.

In *saptapadi* ceremony that follows, the groom takes the bride's right hand in his left hand and leads her around the sacred fire seven times. The bride begins each round by touching her feet to a grinding stone. This signifies her wish that their union may be as firm and steadfast as the grinding stone. The families of the newly weds exchange cloth and other gifts as per their status. The groom accepts puffed rice from the bride's brother and offers it to the sacred fire or *agni*. The blessings of *agni* are sought as fire stands for the divine power and light of God. The bride and groom seek the blessings of the senior members of the family by prostrating in front of them. They also offer them a gift of fruits etc. After the wedding rituals are over, the bride is escorted to the groom's house and is welcomed there.

Telugu Wedding

Telugu language is the mother tongue of people in Andhra Pradesh in South India. The people believe in getting *muhurtham* (auspicious time) determined for the auspicious day from their family priest. The period that is considered auspicious starts from 7 pm and goes on till the next day at about 11 am. Weddings do not usually take place in the months of *Aashad, Bhadrapad* and *Shunya,* the Telugu calendar. The pre-wedding rituals are involved in generally six ceremonies.

In the *pendlikoothuru* ceremony, the bride and the groom are anointed with oil and turmeric before bath. The couple don new clothes followed by bath. The bride wears flowers in her hair. She adorns her forehead with a *bindi* or vermillion dot and wears bangles on her wrists. *Snathakam* ritual is performed at the groom's house before the *muhurtham*. It is a sort of thread ceremony that involves making the wearing of a silver thread on his body. In Kashi *yatra* ceremony, after the recitation of *Vedic* verses the groom pretends to leave for Kashi, a pilgrimage centre to devote himself to God and a life of prayer. He carries a walking stick and other essentials with him, implying thereby that he is not interested in becoming a householder any more. He relents and agrees to the marriage only after he is talked and persuaded by the bride's brother to fulfil his responsibility as a householder.

The bride and the groom must take a *mangala snaanam* or an auspicious bath on the day of the wedding. The bath is believed to cleanse and purify them so as to make them ready for the sacred rights that are to follow. After the bath, the bride and the groom are anointed with oil at their respective homes. Their families perform *aarti*. It signifies a wish of the family that the mind of the bride/groom be illuminated with wisdom. The groom performs Ganesh *puja* to get rid of all the possible obstacles. It is just before the marriage.

During the wedding ceremony, *kanyadaanam* takes place when the girl's family gives the girl to the groom. Her maternal uncle carries the bride in a bamboo basket to the *mandapam*. The bride and the groom are separated by a curtain placed before them. They are not to see each other until after the marriage ceremony. The priest invokes the blessings of the ancestors belonging to the last seven generations of both the families. The bride's parents wash the groom's feet in a gesture that symbolizes the belief that the groom is a form of God to whom they now offer their daughter's hand.

After the priest decides the wedding *shlokas* from the *Vedas* are recited. The bride and the groom apply a paste of cumin seeds (*Jeera*) and *jaggery* on each other's hands. This is known as *Jeelakarra-Bellamu*. The slightly bitter cumin and sweet jaggery, when ground together, turn into an inseparable mixture. This signifies that the bride and the groom are supposed to become inseparable through life's bitter and sweet times. Now, in *madhuparkam* ceremony, the bride wears a white cotton saree with a red border, while the groom dons a white cotton *dhoti*, also with a red border. White signifies purity and chastity, while red is a colour that represents strength.

In *sumangli* ceremony, ten married women (*sumangalis*) accompany the girl. Six of them hold plates full of rice and turmeric powder mixed together. The remaining four women hold plates with small lamps made from the mixture of rice, flour, sugar and milk. Rice signifies abundance and lit lamps represent sweetness and light, two qualities that the bride brings with her to this new phase of life.

In a ceremony that follows, the curtain between the prospective couple is removed at this stage. Prayer is offered as the groom ties the two strings of *mangalsutra* around the girl's neck, each with a golden disc, representing that the three dots represent the strength of their union: physical, mental and spiritual. The groom holds the bride's hand and gazes at the pole star or *Dhruva* with her. The couple also looks towards Vasishta and Arundhati stars. These stars are always visible together and symbolize an inseparable couple. The couple now exchange garlands, and receive blessings from all those present, who sprinkle flowers and turmeric-colorued rice (*akshata*) on them. The couple takes seven steps while the bride's saree and the groom's *dhoti* are tied together at one end in a knot. The groom prays for life-long blessings with each step. With the first step he prays for food that nourishes them. With the second step he prays for strength. With the third he seeks help in honouring the vows. With the fourth he asks for a comfortable life. With the fifth he prays for health of their cattle. With the sixth for a life that survives the seasons. And with the seventh he asks for health in fulfilling religious duties. During this ceremony, sarees, ornaments and other gifts are offered to the couple and to the other family members. The groom slips silver toe rings on the bride's feet. The girl is also adorned with a string of black beads to protect her from the evil effect.

After the marriage ceremony is over, the bride is taken to the groom's home. The two *mangalsutras* are united on a common thread after sixteen days of the wedding. An elder member of the family or the husband himself can unite the two *mangalsutra* with a common thread. A few black or golden beads are slipped between the two plates so that they don't clash with each other. It signifies harmony between the two families. The bride takes a bath and wears a new saree before wearing the *mangalsutra* on this day. Sixteen days are symbolic of the time needed by the bride to understand her husband's family.

What's Common ?

This indeed is the quintessence of the diverse wedding practices in India. Even among Hindus also, the systems vary from region to region. Then there are people who worship different deities and are followers of different religious preachers. However, the Sikhs and Muslims have one thing in common. Both of them perform every rite in the name of their scriptures. The Sikhs go to *gurudwaras* while the Muslims visit mosques. Again, the Sikhs do everything auspicious in the name of *Guru Granth Sahib* while the Muslims take vow in the name of the *Quran.*

Remarriage of Widows

In the olden days, especially among Rajputs in Rajasthan, women were encouraged to burn themselves along with the dead bodies of their husbands. Perhaps, this practice started initially to protect them from falling in the hands of the enemy after their husbands were killed in the battlefield. However, this practice continued among other people as well, who died because of natural death. A number of social reformers like Raja Ram Mohan Roy campaigned against this practice and the first law on the subject was Lord Bentinck's Sati

Regulation of 1829. The tough 1987 law, banning *sati*, was enacted in the background of *Roop Kunwar's* case in modern history.

Remarriage among widows vary from region to region or from one group to another. Generally, lower-ranking groups allow widow re-marriage, particularly if the woman is relatively young. But the highest ranking caste discourage or forbid such remarriage. The strictest adherents to the non-marriage of widows are the Brahmins. Almost all groups allow widowers to re-marry. Many groups encourage a widower to marry his deceased wife's younger sister but never her older sister.

Monogamy

In terms of Indian Christian Marriage Act 1872, the Parsi Marriage and Divorce Act 1865 and the Hindu Marriages Act 1955, the monogamy has virtually become the principle amongst the majority of the Indian population. Only the Muslim law has not undergone any change. Polygamy continues to be in practice only under the Muslim law. The basic approach has been that the demand for reform should come from within the community itself. Marriage is a matter of contract under the Muslim law. The status of marriage lies at the root of the problem of polygamy amongst the Muslims. Abolition of polygamy by law has been taken recourse in Turkey and Tunishia. Other Muslim countries like Iraq, Iran, Syria, Indonesia and Pakistan have also introduced reforms of varying degrees to correct the abuse of polygamy. But in India, implementation of Uniform Civil Codes, as envisaged in Article 44 of the Constitution, has not come about as yet.

While bigamy is an offence under the Hindu Marriage Act, the practice still continues. Non-enforcement of law by the Government, social ostracism of the wife in the event of prosecution of the husband, are the principal reasons for the continuance of the practice of polygamy among Hindus. A number of Hindus started recourse to polygamy through conversion. There has been a very important judicial pronouncement in the context of bigamy by a convert Muslim. In *Sarla Mudgal Case*, the Supreme Court, interpreting the scope and extent of Section 494 (bigamy) of the Indian Penal Code in the context of this case held that "...the second marriage of a Hindu husband after conversion to Islam without having the first marriage dissolved under the law, would be invalid. The second marriage would be void in terms of the provisions of Section 494 IPC and the apostate husband would be guilty of offence under Section 494".

The Practice of Dowry

In many communities throughout India, a dowry is traditionally given by a bride's kin at the time of her marriage. In ancient times, the dowry was considered a woman's wealth. After marriage, she was supposed to have no claim on her natal family's real estate. She was given portable valuables, such as jewelry and household goods, over which she was supposed to have control throughout her life. However, over a period of time, the larger portion of the dowry has come to mean the goods and cash payment that goes to the groom's family.

Giving and taking of such dowries have assumed alarming dimension. Those who can afford are spending lavishly. This creates a feeling of lust among others. It has virtually become a mad scramble. There is no end. As a result, some of the groom's parents insist on more and more cash and goods. A number of women lose their peace of mind in their new house and some even are burnt alive thinking that the second marriage will bring them another dowry. The Government has made it an offence, but still dowry system is continuing. This practice is now prevalent even among the Muslims as well. As a consequence, dowry deaths have been the subject of numerous media reports in India. A number of women organizations have become active to condemn such incidents. The National Capital Territory of Delhi reported 1486 registered dowry deaths in 1987. In 1991, there were around 5000 dowry deaths. The apprehension of becoming victim of dowry has even prompted some young married and unmarried women to commit suicide.

The Dowry Prohibition Act, as amended in 1984, makes subjection of women to cruelty a cognizable offence under Section 304B of the Indian Penal Code. It renders the husband and in-laws liable for punishment in cases of death of a woman preceded by dowry related cruelty or harassment. Causing dowry death has also been made punishable with imprisonment for a period of not less than seven years. Section 113B of the Indian Evidence Act has also been amended to enable courts to draw presumption regarding causation of dowry death in circumstances of precedent dowry related cruelty or harassment.

Divorce & Maintenance

Both the husband as well as the wife amongst the Hindus can seek divorce on common grounds, be it under the Hindu Marriage Act 1955 or the Special Marriage Act 1954. There are some grounds even among the Christians also under the Indian Divorce Act 1899. Amongst the Muslims, the wife has been given restricted rights to dissolve marriage according to traditional laws. She has also rights to dissolution under the Muslim Marriage Act 1939 on stipulated grounds. But the husband has the entitlement to give *talaq* to his wife without assigning any reason, whenever he wishes. While there are different forms of *talaq*, the triple *talaq* is both instantaneous in effect and irrevocable. It has been of much concern to Muslims themselves, especially the Muslim women. The All India Muslim Personal Law Board itself is reported to have taken up this issue for internal deliberations. A Muslim woman is reported to have approached the Supreme Court for quashing the *talaqnama* issued against her by her husband. She urged in her petition that the custom and usage of polygamy and extra-judicial divorce allowed to be practiced by Muslims is a denial of equality, personal liberty and human rights guaranteed to all citizens under Articles 14, 15 and 21 of the Constitution.

Under Section 125 of CrPC, any man who deserts or divorces a wife, who cannot support herself, is liable to pay a stipulated compensation. This protection under the general law was held by the Supreme Court to be applicable in the *Shah Bano Case*, which upheld the maintenance of divorced Muslim women (AIR 1985 SC945). Even earlier, the Court had held that the *Mehr* could not be construed as exhausting a divorced Muslim woman's right to maintenance, especially if the *Mehr* did not tantamount to be adequate maintenance. It has been suggested that the Law of Maintenance should be amended to provide for the obligation of the economically independent women to maintain dependent husbands, to share with them the duty to maintain their children, and to share with her brothers the duty to maintain their indigent parents. It has also been proposed that the ceiling on the maximum amount payable as maintenance should be removed and the term 'wife' should include divorced wife as well. The employer, as in the case of income tax, it has been proposed, should deduct all maintenance, at source and arrears of maintenance shall be recoverable as land revenue or by distress.

8

Hindu Gods and Goddesses

As I have stated earlier, in New Delhi I stayed in Atithi Hotel. One day, I was taken to a nearby temple where I found the images of Krsna, Rama, Hanuman, Durga, Brahma and Siva being worshipped by the devotees. They come at any time in the morning and evening to pay their obeisance and go back. Since Hindus form an overwhelming majority of the Indian population and almost every Hindu is religious-minded, I feel that a knowledge of Hindu gods and goddesses is essential to understand India. Hindu worship is not congregational as in the Christian sense, except in sects, which put great emphasis on devotion. In most of the temples and Hindu houses, it has become customary to recite the *Ramayana* and *Bhagvad Gita*, describing the feats of their heroic characters and referring to the influence that the gods have on their exploits.

The Ramayana and *The Mahabharata*, the two great epics, were written between about 300 BC and AD 300. The stories of the various gods have been woven into the narratives of these epics. It seems that the heroes themselves succumbed to the assimilative powers of Indian popular religion and have thus become deified. The further development of Indian society brought about the corresponding changes in religious concepts and an increase in the size of the pantheon. In this way, numerous gods and goddesses have been identified. To describe their names and description even one book is also not sufficient. I, therefore, describe below some of the prominent deities.

But before this, it may be useful to mention that in Hindu temples, the devotee can employ a priest to carry out a ritual for him or summon the god's attention on his own to hear a supplication or receive an offering made as the result of a vow. *Puja*, however, varies considerably in its details depending on the sect, the size of the temple and its location etc. Domestic worship also varies according to individual's needs and inclinations. A princely household may employ its own domestic chaplin (*purohit*) while others may hire a Brahmin (or traveling *guru*) to perform ceremonies for special occasions. An orthodox believer could rise early and spend most of the day worshipping a deity of which a properly consecrated image in not merely a symbol but the point at which the deity is present. A busy devotee might restrict himself to a prayer and visit a large or small temple perhaps two or three times a year for the most important festivals.

Unlike other religions, Hindus worship a number of deities, particularly the three deities, viz Brahma, Visnu and Siva. Brahma is the creator of this world, Visnu the preserver and Siva the destroyer of evil forces. Gradually, Brahma ceased to be worshipped while Visnu and Siva continued as deities. These and other deities were defined in the *Vedas* together with meticulous descriptions of the ceremonies that were intended to coerce them into bringing about material benefit in this world for the worshipper. Vedic deities were given human form and reproduced as images. In course of time, many of the old deities were assigned to minor positions in the pantheon, others were promoted, and new deities were introduced.

Brahma

There are many myths about the birth of Brahma, that he was born in a golden egg and was, therefore, known as Hiranya-garbha, that he sprang from the waters and the ether, that he took the form of a boar and lifted up the earth from the ocean and that he took the *avatar* (incarnation) of fish. In a temple exclusively dedicated to Brahma, we find the aspect of his name Visvakarma. In this form, Brahma is shown with four heads and four arms. In his hands, there is *akshamala*, a book, a bundle of kusa grass and a *kamandalu*. He is seated upon a swan. A large number of *rshis* with moustaches and *jatas*, carrying in their hands the *akshamala* and the *kamandalu* are seated in the temple of Brahma meditating upon him.

Brahma sits on a lotus attached to Visnu's navel.

Thus, Brahma is a name given to the fiction of a personified creator of an efficient cause (*nimita*) of creation. The Immense Being is also the golden-embryo (Hiranayagarbha) from which the universe develops and the Lord of Progeny (*Prajapati*) who was born before all gods started nourishing and protecting the creation. From the cosmological point of view, Brahma is the golden embryo, the ball of fire from which the universe develops. *The Mahabharata* considers him as born from the embryo, which took shape in the Visnu's mind when he began to think of creation. The scheme of the universe springs from Brahma. Hence, he is the Lord of Progeny (*Prajapati*), the patriarch (*pitamah*).

Brahma is the abode of man (Narayana, a name also interpreted to mean he who dwells in the causal waters—*nara*). All was only water in which the earth was formed. Thence arose Brahma, the self-born. Later, Narayana became almost exclusively an epithet of Visnu. Brahma is also the great lord (*Brhaspati*), the Lord of Speech, the first seer, the god of asceticism. He is the ordinator (*Vidhi*) of *Vedas*, the shaper (*Druhina*) of *Sastras*. He is also the sustainer, the world master, the supreme-ruler, everlasting. He is also called the undivided impulse. After the universal destruction (*pralaya*), Visnu falls asleep floating on the causal water. When creation again arises, Brahma appears on a lotus having been born from the naval-born, lotus. The universe-architect, Visvakarma, is an aspect of Brahma.

Though Brahma had been the God of prime importance and the creator par excellence in the Vedic period and he was honoured much more than other gods or deities of the Brahmanical pantheons, but his popularity gradually declined with the emergence of Saiva and Vaisvanava cults. In the early Buddhist literature, he had been a close associate of Buddha, and according to the Buddhist texts, it was at the behest of Brahma that the Buddha decided to impart to the world the knowledge he had attained after his enlightenment at Bodhgaya.

In spite of various opinions prevailing about the popularity of Brahma in the Indian religious thought from time to time in the past, the presence of Brahma in one form or the other in the Vedic period and in the Brahmanas has been established wherein he has been described as *Prajapati*, Hiranayagarbha and with other epithets. During the *Upanisad* period he has been described as the creator from where all the *devas* and *asuras* were born. In some of the *Upanisads*, he was described as having been born out of the Golden Egg and Svayambhu, while in others he was described as having emerged out of the navel of Visnu or even Krsna seated over a full blown lotus.

Besides, he has been decorated with the title of "first among the gods". In many parts of the country, his worship is in vogue. In the west coast, especially among the Tulus, where the devil worship prevails, Brahma is not only revered as a god, but also as a spirit of *Bhuta*. In *Puranas*, he has been projected as the one who is the embodiment of all knowledge, and the one who impart to the sages whenever the occasion arises. He is approachable by the gods and demons alike, and if the gods get their boons from him, so do the demons. In fact, all castes worship him and he is universally adored. Though, with the development of Saivism, Brahma was relegated to the background to some extent but his worship or importance has not vanished altogether.

Visnu

Visnu happens to be one of the most prominent brahmanical Hindu gods with numerous iconic manifestations and widespread artistic representations to his credit. Since the age of *Rigveda*, he has been considered as an important divine figure. The *Rigvedic* hymns eulogize the essential features of the character of the Vedic Visnu, namely, his taking from the very place where the gods promote man's interests, and the three steps by which he established the broad dimensional actuality of the earthly space in which all being abide. The principle of creation and the hypothesis of the universe, concerned as a whole, come to be the Visnu's epithets.

Visnu, the preserver, floats on Kshirsagar (the sacred ocean), the source of all life. He reclines on hundred-headed leviathan, *Shesh Nag*.

In the *Rigveda*, Visnu is Indra's ally and intimate friend. After Indra slew a board that kept the goods of the *asuras* (anti-gods), Visnu carried the animal with the result that the gods obtained the goods of their enemies. This board, then identified with the creator god *Prajapati*, is also said to have raised up the earth. In the course of time, Visnu fuses with Prajapati, and it is he who saves the overcrowded earth by raising it up. The great fish that delivers Manu, the first human, from the deluge, appears later as a form of Brahma and becomes in the post-epic *Puranas* an *avatara* (incarnation) of Visnu.

In the centuries before the beginning of the common era, Visnu is fused with several divine, mythical and heroic or legendary figures. Among them are the primeval cosmic man (*Purusa*) embodying the idea that creation is the self limitation of the transcendent person, the creator god *Prajapati*; Narayana, a divine figure featured in the narrative of the three ascetics; and Krsna, who, in the *Bhagavad Gita*, in human shape, combine a socially normal life with a prospect of final liberation. Visnu is both the Supreme Being and a deity responsible for particular duties and activities. Brahma, Visnu and Siva, as he creates, preserve or bring the creation to an end.

In the epic period (500 BC-200 AD), Visnu assumed that aspect of the godhead that he holds up to the present day, that of preserver, and protector of the world, Lord and ruler of all. He is usually depicted as a four-armed, dark blue young man bearing in his hands a conch (an auspicious object that represents fertility and is supposed to strengthen the divine power), a discus (his moveable flaming weapon), a mace, and a lotus (indication of the life-supporting power). He wears the miraculous jewel *Kaustubha*, which emerged from the churning of the ocean. The characteristic curl of hair on his chest is called the Srivatsa (favourite of the goddess Sri) and characterizes him as the universal sovereign. These mythological attributes are often used as aids to devotion. The mere presence of Visnu riding the eagle *Garuda*, the thermographic manifestation of his nature and energy, suffices, in myth, literature, and plastic arts, to subdue the demoniac servants.

In the past Vedic period, Visnu's consort is known by two names, Sri and Lakshmi. Originally, there were two different goddesses, the former representing fortune and prosperity, the latter being closely connected with the ripe corn. Like Visnu, Sri Lakshmi is eternal symbol and is said to have risen from the ocean to preside over earthly welfare. It is with the goddess in such form that Visnu is united in all his incarnations. She, as Visnu's *Sakti*, is instrumental and material cause of the universe.

Siva

Lord Siva, also known as Rudra, is one of the eminent ancient Hindu gods. According to *Rigveda*, he appeared as a wild hunter, a flame, his arrow directed against the Creator making love with his virgin daughter, the Dawn (*Usa*). They had the shape of two antelopes. Some of the Creator's seed fell on the earth. Rudra himself as Fire (*Agni*) had prepared the seed, from which mankind was to be born. From a surface of the undifferentiated plenum of the Absolute some of the seed fell on the earth. Rudra's shot failed to prevent its fall. Time, which was about to begin, came in between, in the shape of the flight of his arrow. The Creator, Prajapati, terribly frightened, made Rudra Lord of Animals (Pasupati) for sparing his life. The gods, as they witnessed the primordial scene, made it into a *mantra*, an incantation. Out of this *mantra*, they fashioned Vastospati, "lord of the residue (*vastu*)", "lord of the site (*vastu*)", or "lord of what is left over on the sacrificial etc."

Siva lives atop the Mount Kailash. The River Ganges flows from his matted locks. His vehicle is Nandi (bull), always seen with him in temples. He is seen with his consort Parvati.

On being born, Rudra was invested with the cosmos by *Prajapati*. His eightfold domain consisted of the five elements—earth, water, fire, air and space—together with Sun and the Moon, the measurers of time, and the sacrificer or initiate. Rudra is the totality of manifestation. He did not create the cosmos. He became and is the cosmos. God and the world are one. As the cosmos is a product of Siva's eight forms, so is the human being, the microcosm.

Rudra, the "wild god," is one with Siva, the auspicious, supreme god whose splendour encompasses his primordial form. His being in manifestation is to be meditated upon as a river of five streams from five sources. Five is Siva's sacred number in particular. His *mantra*, "*Namah Sivaya*," has five syllables, and his "body" is said to be constituted of five *mantras*. They evoke the body of God in the five directions of space, in five elements, and in the five senses.

Vedic Rudra, the fierce hunter, is clad in the skins of wild animals. In *The Mahabharata*, Siva is seen by the hero Arjuna, as an archer and as an ascetic. *The Mahabharata* sums up the relation of Siva to yoga, saying that "Siva is yoga and the lord of yogins, and he can be approached by yoga only."

In post-Vedic times, *Prajapati*'s role was taken over by Brahma. Rudra decapitates his father, Brahma. Various reasons for this are given in the *Puranas*. One of them was the lusting of Brahma for his daughter. The head of Brahma clings to Siva's hand. Siva, as a penitent beggar, the skull his begging bowl, goes on a pilgrimage of expiation. After twelve years, the skull falls from Siva's hand in Banaras, and Siva is released from his sin. His pilgrimage takes the god to a pilgrimage in a forest of *deodar* trees. The hermits believe that the young, naked beggar had come to seduce their women and Siva's phallus (*linga*) falls from his body, by his own will or by a curse of the sages. It then arises as a flaming pillar. These events are part of the play (*lila*) of Siva in this world to enable the devotees to recognize God in the guises assumed. The sages apparently fail to identify the begging bowl, Brahma's head or skull (*brahmastras*) in the beggar's hand. *Brahmastras* is also the name of Siva's most formidable weapon, the Pasupati weapon.

Most of Siva's myths are explained in *The Mahabharata*: the myth of Siva, the ascetic, is the theme of his marriage to Parvati, the daughter of Parvataraja, Lord of Mountain. In it is included the story of the destruction and resurrections of Kama, the god of Desire, an archer who aimed his arrow at Siva but was reduced in ashes by a glance from Siva's third eye. Siva's nature is two fold: he is fierce as fire, yet cool and calm as the moon. He is reluctant bridegroom, the indefatigable lover, and the ascetic. He is the Saviour of the world. He swallowed its poison and it left a dark blue mark on his throat. He destroys demons or shows them his grace. He defeats death. He is time and transcends time as eternity. He is a dance, Lord of Dancers, who dances the world in and out of existence. He is a male god inseparably united with his female power (*Sakti*). One image shows him half male, half female. His theriomorphic form is the bull called *Nandin* (Joy). His main attributes are trident, skull, and antelope. His symbol is the *linga* (the phallus), the most sacred object of worship. The linga stands erect in its double significance, full of creative power, and also of the yogic power to develop the seed.

Saivism centers on the worship of the god Siva. In classical Hindu mythology, Siva is the god of destruction of evils, generally portrayed as a yogin who lives on Mount Kailasa in the Himalayas. His body is smeared with ashes, his hair piled up in matted locks. He wears an animal skin and carries a trident. A cobra often serves as his garland and the crescent moon as his hair ornament. He has a third eye, kept closed, in the middle of his forehead. His beautiful wife, Parvati, and their two sons, the six-faced Skanda and the elephant-headed Ganesa, may surround him.

Krishna

Krishna or Krsna, as the human incarnation, showing all the aspects of human development associated with childhood, adolescence, adulthood etc. is revered both within and outside India. His *karma*'s philosophy, as enunciated in the *Bhagavad Gita*, is a torch bearer for the erring mankind.

Although many of the stories about Krsnā concern his super-human deeds he also revealed a marked human capacity for drinking, fighting and amorous escapades. Such stories are mostly found in the *Bhagavad Gita* and the *Mahabharata*. Perhaps, the most popular of these stories are about his skill as a flute player. There are stories about his pastoral character and the impact of his music on the girl cowherds (*gopis*). On hearing the music of Krsna's flute, peacocks dance and other animals stand still and worship him with their glances, celestial maiden flying in their aerial cars above the earth become infatuated with him and shower flowers on him, rivers become smooth running and offer him lotuses. In the heat of the day, clouds let fall on him their cooling rain.

Krsna delivering the message of *karma* to Arjuna in the battlefield of Kurukshetra that forms the epitome of the *Gita*.

In his adolescence, Krsna had a fight with the snake Kaliya, who had previously quarreled with Garuda. After being wounded by Garuda, Kaliya took refuge in a pool of water from which Garuda had been excluded because of one of his own previous misdeeds. Besieged in the pool, Kaliya poisoned it with his potent venom to such an extent that its vapour was as lethal to birds and animals as its water. Even a drop of this water caused instant death. When Krsna heard that his friends, the cowherds and their flocks, had been poisoned in this way he rushed to their aid, revived them, kicked Kaliya almost to death and then danced on him. Kaliya's friends and relations begged for Krsna's mercy and Kaliya was spared to become one of Krsna's worshippers.

Yet, legends of his boyhood bring to light the human side of Krsna's nature. He is described as a mischievous, rather spoilt child whose mother was inclined to overlook the pranks he played on her and their neighbours. He climbed up to the place where jars, containing milk, butter and curds were hung from the ceiling of his house. He broke them and played with the butter that fell out. He and his brother Balram untied the neighbour's calves and let them run away or chased them and held on their tails. They deliberately used their neighbours' newly-cleaned houses as toilets to annoy them. When they complained to Krsna's mother she was reluctant to pay heed to them as her son Krsna looked so innocent and she merely smiled at him.

Krsna, the embodiment of love.

One day, Krsna was caught eating earth. When his mother reproached him he denied that he had done so and invited her to look in his mouth and see for herself. She found not earth but the whole of the universe with its tangible aspects, such as the sphere of the earth with its continents, mountains, oceans, lighting, fire and wind, together with all the planets and stars as well as the intangibles, such as soul, time, nature, mind and destiny. This showed that Krsna is a Supreme God.

Krsna and his female partner, Radha, are associated with ideas of intense romantic love about which many stories and poems, such as the *Gita Govinda of Jayadeva* were written. Illustrations of the Krsna and Radha stories are found more often in painting than sculpture.

Hindus believe that with Krsna the Supreme God among them, a true devotee enjoys a loving, intimate and unique relationship. He constantly pleads, "O my Lord, Sri Krsna! I do not want anything for myself, not material prosperity, not heaven, not even *moksha*; I only want the privilege of serving you in devotion, for ever and ever and ever". Krsna, in turn, is so indebted to and pleased with his devotees for their unconditional love that he totally comits himself to protect them personally under all circumstances, providing for their every need and indeed ever to serve them as of humble servant, as he did in the battlefield of Kurukshetra by becoming Arjuna's charioteer.

Krsna may be the Lord of all that, but He says that He is powerless over his devotees. This aspect is elucidated in the *Srimad Bhagvatam* in the following story. Durvasa Muni was once annoyed with Maharaja Ambarish and he produced a demon from his hair to kill Ambarish. Ambarish was a devotee of Visnu and prayed to him to save him. So, Lord Visnu demolished the demon with his *Sudarshanchakra* and then sent it chasing Durvasa Muni himself who ran first to Brahma and then to Siva for their help. Having failed to get it he hastened to Vaikuntha and pleaded to Narayan, who is none other than Krsna, to save him. But Narayan informed Durvasa that the two could not help him because he doesn't have the power to overrule the actions of his devotees. "I am completely under the control of my devotees", he told Durvasa, and said, "I am not all dependent. I am dependent not only on my devotees but also on my devotee's devotee. The devotees who are unconditionally attached to me in the core of the heart bring me under their full control". He advised Durvasa that the way he could save himself was by seeking Ambarish's forgiveness.

Krsna, it is believed, provides his devotees every need as well. "To those who worship me with exclusive devotion, meditating on my transcendent form—to them I carry what they lack, and I preserve what they have". Krsna's advice to Arjuna, when he refused to fight, as explained in *Bhagavad Gita*, shows the path of action. It is the essence of the *Vedas*. It explains duty of mankind without attachment and without any concern for the result of actions.

As already explained, Krsna also promises to personally protect his devotees. He tells Arjuna in the battlefield of Kurukshetra, "I envy no one, nor am I partial to anyone. I am equal to all but whoever renders service into me in devotion is a friend and I am also friend to him". When a devotee, fully surrenders, asks Krsna for help, the Lord personally comes to his aid. Krsna came to Draupadi's aid as described in *The Mahabharata* and saved her from being disrobed by the Kauravas. He burst out from a stone pillar as an incarnation of Narasimhadeva to save Prahlada when his father Hiranyakashipu taunted Prahlad to prove that Krsna was everywhere. He appeared personally as Visnu to save his devotee Gajendra, the elephant king, who was fighting for his life with his leg caught in the jaws of a crocodile.

Rama, Sita and Lakshman

As described earlier, Ram Navmi happens to be the birthday of Lord Rama, the seventh incarnation of Lord Visnu. Lord Rama was born to rid the world of demons, headed by Ravana, who was creating havoc. It is stated that in *Devlok* (the place where gods live), *Devtas* (gods) ran to Lord Brahma. At the instance of Brahma, Lord Visnu appeared on this earth as the incarnation of Lord Rama. The activities of Lord Rama were explained in the Hindu scripture, *The Ramayana*. Rama and Krsna are believed to be synonyms for Visnu, and Visnu, in turn, meant Rama or Krsna. Born in the Solar dynasty, Rama ruled Ayodhya, the capital of the great kingdom of Kosala, made fertile by the river Sarayu. He was the son of King Dasaratha. For many years, Dasaratha had no son. He consulted his religious master and got *yagya* performed. Contemporaneously with the *yagya* in Ayodhya, there was a conference of the *Devas* in heaven. As already explained, the *Devas* complained to Lord Brahma that Ravana, king of demons, drunk with the power acquired by the boon granted to him by Brahma, was causing them untold misery and hardship. Brahma realized his fateful omission and promised to be born as four sons of King Dasaratha who had then been performing a sacrifice for progeny. As the *ghee* was poured into the fire and the flames shot up to meet it, from out of the flames came a majestic figure, resplendent like the noonday sun, holding a bowl of gold, who told Dasaratha that the *Devas* are pleased to answer his prayer. He gave *paayasam* (sweet liquid) to be given to his wives and the King distributed the *paayasam* to his three wives.

Rama, the epitome of virtue and Visnu's seventh incarnation.

In the course of time, Kausalya gave birth to Rama, Kaikeyi to Bharata, and Sumitra to twins, Lakshmana and Satrughna, as she drank the divine *paayasam* twice. The four sons were given all the training prescribed for princes. At the request of Sage Viswamitra, Rama and Lakshman were sent to protect Viswamitra in the performance of his sacrifice and protect him from *rakshas* (demons). The *rakshas* were then killed. Viswamitra now took the boys to the capital city of Mithila, where the illustrious philosopher King Janak intended to perform a great sacrifice. Janaka's daughter, Sita, was to be the wife of Visnu who had come down on earth in human form. King Janaka, who was childless, had found baby Sita in a field among shrubs. When Sita reached the age of marriage, King Janaka announced that whosoever would string a big bow, kept with him, would marry Sita. A number of kings tried their luck, but ultimately Rama stepped out to the iron bow-case. Opening the box, he lifted the bow effortlessly, as if it were a garland of flowers, and resting one end of it against his toe, he bent and strung it and drew the string back with such irresistible force that the mighty bow snapped with a crash like a clap of thunder. Sita was married to Rama.

Rama and Sita spent twelve happy years in Ayodhya. Dasaratha loved all his four sons and yet he had a special affection for Rama. Rama's graceful frame and virile beauty, his strength, his courage, the purity of his heart, his perfect life, his compassion, sweetness of speech, his serenity, his deep wisdom and his statesmanship were admired by the people and made them eagerly look forward to his becoming king. Considering his own old age, Dasaratha wished to crown Rama as *Yuvaraja* and entrust him with the *de facto* rule of the kingdom. The coronation was to be performed on the next day, but Queen Kaikeyi, on the advice of her maid, Manthara, persuaded King Dasaratha to send Rama to forest for fourteen years and give the throne to her own son, Bharata, in return for the boon he had given to her once in a battlefield. Accordingly, Rama went to forest. His consort, Sita, and brother, Lakshman, accompanied him. King Dasaratha could not bear the agony of separation from his son and expired after Rama, Sita and Lakshman had left for forest.

Bharata was away from Ayodhya when all this happened. On his return, he realized the enormity of the harm wrought by his mother. Overwhelmed by grief and anger, he could not control himself. At the thought of what she had done and the eternal infamy she had incurred, his grief grew wild and he hurled cruel words at her. Among the characters in the *Ramayana*, Bharata is the perfect embodiment of virtue. He took his army and accompanied with his mothers, he went to Chitrakoot to persuade Rama to return but could not. He returned to Ayodhya. On his return, he did not accept the kingdom but installed his *padukas* (sandals) and, deriving his authority from them, he did his duty as a king.

As the years passed, one day, in the absence of Rama and Lakshman, King Ravana abducted Sita. The two brothers searched every mountain, forest and river-bank calling Sita's name aloud. But all in vain. He then learnt from the dying Jataayu that Sita had been carried away by Ravana. Rama's losing health and lamenting in sorrow can be compared to the behaviour of Jesus, nailed to the cross. Passing through the forest, the two princes were suddenly caught by tremendously big *rakshasas*, one after the other, and they killed them one by one. They met Sugreeva. Sugreeva was keen on regaining his kingdom and family and Rama and Lakshman helped them. Sugreeva placed his entire army at Rama's disposal. Sugreeva issued stringent orders to his commanders to send divisions of the army to the four quarters of the earth and make a thorough search for Sita. He advised

Hanuman, son of *Vayu* (air), who possessed the strength and splendour of his father, to undertake search of Sita.

Hanuman learnt that Sita was kept as a prisoner in the land of the *rakshas*, across the ocean. Jambhavan praised Hanuman, reminded him of his strength and roused his dormant courage. At once, Hanuman's form began to swell like the sea in high tide. Flying through the sky and alighting in Lanka, he reached the Ashoka Park where Sita was kept. Ravana approached Sita in the hope of obtaining her consent, but Sita proved to be a faithful wife. Hidden in the branches of the tree, Hanuman watched what went on below. Sita hoped month after month that her lord would discover her whereabouts and come to her rescue. Hidden by the branches, Hanuman sang in sweet and gentle voice the story of Rama so that it fell on Sita's ears. Hanuman met Sita and she narrated to him her story. Hanuman comforted Sita and Sita expressed her unflinching love for her husband. Hanuman demonstrated his powers and jumped off from the platform and began to grow big in size. Sita was pleased.

Taking leave of Sita, Hanuman assumed a huge figure of wrathful menace with a view to create fear psychosis into Ravana. The *rakshasis* quaked with terror at the sight of this stranger and some ran to tell Ravana the news. Ravana was furious on hearing that his favourite park, set apart for his queens, had been destroyed by Hanuman and ordered his bodyguards to go and destroy the monster-monkey. Hanuman showed to them his still formidable figure to scare them. Hanuman struck down and slew the sentries. He uprooted a *sal* tree and, twirling it, flung it and then plucked out a huge iron rod from a temple and aimed it at the chariot and reduced it to splinters and crushed the huge body of Jambumali into a shapeless mass, in which neither head nor limbs could be distinguished. One by one, he also killed *rakshas*.

Hanuman was captured by the mighty force of Ravana. His captors took him to the court of Ravana and placed him in front of the King. Hanuman was warned by Ravana of the consequences. Ravana wanted to kill Hanuman but his brother, Vibheeshana, pointed out that it would be improper to kill a king's envoy. Then Ravana ordered that Hanuman's tail be set fire and he be turned out. His people wrapped Hanuman's tail in rags of all kinds, soaked it in oil and set it on fire making it a huge flaming torch. Bound by ropes and with tail ablaze, Hanuman was taken through the streets of Lanka. Suddenly, he shrank in size and shook off the ropes that bound him, and resuming his huge shape, jumped with his blazing tail to the top of a tall building. He plucked a pillar there and whirled it round, striking terror in all beholders. Then he jumped from mansion to mansion, setting fire to them. In a little while, a strong breeze began to blow and the whole city was in flames.

Hanuman returned to Rama and narrated to him the story and the strength of Ravana's army. Rama and Lakshman resolved to destroy Ravana and rescue Sita. In the battle that ensued, Ravana's brothers and he himself were killed one by one. At the end, Ravana's brother, Vibheeshana, who had helped Rama, was crowned in Lanka. After seeking permission of the new king, Vibheeshana, Hanuman went to Sita and asked Sita's permission to slay the "cruel women" who had troubled her, but Sita said that the noble souls have to be compassionate towards all—sinners as well as good people. These words of Sita are treasured like nectar by generations of pious men, as these *rakshasis*, Sita felt, had carried out their master's order and are not to be blamed. Their king is dead and has paid for his crime and it is unjust to punish these *rakashasis* now. In Ashok Vatika, Sita was taken care of by the *rakashasis* (lady demons). Seated in a *palanquin*, Sita was brought to Rama's camp.

When Sita was brought before Rama, he said, how can a Kshatriya take back a wife who had lived so long in a stranger's house. Lakshman was asked to kindle a fire. She jumped into the flames and the lambent flames were crowded with celestial figures. All the gods came and assembled there. Agni, god of fire, rose in his own body out of the flames and lifting Sita in his arms with all her clothes and jewels untouched and intact, presented her to Rama. Rama accepted Sita fire-proved. It is believed that the one who was abducted by Ravana was not the real Sita. She was only her prototype. The real Sita emerged out of the fire. This ordeal was to satisfy the people. Without it, they would say that Rama, blinded by love, behaved with a strange weakness and broke the rule of well-brought-up men. Rama and Sita were now re-united, ascended the Pushpaka which carried them swiftly in the air with their friends, the *vanara* (monkey) warriors and Vibheeshana, to Ayodhya.

The city of Ayodhya swam in a sea of joy. Rama and Bharata met. Rama was crowned the King of Ayodhya. The whole city was illuminated. The festival of Diwali, every year in October/November, is reminiscent of the happy return and crowning of Lord Rama. Bharata, through his behaviour and actions, showed his spotless mind and unblemished unselfishness. In the same way, Sita, as a true life companion and faithful wife, insisted on accompanying Rama to forest and remain his true life companion through thick and thin. Lakshman too left all the comforts as well as his own wife in Ayodhya and went with Rama as a sincere and faithful brother. For fourteen years till the return of Rama, Bharata installed Rama's *paadukas* and administered the kingdom as a devotional exercise in the service of his brother. Above all, Rama was an incarnation of Visnu descended on earth in human form to play the role model for mankind, *maryadapurushotam* indeed. By adhering to the ideals set by Rama, his consort Sita and his two brothers, one can get guidance as to the right or wrong of a situation when one is confronted with the dilemma in human relationship.

This story has been narrated in the *Ramayana* of Tulsidas. Sita, the female counterpart of the Supreme being, is the embodiment of compassion and grace. Compassion is the Supreme Mother and she is enthroned in the heart of the Lord. When she casts her merciful glance on us, we reach the feet of God. God as Father and God as Mother are not distinct. If the Lord were to be parted from compassion, our plight would be just that of Ravana who separated Sita from Rama. The quality of the Lord's compassion can be understood from the experience of true human love, as narrated through various episodes in the *Ramayana*. *The Ramayana* is not history or biography. It is a part of Hindu mythology. We cannot understand Greek life and Greek civilization without knowing all about Zeus, Apollo, Hercules, Venue, Hector, Priam, Achilles, Ulysses and others. So also one cannot understand Hindu *dharma* unless one knows Rama and Sita, Bharata, Lakshmana, Ravana, Kumbhakarna and Hanuman. Mythology cannot be dispensed with. Philosophy alone or rituals alone or mythology alone cannot be sufficient. These are the three strands of all ancient religions. The attitude towards things spiritual, which belongs to a particular people cannot be grasped or preserved or conveyed unless we have all these three. Even an iconoclast like Bernard Shaw has acknowledged the essentiality of myths.

The stories of Rama, Sita and Lakshman are not only to be read and understood from mythological point of view, they have to offer moral lessons to the younger generation. The stories are repeated in dramatic presentations in *Ramlila* in cities, districts and villages during Dussehra for ten days, invariably in the month of October. On the last day, the effigies of Ravana, Kumbhkaran and Meghnath, the three brothers, are burnt showing victory of good over evil. In the modern day context, when moral values are being ignored, Dusshehra should better be looked not as a Hindu religious festival, it is about the socio-cultural affinity that brings all of us together. The celebration of Dussehra festival is the joint efforts of people of all religions and castes. Both Hindus and Muslims join hands in the dramatic presentation of *Ramlilas* in myriad corners of India, the preparation of fireworks, effigies for burning on the last day and various other activites.

Ganesha

Lord Ganesha, also called Ganapati, has been described as the 'remover of obstacles'. Although Ganesha has been identified with deities mentioned in the Rig *Veda*, his development into his present form took place much later. According to a legend, Parvati created him from the scarf of her body so that he could act as her door-guardian. When he refused to admit Siva, the latter cut off his head. As Parvati was distressed when his son was beheaded, Siva offered to replace it with the head of the first living being that came along, which happened to be an elephant.

Ganesh, the elephant-headed son of Siva, invoked at the start of any auspicious task.

However, according to the *Brihaddharma Purana,* he was conjured out of a piece of cloth by Siva to make a son for Parvati. Later, Siva brought about the boy's death by decapitation and then, in order to placate Parvati, he called on the gods to find him a new head. After much searching, they gave him an elephant's head which had a tusk broken when it was cut from the body.

Another aspect of Ganesa is his appearance. His obesity contains the whole universe, his trunk is bent to remove obstacles, and his four arms represent the four categories into which things—Castes, *Vedas*—can be divided. His companion animal (*Vahana*) is a bandicoot. This illustrates the different ways in which obstacles can be removed to reach religious ends. The elephant tramples down everything in its path, but the bandicoot can creep through small holes and cracks to achieve the same goal. When painted, he is red in colour but in some texts he is described as yellow. Four arms are the usual number but there may be more as in the case of Maha Ganapati who rides on his bandicoot and has a goddess (Siddhi or Buddhi) on his knee. In some images, he may be shown as riding on a lion.

As the remover of obstacles, worshippers, who face a number of calamities frequently, propitiate Lord Ganapati. He is also worshipped while starting any ritual or while beginning a journey. As a god of wisdom, seekers of knowledge invoke him. He is endowed with a gentle and affectionate nature. He is quite popular and his images are found acting as a guarding diety. Ganesh Chaturthi, every year, keeps on reminding every Hindu household the importance Lord Ganesha and the need to worship him. The festival is celebrated for almost ten days with great fervour and enthusiasm in Maharashtra and South India. The images of the god are immersed in river on the concluding day.

Surya Narayana

Surya, personified as Sun, is an important deity of Hindus. He is regarded as the source of light and warmth and even of life itself as well. In Indian mythology, he has been described as the source of all knowledge. He is the origin of solar energy and of the laws that are given in the universe and human society. He is reckoned as the highest of the gods among the agricultural communities, regulating weather and seasons. Thus, he has the power to grant or withhold the ripening of the crops.

Surya Narayana has been described variously. He is shown in northern images as wearing long boots reaching to his knees. In South Indian images, however, he is usually shown bare footed. Whether seated or standing, his main characteristics are the lotuses, held one in each hand at shoulder level. He may also be shown in a chariot, perhaps with only one wheel, drawn by horses, usually seven, that carries him across the sky.

Hanuman

Hanuman is a monkey god and a popular deity who is worshipped all over India. His story is related in the *Ramayana* where he has been described as the perfect devotee of Lord Rama and is the epitome of service and loyalty. When Ravana abducted Sita, the demon king of Lanka, Hanuman's search for her brings to light his superhuman powers. He is confident of his own ability to find her and proceeds with his monkey followers. He heard that Rama's consort, Sita, was

Hanuman is invoked by those who are in need of courage and fortitude.

captured in Lanka. By a prodigious leap, he crossed the channel between India and Lanka. He magically changed his form several times and entered the city. After painful search, he eventually discovered that Sita was lodged in a nearby forest. He was captured and was presented before Ravana. His tail was set on fire, but by his divine power, he escaped and used his tail to burn Lanka. He returned to Rama without Sita and helped him in many miraculous ways to besiege Lanka. When Rama's brother, Lakshman, was wounded in the battlefield he flew to the Himalayas to collect healing grass and herbs. Again, he brought these herbs for his wounded companions in the monkey army. Finally, when the Ravana and all his brothers were killed, he accompanied Rama, Sita and Lakshman to Ayodhya. Sita had to be sent by Rama to Balmiki's hermitage where she gave birth to two brave sons, Love and Kush. Later, Hanuman was sent to Sita and he begged her to return to Rama. After they were reunited it was time for Hanuman and his monkey army to return to their forest home, but his wish to remain as Rama's faithful servant was granted.

Hanuman's image is often available with one head and two arms with a long tail looped over his head. His devotees worship him every Tuesday.

Durga

Durga is a female deity whose relation with her closest male deity (Siva) is sufficiently remote for her to be worshipped in her own right. In 7th or 8th century AD the *Shakti* of the Impersonal Absolute was referred to as Durga in the *Narayana Upanishad* and as being susceptible to worship for the acquisition of material gain in this world and spiritual advancement.

Goddess Durga is invoked for the bestowal of favours for her active and sometime violent assistance against demons, terrors and disasters in the same way that the old gods had used female divinities as their agents in similar struggles. This contributed to the development of a group of fierce-looking female deities in contrast to peaceful ones. Thus, in the *Mahabharata*, a *Shakti* is described as a fierce, black goddess and in *Narayana Upanishad*, Durga is called a flaming goddess.

The deity has eight arms and holds on the left trident, sword, snake and bell, and on the right, drum, shield, cup and water pot. She is seated in *Sukhasana* posture on a double lotus throne and wears a garland of skulls. Next to the lotus throne is the figure of a lion. She is also shown riding a lion.

Durga, riding a tiger, with her deadly arsenal of weapons to destroy evil.

During every autumn, Goddess Durga is believed to leave her Himalayan abode to spend a few days at her parents' in the plains of Bengal. Therefore, when the rest of India celebrates Dussehra festival for the return of the victorious Rama to Ayodhya, West Bengal and the states in its neighborhood celebrate the arrival of the Mother Goddess or Ma Durga. The ten-handed Goddess arrives riding a lion with the children alongside her. Durga *Puja* in October is celebrated to honour her and seek her blessings.

Durga *Puja* involves a strange juxtaposition of faith and festivity. On the one hand, Durga is worshipped as the powerful Goddess, an incarnation of *Shakti*(power) and on the other she is loving, caring mother, who spares some time for her children. It is believed that the festival in autumn was a consequence of Rama's prayer to the Goddess seeking her blessings before venturing out to kill the *rakshas* (demons) and King Ravana.

Durga *Puja* is not merely a religious affair in the post-Independence era, the community *puja* has become an occasion for revelry, irrespective of caste and creed. Non-Hindus are also seen joining the organizing committees and enjoying the pageant. The biggest festival of Bengal has now become a confirmation of cultural and art extravaganza. *Puja* is a money-spinner for some. This is the time when Bengalis go for an extensive shopping, especially for new cloths and furnishings.

The preparations for Durga *Puja* begins months ahead with the *puja* organizers trying to come up with new themes and securing the services of modellers and artists for the purpose. Every year, innovative ideas are evolved. It is said that an organization in north Kolkata, the hub of clay modellers, where 80 per cent of the idols are made, wakes up to frenzy of activities. Occasionally, they make collapsible idols for non-resident Indians to be flown abroad. They start working on the idols as early as in mid-April.

For the three days during the Durga *Puja* festival, Kolkata turns into a "walk-in art gallery". From the elaborate *pandals* to the exploration of themes, every year there is something new to look forward to. In the 1970s, there was a trend of creating the images from mundane things like coins, matchsticks, fish scales etc. A new trend visible since the turn of the century is to revive traditional art forms and explore contemporary social themes.

Kali, wearing a garland of skulls, annihilates evil.

It is not only the interior decorations and the idols, but the *pandals* and illumination which can be mind boggling. During the festivities, Kolkata turns into a mini India when builders of *pandals* are seen recreating monuments from the elaborately sculpted temples of South India to Britain's Windsor Palace or from the Trevy Fountain of Rome to the Space Shuttle Challenger or a Rajasthani temple to the recreation of houseboats and scenery of Kerala. Artists from the various regions are invited to work with the local artists. In this way, a number of people look up to the business boom as their main means of sustenance. Internet and webcam should help Bengalis all over the world to participate in the community *puja* and thus feel the ecstasy of family reunion.

Lakshmi

Lakshmi is Goddess of wealth and the consort of Visnu. Her origin is related to the churning of the sea by Lord Siva. When Vasuki (Basak) nag, king of the serpants robbed Siva of the bowl, which contained the water of immortality, Siva taxed him with the theft and in his fight Vasuki turned the bowl upside down and caused the material to flow into the sea. Visnu infused a portion of his essence into the body of an immense tortoise to aid in producing or recovering the valuable articles, some of which had been lost in the deluge. For this purpose, he stationed himself at the bottom of the sea of milk so that his back might

serve as a pivot for the Mountain Mandara, around which gods and demons twisted the great serpent Vasuki. They then stood opposite each other and using the snake as a rope and the mountain as a churning rod, churned the milky ocean violently till fourteen valuable objects emerged and one of them was the goddess of fortune and beauty, Lakshmi. Lakshmi is said to have existed first as the daughter of Sage Bhrigu. She preferred Visnu's hand in marriage. Being the goddess of light and prosperity she is inextricably connected with Diwali festival. Please also see p. 137.

Saraswati

Saraswati is the goddess of learning and speech. She is said to have initiated Sanskrit language and is the St. Luke of the East as she patronizes art and sciences. She is the consort of Brahma, the creative spirit. Some of her other names are Sarada (giver of essence), Vageshwari (Mistress of Speech), *Brahmni (wife of Brahma)*, Mahavidya (knowledge supreme), Vach (wisdom) and so on.. Saraswati has a dual role in Indian mythology. She is a revered goddess in Hinduism and she governs deity of river Saraswati.

In Vedas, Saraswati and two Ashwini Kumaras from Surya (Sun) are concerned with learning, literature, arts and sciences. As Saraswati is the goddess of learning, Aswini Kumaras are the physicians in the heaven, all-powerful in their divine gifts. There three intellectual divinities function in the realm of the heaven, responsible to Indira, the administrator king of the heaven.

In iconography and painting, Saraswati is shown extraordinarily beautiful and graceful, seated on white lotus with veena (lute) in one hand, plying it with another, symbolizing the need for the cultivation of fine arts. She has a book in the third hand and a necklace of pearls (rosary) in the fourth. The rosary symbolizes spiritual science or yoga, austerities, meditation and japa (repetition of divine names).

Lord Ayyappa

Lord Ayyappa is worshiped particularly by those who belong to Andhra Pradesh, Karnataka, Tamil Nadu and Kerala regions in India. Lord Ayyappa descended on this earth as a relief to *Devas* (the devine personalities residing in Heaven) when *Asuras*(demons living in Hell) made their lives miserable.

There was a quarrel between *Devas* and *Asuras* for sharing the nectar. Devas could not afford to have all the *Asuras* becoming immortal. Therefore, Lord Visnu assumed the form of a beautiful maiden called Mohini to entice *Asuras* away from the nectar. Mohini successfully distracted the *Asuras,* and *Devas* flew from the Heaven with the whole of nectar. Mohini returned to Lord Siva with the victorious news but Lord Siva himself got enticed with her intoxicating beauty. A child, who combined in himself the divine effulgence of the two gods, was born out of the thigh of Mohini. The child was Ayyappa. Ayyappa was born on the last day of the month of *Dhanu,* on Saturday, corresponding to January 13.

Since Ayyappa had to serve in earthly kingdom for a period of 14 years, which was one of the pre-requisites to kill Leela Mahishi, he was abandoned on the banks of river Pampa where he was located by the King and the Queen of Pandalam who had no issue of their own. The boy was named Manikantan. The King believed him to be a god-given child. When he grew up he became expert in the art of archery. He vanquished a Muslim adventurer who became Manikantan's disciple. The festival of *Petta Thullal* has become a symbolic of Hindu-Muslim unity. Manikantan defeated the designs of many other adventurers, one by one. When King Rajasekhara wanted to anoint Manikantan as his successor, the latter said, "I am entering eternal meditation for the betterment of the world. However, every year, at the time of Makara Sankranti, I will wake up from my meditation and open my eyes to see the world. At that time, you adorn my idol with all the ornaments you have made for my coronation ceremony."

To abide by the devine commandment, *Thiruvabharanam* (set of holy ornaments) is brought to Sabarimala every year on Makara Sankranti day during *Petta Thullal,* a mass frenzied dance accompanied by loud music created by traditional instruments of this region. The pilgrims smear color on their faces and bodies. It is said that smearing colors and taking part in this dance is a symbolic step towards shedding one's ego.

The Epilogue

My trip to New Delhi, Agra and Jaipur evoked in me a keen desire to know the land and people of the country. After visiting various places I developed keen interest in the diverse religious systems followed by the people in India, the various festivals and ceremonies the followers of various religions observe, and the progress made in the empowerment of women. The preceding chapters should provide adequate information to understand the country in general. I had an opportunity to see the working of some small and medium scale industries and was impressed with the fast development of the country. But, at the same time, I also came across certain slum areas and have come to the conclusion that but for the growing population, the country could have ranked itself amongst the developed countries.

There was much to be explored and written about the country. One can even cover many aspects of the country—its history, its demographic structure, its political system, functioning of the parliamentary democracy in the country, its social, economic, scientific and technical development, and, above all, the malfunctioning of the Indian society. But, I decided to concentrate only on a few aspects, which should enable the outsiders, like my own countrymen, to understand the land and the people of India.

I have visited almost every country in the world. I found the prices of goods and services in India comparatively cheap while their quality is reasonably good. In India, you can expect goods of every quality depending on your capacity to pay. In Delhi, I found a number of boys and girls from Sri Lanka, Bangladesh, Africa, Iran and Thailand studying in various colleges and universities. In Agra and Jaipur, I also found many tourists from the UK, the USA, France, Switzerland, Germany and Japan. Some of them were seen in temples and Sikh shrines. Why do all such people prefer to come to India? Education in India is comparatively cheaper. The fact that over two billion Indians, including two million in the USA, are engaged in the implementation of different projects the world over, speak for itself the quality of education available in India. Indians are working as doctors, engineers, scientists, teachers, and business entrepreneurs in Europe, USA, in the whole of Africa and the Middle-East. Kalpana Chawla, a space scientist from India, went to space twice, though unfortunately she died during her second mission. The tourists from the developed countries are impressed with Indian art, architecture, philosophy and religion.

While writing this Epilogue, I came across a news item. With a view to bring in peace in the sub-continent through people-to-people contacts, the governments of India and Pakistan resumed bus service between New Delhi and Lahore. Incidentally, one of the passengers in the first trip included a 30-month old Noor Fatima from Pakistan, accompanied with her father, Nadeem Sajaad, and mother, Tayyeba Nadeem. The child had four abnormalities in her heart: two large holes and two defective valves. The bus indeed proved to be a lifesaver for the child. She successfully underwent a 6-hour operation in Bangalore's Narayana Hrudalaya on July 15, 2003. The parents couldn't afford Fatima's treatment in any western country and facilities for such an operation are not available in Pakistan. Fatima is not the only patient who was successfully treated in India, but more than 60 other children from Pakistan and many more from other countries have also benefited from the knowledge and skill of Indian doctors.

This instance underlines the need to rely on India not only as the cheapest source of education, goods and services, but also as the major source which can be relied upon for acquiring necessary managerial and technical skill in establishing small, medium and large industries. Though many people from various countries should have visited India and should have seen for themselves the industrial India, for the benefit of the people in general I am giving below an overview of the progress made in various states and union territories. This should enable the interested entrepreneurs to find out more information from the Indian Embassies and High Commissions in their respective countries and liaise with those with similar interest in India.

I have observed that with the changing pace of time a number of countries are reorienting their foreign policies in the economic interest of their own countries. With a view to alleviate poverty, abolish unemployment, bring in self-sufficiency and prosperity in the respective nations, governments have been looking to new avenues. In November 1980, in my own country, Papua New Guinea, the Government adopted the foreign policy that guided our relationships with many countries of the world. Traditionally, our relationships were with Australia, New Zealand and countries in Europe and North America. Though these relationships were useful, the Government and leaders of Papua New Guinea decided to look elsewhere. It made a small, yet significant amendment to our foreign policy to direct our attention more to the countries nearby, north of Papua New Guinea. They include such countries like Thailand, Malaysia, Singapore, Indonesia, Philippines, (members of the Association of South East Asian Nations or ASEAN), Taiwan, China, Japan, South Korea and as far north west as India. The new addition to the foreign policy is often referred to as 'The Look North Policy'. This simply means that we look at the development in the above countries and, where applicable and appropriate, we adopt them to the development of Papua New Guinea.

There are already some signs of development under that policy but they have not been significant. Since Papua New Guinea is facing increases in economic and social problems, it is now time for us to vigorously pursue that Look North Policy. The only two countries we should start off with are Malaysia and India. If I had my way, I would start with India and look at two areas. First, to work with their government and use volunteers from there to come here and assist us in the training of our youths in the areas of small to medium scale businesses so that they start and run their own businesses. Second, send some of our people to train in selected areas of businesses in India to gain experiences for them to use when they return to Papua New Guinea. Both these ideas would fit nicely with the current Somare/Marat government policy in downstream processing to affect their import replacement policy. Once that is in place, more employment opportunities would be achieved, law and order problems would be reduced, and economic growth would be achieved. After these ideas have been physically achieved, we then move to Malaysia and follow the same plans. If we activate these and other ideas, the Look North Policy will be realized and it will no longer be that for the book only.

What are the areas where the entrepreneurs in various developing countries, in general, and in Papua New Guinea, in particular, should be interested to liaise with their counterparts in India? India is a vast country. Each state or union territory has its own programs or schemes for industrial development. The following brief overview should just give an idea to the readers for forging ahead.

Andhra Pradesh

The State has an area of 275,069 sq km and had a population of 76,111,243 on March 1, 2001. Its capital is Hyderabad. The principal languages are: Telugu and Urdu. There are several major industries in operation in the State. They manufacture machine tools, synthetic drugs, pharmaceuticals, heavy electrical machinery, fertilizers, electronic equipment, aeronautical parts, cement and cement products, chemicals, asbestos, glass and watches. The State has the largest deposits of quality chryasolite asbestos in the country. Other important minerals found in the State are copper ore, manganese, mica, coal and limestone. The Singarenic Coal Mines supply coal to the entire south India. By the year 2002, the State had 3,111 large and medium scale industries providing employment to 802,878 persons. Besides, the State had 329,444 tiny industries employing 2,809,468 persons. There are 22 universities in Andhra Pradesh.

Arunachal Pradesh

The State has an area of 83,743 sq km and had a population of 1,096,702 as on March 31, 2001. Its capital is Itanagar. The principal languages in the State are: Monpa, Miji, Aka, Sherdukpen, Nyishi, Apatani, Tagin, Hill Miri, Adi, Digaru-Mismi, Idu-Mishmi, Khamti, Miju-Mishmi, Nocte, Tangsa and Wancho. At present, there are 88 crafts and weaving centres, 18 medium scale industries, 5224 registered SSI units besides one mini-cement plant, a fruit processing plant and a citronella oil distillery. The State has only Arunachal University, located in Itanagar.

Assam

The State has an area of 78,438 sq km. As on March 31, 2001 its population was 26,638,407. Its capital is Dispur and the principal language spoken is Assamese. Tea occupies an important place in the State. There are four oil refineries in Assam, including the one at Digboi. A Central Institute for Plastic Engineering Technology has been established at Amingaon near Guwahati. Assam has always enjoyed the highest reputation for her arts and crafts associated with her cottage industries. Cottage industries include handloom, sericulture, cane and bamboo articles, carpentry, brass and bell-metal crafts. Assam produces varieties of silk, Endi, Muga, Tassar, etc. Production of Muga silk in the world is done only in Assam. There are 6 universities in Assam.

Bihar

Bihar state, with Patna as its capital and Hindi as the language had a population of 82,878,796 in 2001. Bihar has cotton spinning mills, jute mills and leather industries. It is also famous for the production of tusser. It has 5 power projects and 13 universities.

Chattisgarh

This newly-carved State, with its capital of Raipur, has an area of 135,133 sq km and population of 20,795,956 as per 2001 census. Its principal language is Hindi. It is famous for 400,000-tonne Bhilai Steel Plant in the public sector. It has eight sponge iron plants, 13 ferro-alloy plants and 125 steel rolling mills, all in the private sector. Chhatisgarh has nine major cement plants besides iron casting units, engineering and fabrication units, agro-based food processing, chemical and plastic industries. One of the largest aluminum plants in India is BALCO in Korba. The State manufactures 100 per cent of the rail track in the country, and 20 per cent of the cement in India. It has several foremost industrial parks in the country, the prominent ones being in Bhilai and Korba. The thrust sectors in the new State are agro-based and forest-based industries, mineral based and sunrise industries, such as infotech, biotech, infotainment and tourism. It is one of the richest states in the country in terms of mineral wealth and is a home of 28 major minerals, including diamonds. It contributes one fifth of the country's total iron ore. The State has deposits of base metal, gold, beryl, garnet, amethyst, rock crystal and alexandrite, one of the rarest gemstones. The State has three universities.

Goa

The State has an area of 3,702 sq km and its population, as per 2001 census, was 1,343,998. Its principal languages are Konkani and Marathi. The State has 5,765 small-scale industrial units with an employment potential of 39,432 persons in large and medium sectors. There are 16 industrial estates besides a new electronic city coming up in the State. Mineral products are: ferro-manganese, bauxite and iron ore, contributing substantially to the economy of the State through exports. It has only one university, i.e Goa University.

Gujarat

The State has an area of 196,024 sq km and a population of 50,596,992 as per 2001 census. Its principal language is Gujarati. The industrial structure in the State has been gradually diversifying with the development of industries like chemicals, petrochemicals, fertilizers, engineering, electronics, etc. The number of registered working factories in the State were 20,050 at the end of the year 2000 with an employment potential of 868,000. The number of small-scale industrial units in the State was 263,564 in 2001. 12 universities are functioning in Gujarat.

Haryana

The State jointly shares Chandigarh as the capital city. It has an area of 44,312 sq km and population, as per 2001 census, is 21,082,989. Its principal language is Hindi. It has ambitious expansion programs for industries. Many IT units have been set up, particularly in the Gurgaon region. Almost all the major IT and related companies, including multinationals and Indian IT corporations, have established their units in the Gurgaon region. A Cyber City and a Cyber Park in the private sector is being developed in Gurgaon. Software Technology Park of India is setting up a dedicated Earth Station at Gurgaon to provide high-speed data communication facility for IT Industry. Major private organizations, like Bharati Telenet and Reliance, have taken up the projects of laying optical fiber in the State. Ambala city has become famous for laboratory and scientific equipment. Faridabad is yet another Industrial City in the State. The major industries are cement, sugar, paper, cotton, textiles, glassware, brassware, cycles, tractors, motorcycles, timepieces, automobile tyres and tubes, sanitaryware, television sets, steel tubes, handtools, cotton yarn, refrigerators, vanaspati, *ghee* and canvas shoes. Hindustan Machine Tools, producing tractors, is located at Pinjore. Maruti Udyog, which produces small cars, is located in Gurgaon. At the end of 2000-01, there were 1,077 large and medium industries and 74,128 small-scale units in the State. 6 universities are functioning in the State.

Himachal Pradesh

With Shimla as its capital and population of 6,070,305, as per 2001 census, the principal languages of the State are Hindi and Pahari. The State has made significant progress in the field of industrialization in the past few years. It has 191 large and medium and about 29,200 small scale and industrial units. It has three universities.

Jammu & Kashmir

The State has an area of 222,236 sq km. Its population, according to the latest census, is 10,069,917. The principal languages in the State are: Urdu, Kashmiri, Dogri, Pahari, Balti, Ladakhi, Punjabi, Gujri and Dadri. Handicrafts form the traditional industry of the State. Handicrafts include paper, wood carving, carpets, shawl-making, embroidery, etc. It particularly includes carpets which has an employment potential of 0.329 million artisans. The number of handloom weavers in the State is in the range of 40-50,000. There are three universities in Jammu & Kashmir.

Jharkhand

This newly-carved State has an area of 79,714 sq km. Its capital is Ranchi. The State, as per 2001 census, has a population of 26,909,428. Its principal language is Hindi. Jharkhand has the country's two biggest steel plants at Bokaro in the public sector and Tata Iron and Steel Company (TISCO) in Jamshedpur in the private sector. Other important industries are: Tata Engineering and Locomotive Company, Sriram Bearings, Usha Martin, Indian Tube Company, etc. The State is abundantly rich in minerals like copper, coal, iron, manganese, mica, chromite, bauxite, etc., and has the potential of becoming one of the most prosperous states of India. It has nine universities.

Karnataka

Spread over an area of 191,791 sq km, and Bangalore as its capital city, the State has a population of 52,733,958. Its principal language is Kannada. Karnataka contributes 4 per cent of the national production in the industrial sector and 20 per cent to the State income. Public Sector undertakings include Bharat Earth Movers, Bharat Electronics, Bharat Heavy Electricals, Hindustan Aeronautics Limited, Hindustan Machine Tools, Indian Telephone Industries, Wheel and Axle, New Government Electric Factory and Mangalore Chemicals and Fertilizers. There are many factories under joint and private sectors in addition to small-scale industries. Some of the manufactured items include aircraft, rail coaches, telephone instruments, electronic and telecommunication equipment, glass, batteries, spark plugs, electric motors, textiles, silk, sandal oil, electrical goods, porcelain, sugar, caustic soda, paper including newsprint, capacitors, mining metal tools, cement, motor cycles, fertilizers, etc. The Visveswaraiah Iron and Steel Limited, Bhadravati now owned by SAIL, produces special steel, alloy and ferro silicon. There are more than 223,000 small-scale industrial units with an employment potential of 1.5 millions people. Karnatāka stands first in the production of electronic equipment and raw silk. The State is famous for its sandal soap and sandalwood oil. There are 16 universities in Karnataka.

Kerala

Kerala with 90.92 per cent literacy rate, spread over an area of 38,3633 sq.km, has a population of 31,838,619. Its capital is Thiruvanthapuram. Kerala is a major producer of coconut, rubber, pepper, cardamom, ginger, cocoa, cashew, arecanut, coffee and tea. Tree spices, like nutmeg, cinnamon, cloves, etc. are also cultivated. Rice and tapioca are important food crops. Kerala is rich in industrial potentialities and infrastructure facilities, such as hydro-electric power, rich forests, rare minerals like ilmenite and monozite and the different systems of transport and communications. The State has traditional industries and the efficient system of transport and communications.

Traditional industries are handloom, cashew, coir and handicrafts. Other important industries are rubber, tea, ceramics, electric and electronic appliances, telephone cables, transformers, bricks and tiles, drugs and chemicals, general engineering, plywood splints and veneers, beedi and cigar, soaps, oils, fertilizers and *khadi* and village industry products. A number of manufacturing units have also sprung-up for production of precision instruments, machine tools, petroleum and petroleum products, paints, pulp paper, newsprint, glass and non-ferrous metals. As of 2000, there were 18,710 registered working factories in the State comprising of 18,160 private and 550 public factories. The total employment in those factories was 440,083 during the year 1999-2000. There was a total of 589 large and medium industrial units functioning in Kerala as on March 31, 2001, which consisted of 19 central sector units, 63 state sector units, 60 in the cooperative sector, 29 in the joint sector and 402 in the private sector. There are 110 public sector undertakings in the State. 27 Software Technology Parks of India have running complexes in Thiruvanthapuram, the capital of the State, with 17 units functioning under its umbrella directly and three other units in private premises, all engaged primarily in the export of computer software. Nearly 191,670 persons are employed in the Khadi and Village Industries Sector in the State. There are 8 universities in Kerala.

Madhya Pradesh

The State, with its capital in Bhopal, has a population of 60,385,118, as per 2001 census. It has an area of 308,000 sq km. Its principal language is Hindi. Madhya Pradesh is one of the leading states in India in mineral production. Coal, bauxite, iron-ore, manganese-ore, rock phosphate, dolomite, copper-ore, limestone are being mined on a large scale. The State is famous for its traditional handicrafts and handloom cloths manufactured at Chanderi and Maheswar. A large number of automobile industries have been established at Pithampur near Indore. Prominent industries in the public sector in the State are Bharat Heavy Electricals Limited at Bhopal, Security Paper Mill at Hoshangabad, Bank Note Press at Dewas, Newsprint Factory at Nepanagar and Alkaloid Factory at Neemuch. During 1999-2000, 81.13 million metre cloth was manufactured in the handloom sector and 131.59 million metre cloth by the power looms. Total production of saleable steel in 1998-99 was 3.35 million tonnes while that of aluminium was 91.8 thousand tonnes. Production of cement touched 11.24 million metric tonne mark. The State produced about 58.4 thousand tonne newsprint. 16 universities are functioning in Madhya Pradesh.

Maharashtra

The State has an area of 307,713 sq km. According to 2001 census, its population is 99,752,247. Its capital city is Mumbai and the principal language is Marathi. Maharashtra has been identified as the country's powerhouse and Mumbai as the central point of India's financial and commercial markets. Industrial sector occupies a prominent position in the economy of Maharashtra. Food products, breweries, tobacco and related products, cotton textiles, textile products, paper and paper products, printing and publishing, rubber, plastic, chemical and chemical products, machinery, electrical machinery, apparatus and appliances, and transport equipment and parts contribute substantially to the industrial production in the State. Maharashtra is a major producer of oilseeds. Groundnut, sunflower, soyabean are major oil seed crops. Important cash crops are cotton, sugarcane, turmeric and vegetables. There are 31 universities in Maharashtra.

Manipur

The State has an area of 22,327 sq km, of which 17,384 sq km is under forest. Its population, according to 2001 census, is 2,388,068. Its capital is Imphal and the principal language is Manipuri. Manipur continues to strive forward for rapid industrialization of the State. Agriculture is the single largest source of livelihood of the majority of the rural masses and is also the mainstay of the State's economy. The State Government has taken up steps to revitalize a few industrial corporations in the priority areas and to wind up or privatize the remaining ones.

Steps are being taken to invigorate industrial development in the State. Manipur has two universities.

Meghalaya

The State has an area of 22,429 sq km and its population is 2,306,069 as per 2001 census. Its capital is Shillong and the principal languages are: Khasi, Garo and English. Meghalaya is basically an agricultural State in which about 80 per cent of its population depends primarily on agriculture for their livelihood. A number of industrial projects have been set up for the manufacture of iron and steel materials, cement and other consumer products. Only Nehu-North Eastern Hill University in Shillong is functioning in Meghalaya.

Mizoram

The State has an area of 21,087 sq km and its population is 891,058. Its capital city is Aizawl and the principal languages are: Mizo and English. It is a mountainous region. The entire Mizoram is a Notified Backward Area and is categorized under 'No Industry District'. However, concerted efforts were made in the last decade to accelerate the growth of industries in Mizoram. Mizoram University came into existence in July 2001. Nehu-North Eastern Hill University has its campus in Aizawal.

Nagaland

The State has an area of 16,579 sq km and its population is 1,988,636. Its capital is Kohima and the principal languages are: Angami, Ao, Chang, Konyak, Lotha, Sangtam, Sema and Chakhesang. Agriculture is the main occupation of the people in Nagaland. The process of industrialization in the State is in its infancy. The Nagaland Sugar Mill at Dimapur has an installed capacity of 1,000 tones per day. There is a pulp and paper mill at Tuli and a plywood factory at Tizit. Handloom and handicrafts are important cottage industries, which are mainly being managed by cooperative societies. The mini-cement plant at Wazeho has commenced production. The fruits and vegetables processing and cold storage Plant at Dimapur has an installed capacity of 5 MT per day. Nagaland University is functioning. Nehu North Eastern Hill University has its campus in Kohima. Nagaland Central University at Lumamii is being set up.

Punjab

The State has an area of 50,362 sq km and its population, according to 2001 census, is 20,281,969. Chandigarh is the joint capital of Punjab and Haryana. The principal language is Punjabi. Agriculture is the mainstay of Punjab's economy and nearly 86 per cent of the total geographical area of the State is under cultivation. There are 20.2 million small-scale units in the State. These units produce bicycle parts, sewing machines, hand tools, machine tools, auto parts, electronic items, sports goods, surgical and leather goods, hosiery, knitwear, nuts and bolts, textiles, sugar, vegetable oil, etc., giving employment to 0.909 million persons. As of March 31, 2002, there were 620 large and medium scale units providing employment to about 0.256 million persons. A large number of Information Technology and Software Development companies are coming up in the State. With the setting up of Earth Station in Mohali and with the laying of fiber optic backbone in the State, basic infrastructure has been established for the growth of Information Technology industry. An Information Technology Park is also being set-up in Mohali. There are 8 universities in Punjab.

Rajasthan

The State, with an area of 342,239 sq km, has a population of 56,473,122. Its capital is Jaipur and the principal languages are Hindi and Rajasthani. Rajasthan is endowed with a rich culture. It is also rich in minerals and is fast emerging on the industrial scenario of the country. Some of the important Central undertakings are: Zinc Smelter Plant at Devari (Udaipur), Copper Plant at Khetri Nagar (Jhunjhunu) and Precision Instrument Factory at Kota. Small-scale industrial units, numbering

2.297 million, provided employment potential to about 0.886 million persons in the State in January 2002. Major industries are: textiles and woolens, sugar, cement, glass, sodium plants, oxygen, vegetable dyes, pesticides, zinc, fertilizers, railway wagons, ball bearings, water and electricity metres, sulphuric acid, television sets, synthetic yarn and insulating bricks. Precious and semi-precious stones, caustic soda, calcium carbide, nylon and tyres etc. are other important industrial units. The State has rich deposits of zinc concentrates, emerald, garnet, gypsum, silver ore, asbestos, felspar and mica. It abounds in salt, rock phosphate, marble and red stone deposits. The first Export Promotion Industrial Park of the country has been established and made operational at Sitapura (Jaipur). There are 8 universities in this State.

Sikkim

The State has an area of 7,096 sq km and its population is 540,493. Its capital is Gangtok and the principal languages are: Lepcha, Bhutia, Nepali and Limbu. Its economy is basically agrarian. It has been declared industrially backward State. The emphasis of the Government has been on the promotion and development of various small-scale industries. There are three public sector undertakings in Sikkim. The State government owns Sikkim Time Corporation. It assembles watches, manufactures digital watches and MIC chips. Sikkim Jewels Limited is one of the sophisticated and precision oriented industries for the manufacture of jewel bearings for electric meters, water meters and other measuring instruments like watches and clocks. Ten ancillary units have been set up to manufacture watch jewels. Only Sikkim Manipal University of Health, Medicals & Technological Sciences is in Gangtok.

Tamil Nadu

This State, with Chennai as its capital, has an area of 130,058 sq km. Its population is 62,110,839 as per 2001 census. Its principal language is Tamil. Agriculture is the major occupation of Tamil Nadu. Major industries in the State are: cotton, heavy commercial vehicles, auto components, railway coaches, power pumps, leather tanning industries, cement, sugar, paper, automobiles and safety matches.

Knowledge based industries like I T and Biotechnology have become the thrust area in the industrial scene in Tamil Nadu. TIDEL, a software technology park, has been established in Tharamani, Chennai. Chennai has currently about 32,000 software professionals employed in 767 IT companies. Global auto majors Hyundai Motors, Ford, Hindustan Motors and Mitsubishi have commenced production with expansion plans of Ashok Leyland and TAFE in Chennai. Main mineral wealth of the State is granite, lignite and limestone. The State is an important exporter of tanned skin and leather goods, yarn, tea, coffee, spices, engineering goods, tobacco, handicrafts and black granite. The strong engineering base consists of a network of nearly 3,000 units, employing a skilled workforce of more than 0.25 million. The State contributes to 70 per cent of the tannery industry in India. Chennai Refinery Limited has given rise to several petro-based units. Major chemical and fertilizer plants have been established at Cuddalore and Tuticorin. Tamil Nadu has 23 universities.

Tripura

The State, with capital city of Agartala, and population of 3,191,168, has an area of 1,049,169 sq km. Its principal languages are: Bengali and Kokborak. Tripura is abundant in natural gas and a number of gas-based industries have sprung-up. There are 809 small-scale industrial units in the State. Handloom is the single largest industry and it is essentially a tribal household industry. Only Tripura University in Agartala is functioning in Tripura.

Uttaranchal

This newly carved State has an area of 53,484 sq km and its population is 8,479,562. Its capital is Dehra Dun and the principal languages are: Hindi, Garhwali, and Kumaoni. About 90 per cent of the population of Uttaranchal depends on agriculture. The State is rich in mineral deposits like limestone, rock phosphate, dolomite, magnesite, copper greyphyte, soap stone, gypsum, etc. The number of small-scale industries is 41,216 providing employment to 153,229 persons. 191

heavy industries in the year 2001 employed 50,802 persons. Most of the industries are forest-based. There are seven universities and university level institutions in Uttaranchal.

Uttar Pradesh

The State with an area of 238,566 sq km has a population of 166,052,859. Its capital is Lucknow and the principal languages are: Hindi and Urdu. Agriculture is the main occupation of 78 per cent of the population of the State. By the end of March 1998, there were 2,616 medium and large industrial undertakings with employment opportunities for 738,582 persons. Besides, there were 401,372 small-scale industrial units with an employment potential for 1,552,000 persons. About 4.6 million tones of sugar was produced in the State. There were 68 textile units. 32 automobile units provided jobs to 20,280 persons. The New Okhla Industrial Development Authority (NOIDA) is planning development of 102 sectors by the year 2011. It includes industrial sectors, housing sectors, group housing sectors, residential buildings, commercial assets and institutional sectors. Steps have been taken to develop other industrial areas in the State on the pattern of NOIDA and Greater NOIDA. A Software Technology Park has been set up in Kanpur while five more Software Parks are proposed to be set up. Under the public sector, mining of limestone, magnesite, coal, rock phosphate, dolomite and silicon-sand is carried out. Important mineral-based industries include large cement plants in Sonebhadra. Uttar Pradesh has 25 universities.

West Bengal

The State, with capital city of Kolkata (formerly: Calcutta), has a population of 80,221,171. Its area is 88,752 sq km. Its principal language is Bengali. Agriculture plays a pivotal role in the State's income. It is one of the major industrial states in India. In 1998, it registered 11,416 factories, excluding defence factories. The number of registered small-scale industries at that time was 453,831. Durgapur and Burdwan have steel plants. Major industries include engineering, automobiles, chemicals, pharmaceuticals, aluminium, ceramics, jute, cotton textiles, tea, paper, leather, footwear, bonemeal, bicycle, dairy, poultry and timber-processing. Central public sector undertakings include locomotive, cable, fertilizer, shipbuilding and ordnance. Coal and china clay are two important minerals being exploited. There are 14 universities and university level institutions in West Bengal.

Andaman and Nicobar Islands

It is a Union Territory. There are 36 inhabited islands including 25 in the Andaman district and 13 in the Nicobar district. The original inhabitants of the islands lived in the forests for hunting and fishing. There are four Negrito tribes, viz, the Great Andamanese, Onge, Jarawa and Sentinalese in the Andaman group of islands and two Mongoloid tribes, viz., Nicobarese and Shompens in the Nicobar group of islands. Sentinalese are still hostile. Even now they are keeping a separate entity and have not yet learnt the concept of covering their bodies. Forests cover 7,171 sq km of the total area of the islands. There are 1,421 registered small scale, village and handicrafts units. Two units are shell and wood based handicraft units. Small-scale industrial units are engaged in the production of polythene bags, PVC conduit pipes and fittings, paints and varnishes, fibre glass and mini flour mills, soft drinks and beverages, etc. Small scale and handicraft units are also engaged in shell crafts, bakery products, rice milling, furniture making, etc.

Chandigarh

Chandigarh and the area surrounding it were constituted as a Union Territory in 1966. It serves as the joint capital of both Punjab and Haryana states. There are 15 large and medium and about 3,026 small-scale industrial units offering employment to about 29,400 persons. It exports goods to the tune of Rs.600 million annually. The neighbouring states have developed industrial estates right next to the city. As a result, industries have been set up on a large scale in Parwanoo, Baddi, Derabassi, Mohali and Panchkula. Punjab University and Post Graduate Institute of Medical Sciences & Research, a deemed university, are the two biggest educational institutions in Chandigarh.

Dadra and Nagar Haveli

This Union Territory consists of two pockets, namely, Dadra and Nagar Haveli. Its total area is 491 sq km and its population is 220,451. The capital city is Silvassa and the principal languages are: Gujarati and Hindi. It is predominantly a rural area, having about 70 per cent population of tribals. Three government industrial estates have been developed at Silvassa, Masat and Khadoli. By March 2002, there were 1,317 industries which include cottage, village and small scale industries and 383 medium-scale industries in textiles, engineering, plastics, electronics, chemicals, pharmaceuticals, etc., employing more than 37,000 persons.

Daman and Diu

Daman and Diu along with Goa formed a colony held by the Portuguese even after Independence in 1947. In 1961, it was made an integral part of India. After conferring statehood on Goa on May 30, 1987, Daman and Diu was made a separate Union Territory. Its total area is 112 sq km and its population is 158,059. Its capital is Daman and the principal language is Gujarati. There are 1,700 small scale and medium scale industries in Daman and Diu. Omnibus Industrial Development Corporation at Daman has developed two industrial areas. The other industrial areas are: Dabhel, Bhimore and Kadaiya.

Delhi

Delhi, the capital city of India and spread over an area of 1,483 sq km, is not only the largest commercial centre in northern India but is also the largest centre of small industries. It has a population of 13,782,976 according to 2001 census. The principal languages are Hindi, Punjabi and Urdu. In 1991, it became a National Capital Territory and got a Legislative Assembly. A wide variety of items like television, tape recorders, light engineering machines and automobile parts, sports goods, bicycles and PVC goods, including footwear, textiles, fertilizers, medicines, hosiery, leather goods, software, etc. are manufactured in Delhi. Delhi's new millennium industrial policy emphasizes the setting up of high-tech and sophisticated industries in electronics, telecommunications, software industries, IT enabling services, etc. The industries, which are non-polluting and encourage high-value addition and depend largely on skilled manpower, will be promoted. For the purpose of relocating industrial units functioning in residential non-conforming areas, the government of

National Capital Territory of Delhi took possession of 1,065 acres of land in villages of Bawana, Holambi Kalan and Holambi Khurd for developing new industrial estates. 14 universities and university level institutions exist at present in Delhi.

Lakshadweep

It is a group of coral islands consisting of 12 atolls, three reefs and submerged sand banks. Of the 36 islands, only 11 are inhabited. Spread over an area of 32 sq km, and with population, as per 2001 census, is 60,595. The capital city is Kavaratti and the principal languages are: Jesri and Mahl. Coconut fibre extraction and conversion of its fibre products is the main industry in the islands. Under government sector there are seven coir fibre factories, seven coir production-cum-demonstration centres and four fibre curling units, functioning under coir sector. These units produce coir fibre and coir yarn in addition to other coir products like curled fibre, corridor mat, mat and mattings. Small coir units are also functioning under private sector in different islands.

Pondicherry

The territory of Pondicherry comprises of the former French establishment Pondicherry, Karaikal, Mahe and Yanam. It is a Union Territory. Its total population is 973,829 and the area is 492 sq km. The principal languages are: Tamil, Telugu, Malayalam, English and French. 6,760 industries were providing employment to 79,179 persons as on March 31, 2002. The number of industrial units registered up to May 2002 is 6,778 units. The units are manufacturing items like textiles, computers and peripherals, UPS and other electronic products, consumer durable, fast moving consumer goods, pharmaceuticals, leather goods, earth moving equipment, sugar, yarn, spirit, beer, potassium chlorate, rice-bran oil, auto parts, disposable syringes, roofing sheets, washing machines, bio-polymers, steel tubes, LPG cylinders, etc. Only Pondicherry University is functioning in Pondicherry.

Index

Bibliography

Arya, Anita, *Indian Women*, New Delhi, Gyan Books , 2000

Bezbaruah, M P, *Fairs and Festivals of India,* 5 vols, New Delhi, Gyan Books 2003

India: A Reference Anuual, New Delhi, Publication Division, Ministry of Information & Broadcasting, 2003

Isser G P, *Changing Face of Poverty and Globalization,* New Delhi, Gyan Books, 2002

Kumar, Nagesh, *Indian Economy Under Reforms*, New Delhi , Bookwell, 2000

Mathew M, *Manorama Yearbook 2003,* Kottayam, Malayala Manorama Co. Ltd., 2003

Panchamukhi, *Indian Classical Thoughts on Economic Development and Management,* New Delhi, Bookwell, 2000

Pillai, J K, *Women and Empowerment,* New Delhi, Gyan Books, 1995

Ralhan O P, *Encyclopedia of Political Parties,* 101 vols., New Delhi, Anmol Publications, 2002

Shashi, S S, *Encyclopedia Indica,* 130 vols, New Delhi, Anmol Publications, 2003

Singh, Nagendra, *International Encyclopedia of Buddhism,* 75 vols, New Delhi, Anmol Publications, 2003

Singh, Nagendra, *Encyclopedia of Gods and Goddesses,* 15 vols., New Delhi, Anmol Publications, 2001

Tharoor, Shashi, *India: From Midnight to the Millennium,* New Delhi, Penguin, 2000

Tiwari, Satish, *Encyclopedia of Indian Government,* 40 vols. New Delhi, Anmol Publications, 2000